FAVORITE MOVIES

Favorite Movies

CRITICS' CHOICE

Edited by PHILIP NOBILE

Macmillan Publishing Co., Inc.

NEW YORK

ACKNOWLEDGMENTS

*I acknowledge my contributors who worked for scale
so that this book might be, and my editor Ray Roberts,
without whose high enthusiasm this book
would not be.*

Macmillan Publishing Co., Inc.
866 Third Avenue, New York, N.Y. 10022
Collier-Macmillan Canada Ltd., Toronto, Canada

Library of Congress Catalog Card Number: 73-2327

First Printing 1973

Printed in the United States of America

FOR

Pietro Germi

AND

Paolo Sannella

Contents

Introduction

PHILIP NOBILE

MOVIE CRITICISM IS in a shambles. The devout filmgoer in search of some semblance of critical harmony will not be rewarded. In the first place, those who write about films can't seem to get their superlatives straight: works like *The Damned, The Discreet Charm of the Bourgeoisie, The Last Picture Show, Greaser's Palace, Play It As It Lays* and *Such Good Friends* pop up on year-end ten best as well as ten worst lists!

This dismaying aesthetic distance runs roughly parallel to the distinction drawn between (highbrow) critics and (middlebrow) buffs or reviewers. Whereas the former are strictly interested in art, the latter can content themselves with trash. So-called critics refer to buffs as pedants and supposed buffs slap critics for being too bookish. For example, critic Charles Thomas Samuels of *The American Scholar* has the following to say about *Village Voice* buff Andrew Sarris:

> Habitually, he discusses a film he likes by comparing it to all those it resembles or by which it may have been influenced; if he can find no other way to show his total recall, he merely imagines how another director would have shot the same subject. Plainly, here is a man who

1

has seen everything and retained it all, while he avoids the troubling question of what is worth knowing in the first place. . . . Perhaps, as with most pedants, one should go to Sarris for information rather than judgment (*Modern Occasions*, Fall, 1971).

And Sarris would riposte:

Part of my intransigence may be attributed to the relative ignorance that my generally bookish attackers displayed in the movie medium. . . . Unfortunately, too many bookish film critics have perverted the notion of ecumenical erudition by snobbishly subordinating film to every other art. Whereas the late James Agee discovered cinema through his love for movies, too many of his self-proclaimed successors chose to abuse movies in the name of Kultur (*Confessions of a Cultist*).

These polemics are uncommonly polite. When aroused movie critics turn on each other, the spectacle is usually bloody. And the original disharmony increases.

Critics and buffs are so disputatious that they even debate the name of what we see on the screen: is it a movie or a film? For the uninitiated either description will do. Yet John Simon makes a federal case for "film" in his recent collection *Movies into Film*. "There is, obviously, no harm in calling films movies, or cinema, or flicks, or anything else," he insists. "But a diminutive is not what one usually applies to an art. Not only are books not printies, but a non-motion picture is not a paintie, and a work of architecture is not an Archie, and so on. To call film movies is, however fondly, to derogate from it; or, more precisely, to view it as an entertainment rather than as an art."

Where do we go from here? Clearly, the field of film criticism wants for unity of a sort, and that's what *Favorite Movies* is about. By gathering together a broad range of critics, buffs, or whatever, and having them answer the same question in the same location, this book hopes to provide a start toward a comparative aesthetic of cinema. But how to nail down the premises at play in criticism? What is the proper question? I decided to ask: What is your favorite movie? This phrasing purposely avoids summoning forth knee-jerk essays on the "greatest movie." One's "favorite" goes deeper into film and deeper into criticism by demanding an exceedingly personal response.

Although the question was direct, the answers were left entirely up to the contributors. Some settled on a single favorite; others had a handful and still others chose a wide assortment. Of the twenty-seven contributors, only two chanced upon the same film (Molly Haskell and Peter Harcourt on *Madame de*); in addition, only six featured the same director (Richard Roud and Roger Greenspun on Jean Renoir, Charles Thomas Samuels and Richard Gilman on Michelangelo Antonioni, and Andrew Sarris and Robin Wood on Kenji Mizoguchi).

The diversity of taste expressed in this volume reflects a pretty mixed lot of respondents. They differ much in age, rank and place of aesthetic origin. Established critics/buffs like Dwight Macdonald, John Simon, Andrew Sarris, Richard Roud, Judith Crist and Richard Schickel are lined up alongside talented but lesser-knowns like Joseph McBride, Peter Harcourt, Robin Wood and Colin Westerbeck. Most of the major outlets of film criticism are represented here, including the *New York Times, Time,* the *Village Voice, Esquire,* the *New York Review of Books, Commentary,* the *Atlantic, Film Comment* and *Film Quarterly.* No major voice in American film criticism was overlooked. Stanley Kauffmann, Vincent Canby, Richard Poirier and Roger Ebert were once committed to the project before dropping out for various reasons. Pauline Kael and Rex Reed said they didn't have the time. Neither Manny Farber nor Hollis Alpert replied to invitations. Penelope Gilliatt was somewhat disposed to doing her favorite but became incommunicado after the appearance of *Sunday, Bloody Sunday.* Renata Adler did not complete her piece. And Wilfrid Sheed retired from the trade.

I polled several contributors on the matter of (1) the extreme polarization of views in film criticism and (2) the vehemence with which critics/buffs tend to pursue their fellows. A sampling of replies goes a long way toward explaining the chaos that *Favorite Movies* means to put in partial order.

Q. Why is film criticism so polarized?

STUART BYRON:

A. Film critics have such a broad range of opinions compared to the other arts because of the absurd notion that anyone can be a film critic. Nobody would hire a book, music or art critic unless he were an expert in the field; yet the impression persists in the land that anyone can review films. Thus perennial amateurs become household names, and their subjective opinions, based on no expertise whatsoever, are taken seriously.

JOHN SIMON:

A. Because, more patently than in other forms of criticism, there are two ways of approaching film: the low road, coming from movies as pure entertainment, film buffery, the Loew's as an escape from and a substitute for education, learning, work, thought, living; the high road, coming from a view of film as an art among and involving other arts, having a similar potential and making like demands as the best of literature, music, fine arts, etc., and having the same responsibility aesthetically, ethically, humanly. The movie reviewer as escapist and lowbrow (or highbrow with *nostalgie de la boue*) or rationalizer of his immature tastes left over from childhood will, obviously, have little in common with the film critic as intellectual, aesthete, scholar and responsible human being.

CHARLES THOMAS SAMUELS:

A. I'm sure that film criticism is polarized for reasons I know nothing about, being up here in the provinces. So far as I'm concerned, the one serious (not political) cause of polarization is the status of film as an art. Most people who write on the subject—either through lack of education, pop cult mentality, or excessive fondness for "entertainment"—celebrate in movies what no respectable critic would find worthwhile in the other arts. For me, the most significant difference between one film critic and another is that between men of general culture who believe that some films are part of culture and those who don't care whether what they write about is art or trash.

There is not even the basic agreement that obtains among literary critics about the difference between best sellers and serious novels. There are no accepted classics because there is no agreement on the desirability of applying to film the standards that underlie the very conception of a classic. There are no accepted reference works or bibliographical tools. There is no distinction between journalism and criticism, or even between gossip and biographical or historical data that can be legitimated through its contribution to critical understanding.

STEPHEN FARBER:

A. There is no established body of criticism with regard to films, and even more significantly, there is no "great tradition" of screen classics that all major critics can agree on. The *auteur* critics have tried to *create* a great tradition, but their preferences seem hopelessly arbitrary, unsubstantiated by a coherent rational theory. Everyone does agree on major poets or painters, but many of the films considered classics—for example, Griffith's *Intolerance*, Eisenstein's *Potemkin*, Murnau's *The Last Laugh*—seem to me primitive and hopelessly inadequate as touchstones on which to base an aesthetic. If the classics are still in doubt, it is not surprising to find radical disagreement about contemporary films. Nothing can be taken for granted. Everything remains to be proved, and this is one of the things that makes movie criticism exciting. The territory is still wide open. Nevertheless, I would like to see several critics engage in a systematic, unsparing revaluation of major directors—an attempt to write a viable history of film by defining the truly valuable achievements. That will not eliminate all differences among critics, but it may encourage a critical dialogue that at least shares some of the same assumptions.

ANONYMOUS:

A. My short, spontaneous, ill-tempered response to your first question is simply that film criticism, growing as much as films themselves out of bastard origins, *is still a field dominated mainly by assholes and axe-grinders. And maybe this will always be the case, at least until films are wholly absorbed into academic respectability (a prospect I dread) and a tradition established comparable to that in the study of literature.* Until that time, film remains everybody's property, each man his own film critic. What critics are we talking about, anyway? Most of my distinguished colleagues in the National Society of Film Critics are people whose writing I find wholly irrelevant to my interests in films; I can't even get angry about it. Why is there such a polarization between my judgments and theirs? Why are eggs different from apples?

The assholes can be dispensed with; it's the axe-grinders who are more problematical. The posture of a John Simon or Stanley Kauffmann is easily identified by Warshow's dichotomy of those saying, "It's not I who go to the movies, it's their audience," and those others who say, "It's not the movies I go to, it's art." Clearly, a Kauffmann and Simon are among the latter, and, this being so, I tend to think they've simply found the wrong subject: that the great majority of films, including many of the most interesting ones, will of necessity elude their grasp.

With Sarris (and especially with Roger Greenspun), motives become less clear. The *auteur* controversy has always seemed to me a lot of obfuscation; everyone agrees with the proposition that a good director's work has a continuity of theme and style; the disagreement is over which directors are good and which aren't. And, in Sarris's case, I've increasingly come to believe his opinions are intimately bound up with his real or imagined slights by the literary Establishment. This is why a Douglas Sirk or Blake Edwards is elevated to prominence: so as to create a mystique-laden specialized province (the Visual) beyond the literary critic's pale and invulnerable to the obvious accusations that these directors' films, whatever their merits, are fundamentally trashy by traditionally applicable criteria. The professors have been condescending toward the very real artistic achievements of past films and toward an enthusiasm for movies generally; OK, let's put the professors on the defensive. I think the attitudes expressed in Sarris's extraordinary introduction to *Confessions of a Cultist* are very self-revealing in this regard.

JOSEPH McBRIDE

A. Why is movie criticism so polarized? Primarily because it lacks the benefit (or onus) of an academic tradition. This makes the field a very exciting one, because we're all pioneers; but it also makes for a lot of stridency on all sides. Literary critics agree that, say, Hemingway deserves serious consideration, even though they don't all agree on his merit. The same isn't true for a director of the stature of John Ford (a lot of others could be mentioned—Hawks, Hitchcock, Mc-Carey, etc.). Someone like Pauline K. can kiss off *Liberty Valance* with a snide line or two and not have to worry about justifying her attack. Conversely, many of us *auteur* critics tend to assume that a film we like is great, or good, or worth discussing, without justifying our esteem for it. I wouldn't want to analyze a film without at least implicitly answering the question of, "How good is it? And why?" As Robin Wood has said, film criticism has to confront the question of value. There is also the old bugaboo of commercialism; people are still hung up on arguing whether films are art, and whether Hollywood is anathema to art. . . . Some non-*auteur*ist critics have worked out distinctive approaches. Stephen Farber can't write three lines without using the word "America"; his could be called the hate-America school. Pauline K. can't write three words without using the pronoun "we" to create the snobbish impression that "we" all agree. . . .

Stephen Farber has learned much from Kael—his writing often sounds like a parroting of hers—and I suppose she and her adherents can be described as a school. What I once described as "reviewing the audience" rather than reviewing the film. The value of *auteur*ism, to me, is that it gets rid of much of the rampant egocentrism that afflicts American reviewing and criticism. *Auteur*ism looks at the film and tries to see it for what it is, rather than what the reviewer or critic would like it to be.

Manny Farber is probably the best American movie critic, and his approach is completely idiosyncratic. His painter's personality certainly comes through in his feeling for visual style, and his writing is by far the most colorful of any critic's. His weakness, I think, is his tendency to write impressionistically rather than logically, but his insights more than make up for that. In the last couple of years my criticism has been influenced a lot by Farber. . . . One thing I've picked up from him, and have been trying to work on, is his sensitivity to the nuances of acting, and how an actor retains his personality even under the influence of a dictatorial director.

PARKER TYLER:

A. The two queries are necessarily interrelated and my contribution here touches closely upon the cause of what you call "polarization" in film criticism. I identify the cause as the absence of a body of applied aesthetics that would have established basic order and rank in the history of filmic achievement. This lack is owed, I think, to an original split in the public attitude toward the movies. Long ago they were roughly divided into entertaining or educational factuality (documentarism) and more or less "entertaining" art. Unfortunately, film theory itself (see Faure, Kracauer and Langer) has tended to italicize rather than mend the enduring split. Because of the intellectual condescension bred by this situation, the vocation of film critic has lacked ready prestige from the literary viewpoint. Hence, anyone presuming to be a man of letters feels he must somehow vindicate his choice of film criticism as a medium and may begin by attacking those (such as myself) who have tacitly "held back" the movies' prestige by satirizing them and viewing them beyond strict aesthetic categories. I believe such repudiation of freewheeling critical activity is narrow and more political than it is intelligent or "aesthetic." An upcoming young critic (William S. Pechter) once observed that I, among others, have more than adequately shown how a movie could be criticized as something other than a movie. What might be a valid distinction *if available standards existed* becomes only a facile mystique to be used as a polemical weapon. Recently, an aggressive practitioner of journalistic criticism branded me with an epithet garnered from another critic who was engaged in defending my point of view in my early books. The first critic (Richard Schickel) had used the term "idiot savantry" to describe the enthusiasms of Myra Breckinridge, the heroine who explicitly parodies my attitude toward Hollywood films in Gore Vidal's novel; the second critic (John Simon) then seized on the epithet, "idiot savant," to discredit me directly and personally. Paradoxically, another section of critical opinion deems all my work both highbrow and aesthetic. Such blatant contradictions could not exist in a body of criticism with any coherent and acknowledged canons. Reigning disorder always tempts the opportunist and the journalist and develops the worst in everybody.

RICHARD SCHICKEL:

A. Obviously the major intellectual issue among critics right now is *autuer* theory. In some respects it is a useful theory. It has served the worthwhile function of restoring reputations, particularly of action directors as Wyler and Stevens. It leads, however, to a certain idiot and Minelli. It has also, happily, helped to deflate such Academy directors as Wyler and Stevens. It elads, however, to a certain idiot savantry and to rather too rigid categorizations, which seem to me to interfere very often with the perceptions of the critics who hold with the theory. The opposition, which might be termed "the Humanists," have other problems. In the notable instance of Pauline Kael, for example, they have been doing a good deal of speculation (often disguised as reportage—anyway it *sounds* very authoritative) about the motives of the people who make movies. She has been very quick, for instance, to apply the term "fascist" to works that are, I agree, deplorable, but are probably undeserving of such a phrase. I do think moral judgments are part of criticism—see Orwell on Dali— but you gotta be careful about them.

ROGER GREENSPUN:

A. The artistically elusive nature of the medium has posed special problems for film critics (and created special anxieties), but it's worth remembering the polarization in English studies over the reputation of John Milton not too many years ago. There is a difference in that, whether in or out of favor, Milton remained part of the curriculum. There is no such "curriculum" for films as yet—but there will be, I suspect in less than a dozen years, and that will make for a kind of continuity that you don't see at the present.

All this, of course, has very little to do, with the history of moviemaking, which is—quite properly—more affected by audience taste and technology than by critics' opinions. I should guess that by the turn of the century we'll be seeing movies (somebody will be seeing movies) as a much more cohesive historical endeavour than most people are willing to grant now.

Q. Why do film critics/buffs go after their fellows with such vehemence?

DWIGHT MACDONALD:

A. My objections to some other critics aren't based on personalities, but on profound differences of opinion. They're not critics and represent a whole Philistine trend—the lower middlebrow stuff. I just get angry at their violations of taste and cultural decency.

STUART BYRON:

A. Partly because of the industrial nature of the medium: it costs a lot to make a feature film. Therefore relatively few of them are made, and those few (three hundred to five hundred a year) are seen by many. Argue about a new novel and you're arguing about something read by a few thousand; argue about a film and you're addressing a large common audience which has seen what you're talking about. Also, the art of criticism of film is only a few years old compared to criticism of other arts; therefore positions are just beginning to be assumed. It's the adolescent period in the field, and adolescents, as we all know, argue constantly.

JOHN SIMON:

A. Film is a new art and film criticism an even newer discipline, having as yet no ground rules, canons, traditions, minimum requirements. Film criticism, moreover, is not yet sorted out into upper and lower, like literary criticism, where the same medium and practitioner are unlikely to concern themselves both with James Joyce and Jacqueline Susann. In film criticism, everything is still unstratified, thrown together pell-mell. The film critics for *Hudson Review* and the *New Republic*, for instance, are in the same arena with the reviewers for *Cosmopolitan* and *Cue*. This makes for increased acrimony.

There is also the matter of the dearth of serious and respected film critics; their number is so small that each of them can easily delude himself or herself into believing that uncontested hegemony in the field is only a question of demolishing a few measly rivals. When film criticism becomes more established, widespread and diversified, the individual practitioner will not so readily be tempted by omniscience and omnipotence. Meanwhile the ideological warfare is not necessarily damaging: it makes both film and film criticism more conspicuous—more talked and, possibly, even more thought about—and a more accepted part of the culture. And we know from history that such ideological conflicts as were engendered by the Reformation and Counterreformation, for all their political ferocity, greatly benefited the arts and humanities.

CHARLES THOMAS SAMUELS:

A. Movie critics are at each other's throats for lots of silly reasons— vanity, chief among them. Where they oppose each other because of passionate differences in aesthetics or critical judgment, I think the rivalry is a good thing. In that case, rivalry becomes controversy, which is the main vehicle for arriving at the truth. For me, power is not the issue. I am not trying to grab power from Pauline Kael (which, given my rate and place of publication, would, in any case, be an absurd aim). I am trying, when I attack her, to convince people that her ideas are dangerous. This they are, first of all, because she is a talented and intelligent critic. Being so intelligent, why does she devote herself to convincing her readers that movies should be treated not as if they purported to represent life but rather as a diversion from the fundamental concerns of daily living? I don't want to go on about this subject since I've written about it elsewhere.

STEPHEN FARBER:

A. The first obvious reason for these critical squabbles is ego. Because of their own insecurity, many critics resent the attention that their colleagues are receiving, and want to cut them down to size. However, there is a healthy side to this infighting. Something more than petty jealousy is involved. In a field where so little has been established, many bewildered moviegoers try to make things easier for themselves by aligning themselves with a major critic, whether Kael or Sarris (by far the two most influential) or Crist or Canby or Simon or Kauffmann. In effect they let the critic do the work for them, and they slavishly mimic their mentor's pronouncements. Major critics now have their dutiful disciples—young critics who never deviate from the received opinion of St. Andrew or St. Pauline. One advantage of the constant critical skirmishes is that they may help to discourage a few people from regarding any superstar critic as infallible. I deplore the personal, vicious tone of much of this infighting. But I am in favor of fierce intellectual battles in which critics attack the arguments of their peers with all the reasoning skill at their disposal. Nothing is more dangerous than party-line thinking. Intelligent debate that concentrates on issues rather than on personalities can help keep the lines open.

ANONYMOUS:

A. The contribution of film critics to the hallowed tradition of such invective lies not in making it more personal, but in bringing to it—as to everything else—an increased crudity (with the Simon-Sarris mudslinging in the *New York Times* probably setting a new standard in this which will long endure). Where, anyway, does a critic's personality end and his body of work begin? Admittedly, my last reply to Sarris was nothing but a personal dig (of a kind in which I wouldn't engage in an actual piece); but, then, he asked for it . . . a Stanley-Kauffman-above-the-battle attitude temperamentally doesn't suit me.

JOSEPH McBRIDE:

A. Why are critics so vicious? For some reason, in America at least, critics of movies aren't taken seriously unless they are snotty. This has something to do with the commercialism hang-up. If a critic doesn't look down on the vast majority of movies, he is considered a flack.

Another reason critics are so vicious is that movie buffs tend to be highly neurotic people; *I'm* pretty cuckoo and so are most of the buffs and critics I've met. Books also attract neurotics, but I think it's a more gentle, more passive kind of neuroticism—more withdrawn. Movie freaks tend to be the loud and obnoxious type, and that helps explain why so much criticism is loud and obnoxious. (Perhaps we should clearly differentiate between reviewers and critics; I find it hard to take more than a handful of reviewers seriously. As Walter Kerr put it, a reviewer writes for someone who hasn't seen the work in question, and a critic writes for someone who has. I don't see much point in writing for people who haven't seen the movie, because then you're just writing tout sheets.) Another big hang-up is that critics want personal publicity or notoriety; John Simon the Bad is a perfect example. He put *The Last Picture Show* on his Ten Worst of the Year list simpy because everybody else had it on their Ten Best lists. Since movies are such a popular art, and since so much money is at stake with each film, critics tend to assume a Messiah complex.

RICHARD SCHICKEL:

A. Rivalries exist because in the last decade or so movies have ceased to be a mass art and are an essentially middlebrow art. Critical opinion weighs heavily with this new smaller audience and critics have become demi-celebrities. Careerism is rampant, the audience loves to watch them squabble, defend their turf (and try to expand it). The critics have become as temperamental as a bunch of ham actors and about as tedious in my view. Indeed, I've virtually ceased reading any of them because it appears to me this celebrity tripping has distorted nearly every major critic's perceptions. None of them are just seeing movies and bringing their best intelligence to bear on whatever work is at hand. They're sending private messages back and forth in their columns and, at the same time, playing to the galleries. At the moment the whole business disgusts me. Fortuitously, I am at the moment doing less criticism than I was when *Life* was in business, just enough to keep my hand in. Moreover, I'm *reviewing* briefly (and I hope unpretentiously) for *Time* on an occasional basis, trying as hard as I can to just see the picture and sketch an impression of it— no more than that. Mostly, I find I don't like modern films, which I find almost as self-conscious and self-indulgent as their critics. More and more my work is historical in nature and it is a great relief to mostly leave Kubrick and that bunch to the new critics and the new audience. They all deserve each other and I'm only sorry, as Manny Farber said, at the beginning of this era, that movies aren't movies anymore.

ROGER GREENSPUN:

A. The matter of visibility probably accounts for the profession of vehemence of somebody like John Simon—but Simon, when you stop to think of it, is almost unique. In general, the more intellectual the critic, the more pugnacious he is likely to be. But I've recently come to realize that intellectuals earn at least some of their importance by talking louder (or writing louder) than anyone else, and for them pugnacity must be a matter of style.

The previous statements are not in the least harbingers of harmony. When and if that state comes to pass through the adoption of somewhat common standards and practices, there will be signs. Charles Thomas Samuels will remove the quote marks from "film critic" in reference to Stuart Byron, a buff-protégé of Andrew Sarris (*Modern Occasions*, Spring, 1972). And Sarris won't cite Dwight Macdonald, Stanley Kauffmann and John Simon as "Horsemen of High-Browism," nor Samuels as one of their "stable boys" (the *Village Voice*, January 4, 1973).

1. My Favorite Movies

DWIGHT MACDONALD

Editor Philip Nobile has asked me to write about "My Favorite Movies" and I respond as I did to similar demands in my schooldays for compositions on "How I Spent My Vacation," "Who I Am" and—really fun—"The Adventures of a Penny." I've never been a drop-out.

"Favorite" I take to mean not the movies I'd stamp, objectively, like a cultural customs officer, "Approved for Entry to Posterity." But rather the ones I've enjoyed the most—and still do, after a half-century of experiencing cinema.

The objective-subjective categories should largely overlap, else one becomes uneasy if one is, like me, a central-minded, classicist kind of critic—as against solipsistic romantics like Parker Tyler, Jonas Mekas (really a fan not a critic) or the early Andrew Sarris, before he kicked that *politique-des-auteurs* monkey off his back. In theory the coincidence should be 100 percent, but in practice I'd find this suspicious: either a computer programmed to reflect the taste consensus of the historical present (which may be very objective but isn't very conclusive, historically) or else the reactions of Pangloss types like Arthur Knight, Richard Roud and his Lincoln

13

Center press-gang, who are self-programmed to appreciate every-thing that's going—at the trendy moment.

My own objective-subjective coincidence is, right now, only about 75 percent because of idiosyncratic allergies to Dreyer (especially that silent "classic" which still turns up on "ten-best-of-all-time" lists, *The Passion of Joan of Arc*—pretentious kitsch, manneristic and sentimental—which I saw through forty years ago), Bresson (except for *Les Dames du Bois de Boulogne*), Godard (except for *Breathless* and *Weekend*, all of Visconti (especially *La Terra Trema*), the portentous aspect of Bergman (especially *The Seventh Seal, Winter Light* and *Persona*) and most of the Weimar-silent Germans.

All art is enjoyable, though all that is enjoyable isn't art (law of the excluded middle). Unenjoyable movies are not art but either (a) fodder for Ph.D theses, or (b) excuses for arcane invocations by *Cahiers de Cinéma* hierophants, or (c) occasions for respectful and uncomprehending (and nonenjoying) awe by culturally de-prived masses trying to "better themselves" by following not their own tastes but those imposed on them by the critical establishment —or rather by what they take for such.[1]

While, as noted, one characteristic of a work of art (not the only one) is that it gives pleasure, the degree of pleasure varies with the historical moment—and with the individual. The Philistines say "It's

[1] Like the millions of New Yorkers who, a few years ago, patiently stood in line at the Metropolitan to glimpse (three seconds full view, then "Move along, please!") a painting whose frame is greater than its quality. A great many Re-naissance works are more important—and more interesting—than Da Vinci's *Mona Lisa*. But she's had the publicity breaks, beginning in 1873 when she was known as *La Gioconda* and Walter Pater, of all unlikely pitchmen, wrote his famous love letter: "She is older than the rocks among which she sits; like the vampire, she has been dead many times and learned the secrets of the grave; and has been a diver in deep seas and keeps their fallen day about her; and trafficked for strange webs with Eastern merchants; and, as Leda, was the mother of Helen of Troy, and, as Saint Anne, the mother of Mary...." Quite a heavy charge to lay on one small portrait—no wonder she's smiling ambiguously. I suppose it meant something to the more intense among Victorian aesthetes, and the message seems to have survived to our day—a little pot would make it perfectly clear. To me it means what the editor of *Captain Billy's Whizz-Bang*, a twenties precursor of *Mad*, meant when he subtitled his journal: *An Explosion of Pedigreed Bull*. It also recalls Truffaut on Hitchcock and the vaticinations of his *Cahiers* colleagues on Robert Aldrich, Nicholas Ray and Joseph Losey. But it's undeniably the stuff for the troops, midcult division, The Big M, as those lines at the Met and Lincoln Center demonstrate.

just a matter of taste" (though why "just"?), and they've been saying it a long time. Like the poor, the Philistines are always with us. *De gustibus non est disputandum* is how their Roman soul-brothers put it, and there's doubtless an earlier Sanskrit, if not Cro-Magnon, saw to that effect. But actually it is precisely tastes that can be, should be and in fact are argued about—endlessly. Indeed, tastes are about all that *can* be disputed profitably. An argument about facts is a waste of time, also a contradiction in terms, since once the facts have been established—which is a matter of research, not argumentation—both sides must accept them, and the dispute degenerates into compulsory agreement. Art and morals, aesthetics and ethics—these are the two areas where subjective value judgments cannot be reduced to objective scientific agreement, hence the areas in which the disputants can and must deploy imagination, sensibility, wit, logic, rhetoric and the other imponderables that make a discussion interesting and sometimes even useful.

Not the least important job of a critic is to demonstrate how absurd (if he's in a genial mood, how pathetically misguided) are all value judgments than run contrary to his own. A critic's success is measured by his ability to convince his readers (by reasoning, persuasion, knowledge of the field and *explication du texte*) that tastes *can* be disputed and that he's the boyo to do it. Bernard Shaw was very good at it, which is why his dramatic and musical criticism can still be read with profit—and pleasure—a century after he dashed off his reviews of long-forgotten plays and concerts for long-forgotten London weeklies like *The Star, The World* and *The Saturday Review*. (His successor as drama critic on the last was Max Beerbohm, who wasn't bad at it either.)

The ultimate confoundment of the *non-est-disputandum* untruism comes when, after a period of arguing about taste (it used to take a century or two, but our modern tempo is closer to fifty years), everybody, *including the Philistines,* arrives at pretty much the same consensus. Goethe wasn't the only critic of his day who seriously compared the *Waverly Novels* with Shakespeare. And the tough-minded Byron could write in *Don Juan,* the masterpiece of his maturity: "Scott, Rogers, Campbell, Moore and Crabbe will try/ 'Gainst you the question with posterity." The "you" was one-third Southey—who proved to be as spavined an entry in the posterity sweepstakes as Scott, Rogers et al—but the other two-thirds were Wordsworth and Coleridge, who didn't. So, who knows, maybe I'll be proved right—around, say 2001—about Bresson, Godard, Dreyer et al. Stranger things have happened in the history of taste. I'll bet there were a few seventeenth-century wisenheimers who ventured to argue—just among friends, of course; they weren't about to make fools of themselves in public—that Abraham Cowley just might not be as great a poet as that crude, old-fashioned Shakespeare, and maybe not even as good as Cowley's then neck-and-neck contemporary rival, John Milton.

In cinema, a peculiar new twentieth-century art whose history is typically speeded up until its "periods" cover not centuries but decades; an art whose basic vocabulary, uniquely in cultural history, was invented by one man, D. W. Griffith, in a couple of years, 1908-1910—it's actually younger than I am—in such an art, critical judgments are more problematical than in the more leisurely development of the traditional arts. Cinécritiques are provisional, horseback judgments—and a bucking bronco at that!

Thus in 1952, 1962 and 1972, the British Film Institute asked critics throughout the world to list the ten movies they considered the greatest of all time. Only three appear in all three lists—that is, survived for twenty years; two others on the first list lasted till the second and then were dropped; the remaining seven on the 1952 list (ties brought the number to twelve) didn't last even ten years. (See Appendix at the end of this chapter for these lists plus comments.) Marshy ground on which to erect final, definitive, "objective" judgments.[2]

[2] I myself kept insisting in the thirties and forties, for example, that the addition of sound was an aesthetic disaster because it made montage technically difficult and also seduced directors back into theatrical realism. My assumption was that montage was "the" structural basis of all "true" cinema. I had a point: in the first twenty years after sound was added, cinema in general was aesthetically regressive, less creative and less interesting. (Though I would have given more credit to exceptions like Clair, Vigo, Renoir and Welles had I not been blinded by my preconceptions—or, more bluntly, prejudices.) Then Bergman, Kurosawa, Antonioni, Fellini, Resnais and Truffaut came along and taught me what I should have known: that there is no one "true" kind of cinema or any other art, and no "the" principle but only various "a" principles. They used montage sparingly, if at all, and yet created movies I had to admit—was glad to admit, I've always rolled with the experimental punch in aesthetics as in politics—again achieved the heights of what I call the "Silent Classic" period. Like the earlier Renaissance, this one built on and was stimulated by a rediscovery of the classical past.

DWIGHT MACDONALD

So I think the subjective category, "favorite," is more useful—
and certainly more interesting—than the objective "best" in dealing
with such a fast-moving, chancey, Protean art.

Let me begin by setting down the movies I remember as of now
(October 5, 1972) as the most enjoyable during the half-century
I've been looking at and writing about films. My criterion is that I'd
like to see them again tomorrow (October 6), not for reasons of
historical instruction or critical duty, but simply for my own self-ish
pleasure. They are given in chronological order (an asterisk indicates my favorite favorites).

*Griffith *The Birth of a Nation* (1914). (Second feature: *Intolerance,*
1916)

Chaplin-Sennett: the early two-reelers (1915-1918) such as *The
Tramp, The Pilgrim, The Immigrant, Easy Street, The Pawnshop,
One A.M., Charlie at the Show* and *Shoulder Arms*

*Wiene-Zuckmayer-Janowitz: *The Cabinet of Dr. Caligari* (1919)

*Keaton: *Sherlock, Jr.* (1924). (Second feature: *The General,* 1926)

*Eisenstein: *Ten Days That Shook the World* (1927). (Second feature: *Potemkin,* 1925)

Pudovkin: *The End of St. Petersburg* (1927). (Second feature:
Storm Over Asia, 1928)

Vigo: *Zéro De Conduite* (1932)

Wellman: *The Public Enemy* (1931)

*Lubitsch: *Trouble in Paradise* (1932)

Riefenstahl: *Triumph of the Will* (1934). (Second feature: *Olympiad,* 1936)

*Renoir: *La Grande Illusion* (1937). (Second feature: *Rules of the
Game,* 1939)

Donskoi: *The Childhood of Maxim Gorki* (1938)

Hawks: *Bringing Up Baby* (1938)

*Huston: *The Maltese Falcon* (1941)

*Welles: *Citizen Kane* (1941). (Second feature: *The Magnificent
Ambersons,* 1942)

*Carné: *Children of Paradise* (1944)

Cocteau: *Beauty and the Beast* (1945)

*Ophuls: *La Ronde* (1950)

*Ozu: *Tokyo Story* (1953)

Kurosawa: *The Seven Samurai* (1954). (Second feature: *Rashomon,*
1950)

My Favorite Movies   **17**

*Bergman: *The Naked Night* (1954).[3] (Second feature: *Wild Strawberries,* 1958)

*Antonioni: *L'Avventura* (1959). (Second feature: *Le Amiche,* 1955)

  Buñuel: *Viridiana* (1961). (Second feature: *L'Age d'Or,* 1931)

*Renais-Robbe Grillet: *Last Year at Marienbad* (1961)

  Truffaut: *Jules et Jim* (1961)

*Fellini: *8½* (1963). (Second feature: *Nights of Cabiria,* 1957)

  Monicelli: *The Organizer* (1964). (Second feature: *Big Deal on Madonna Street,* 1961)[4]

A few personal remarks on the above list:

1. I'm interested to find almost half (eleven) are in the early-sound period of the thirties and forties that I tirelessly attacked at the time (on theoretical principles, or prejudices, as explained in footnote 3) as a decadent comedown from the classic-silent period (only six titles from that now).

2. The only movie on the list that I saw after I gave up my monthly *Esquire* reviews in 1966 is *Tokyo Story.* Granted I didn't see as many after 1966 (to put it mildly—one reason I gave up the column was I saw so few good ones after 1964). But I have caught some of the more highly praised by my ex-colleagues, post-1966 pictures such as *A Clockwork Orange, Midnight Cowboy, The Graduate, Fellini Satiricon, Roma* (also by Fellini), *Joe, Klute, Mr. McCabe and Mrs. Miller, Persona, The Last Picture Show* and

---

[3] Also known as *Sawdust and Tinsel,* and best and most literal title, *The Clown's Evening.*

[4] The reader may be disturbed, as I am, to find the above list contains not twenty-five but twenty-seven titles. Twenty-seven is not the kind of number one expects in such lists, for some instinctual reason. Messy, somehow. "My ten favorites," OK; "my twenty-five," OK; but not "my nine" or "my twenty-seven." Actually I aimed at ten originally, but this proved too cramping for my anarcho-catholic tastes. I kept thinking of more and more films I couldn't bear to omit, and so I edged it up to a conventional twenty-five, which I reached four days ago. But tonight (October 10) as I retype the piece, I thought of two more movies, *The End of St. Petersburg* and *Zéro de Conduite,* that I would like to re-experience tomorrow as much as and possibly more than—discrimination gets tricky and a bit absurd when you get down to such fine calibrations—two already on my October 5 list: *Public Enemy* and *Beauty and the Beast.* What to do? Omit and substitute to retain that instinctually neat twenty-five? Or shove them in for an untidy bulging twenty-seven that would better reflect my taste as of the moment (which is by now 3:30 A.M., October 11)? As always, I chose truth over order. Revisions could go on forever, of course, but time must have a stop and even the weariest article winds somewhere safe to a deadline.

DWIGHT MACDONALD

Frenzy (none of which I liked much and most of which I disliked very much). I also saw some I liked, but not enough to put them on the list: *Bonnie and Clyde, Rosemary's Baby, Blow-Up* (what a relief to get away from The Miseries of Monica!), *The Year of the Pig, The Sorrow and the Pity, 2001, Clowns, The Garden of the Finzi-Continis* and *Play It Again, Sam.*[5]

3. My tastes have changed over fifty years—and, I hope, are still changing.

I don't admire Stroheim as much as I used to. *The Wedding March*, which I rhapsodized over in 1933 ("as vast in emotional scope as *The Birth of a Nation* is vast in physical scope"—I was only twenty-seven, your honor) looked like a ghost in 1966, a slow-moving and tediously insistent wraith. *Greed* was still impressive on a second viewing in 1962—impressive by sheer brute accumulation of realistic detail, like a Dreiser novel, slow but sure, and with unexpected outbursts of high baroque fantasy. But while I'd put it on my All-Time Ten-Greatest List, I don't want to re-view it tomorrow.

Von Sternberg now seems not the master he once did. *The Blue Angel* was actively depressing on a re-viewing two years ago, its naturalism striking me as both meanly antihuman and melodramatically exaggerated, Zola-cum-showbiz. *Underworld* is no longer "high-powered" but rather "low-geared," though it may well be, as I put it in 1933, "the ancestor of all gangster films"—an example of a historically important pioneer breakthrough which looks faded later on—more recent examples are *Breathless* and *Hiroshima, Mon Amour*. (Kyd's *Spanish Tragedy* is, after all, the "ancestor" of the Elizabethan drama.) Only *Docks of New York* has lasted, for me, as a *tour de force* of lighting and camera angles that still works in a narrowly stylized way. As for those later Dietrich visual orgies: Marlene was as fatal to Sternberg's development as Monica was to Antonioni's.

Cocteau's *Blood of a Poet* I thought major when I first saw it in the early thirties and at several re-viewings later. I compared it to Eisenstein because of its exuberant use of montage, and I had a point; what I overlooked, and what only became clear to me re-

[5] For explications on these recent film-viewing experiences, plus other excursions, see Tony Macklin's interview with me in the Spring 1972 *Film Heritage*.

cently, is that Eisenstein used technique to make serious statements about large subjects, while Cocteau was just self-indulgently fooling around about campy trivia. When I screened it four years ago at the University of California (Santa Cruz), I had a drastic reversal of taste: it looked withered, empty, pretentious, dated and in general phony-avant-gardist. I had to apologize to the class.

On the other hand, Buñuel's *L'Age d'Or,* an avant-garde film of the same period but a genuine one, repelled me so much when the New York Film Society—which I'd helped found—insisted on showing it in 1931, that I resigned as treasurer. I thought at the time my objections were aesthetic, but I now believe they were moralistic. *L'Age d'Or* now fascinates me. Nor does its cynical brutality bother me, maybe because I've become less priggish, certainly because it's mild stuff compared to what one endures in rear-guard movies today.

My greatest reversal of taste has been about *Caligari*. In the twenties, when I lusted after the *plein air*, socially exciting and dynamically montaged Griffith-Eisenstein cinema, I despised *Caligari* as static, claustrophobic, artificial, "uncinematic" and perversely manneristic—all of which it was, and is. The difference was there all right, but my value judgment was too narrow, aesthetically and ideologically. After re-viewing *Caligari* a half-dozen times since then, I have gradually come to delight in it as one of the few perfect works of art the cinema has produced—perfect in its own terms, that is to say, which are almost a hundred percent antithetical to almost every theory of the "real" or "true" nature of cinema.[6] My recent interest in Poe may also be involved—Poe's ghost created *Caligari* via demoniac possession of those three Germans who were unable to make another significant movie once the spirit of Israfel had departed from them. It's interesting that the young nowadays also seem to dig *Caligari,* despite its art-for-art's-sake expressionistic "irrelevance." Perhaps, like cattle needing salt, they feel a craving for the irrelevant in this all too socially serious time. Or perhaps, on the contrary, its mood of irrational, sinister, authoritarian menace in "extreme situations" has now become "relevant" for them in the age of Vietnam, Bangladesh, Uganda, Ulster and our own little domestic horrors like Kent State and the oratory of Spiro Agnew. (They also

[6] For details, see *Dwight Macdonald on Movies* (New York: Berkeley Pub., Medallion Books [paperback], 1971), pp. 19–20.

DWIGHT MACDONALD

dig Poe, as I've discovered from teaching courses in him lately.) Whichever the reason—it's probably an unstable mixture of both; contradictions don't bother the young, or life—they do seem to take to *Caligari*. When I polled the 250-odd students in a history-of-cinema course I gave two years ago at the University of Wisconsin (Milwaukee) as to the "most liked" movie in the course, I was pleasantly surprised that *Caligari* came in fourth, after *Sherlock, Jr., Children of Paradise* and *Kane*, but ahead of *Jules and Jim, Birth of a Nation, Potemkin* and *Rules of the Game*.

If I had to choose one favorite movie of all time, I'd pick Fellini's *8½*. It's not, of course, "better" than the other twenty-six—it's idle to talk about "better" or "worse" when you're considering great works of art: is Titian "better" than Veronese? Mozart than Beethoven? Tolstoy than Jane Austen? I'd guess that *8½* is my favoritest favorite because I'm a critic and I found more to say about it than any of the others. Also, again as a critic, I was amazed to find that many of my colleagues, including several I respect, were either contemptuous or (at best) condescending about *8½*. This led me to examine my own critical values *re* cinema and to become conscious of what they are—personally.

Let me conclude with some excerpts from my review, "*8½*, Fellini's Obvious Masterpiece," in the January, 1964, *Esquire*:

This portrait of the artist as a middle-aged man is the most brilliant, varied and entertaining movie I've seen since *Citizen Kane*. I saw it twice in as many weeks, and the second time I discovered many points that had escaped me in the first viewing, so headlong is its tempo, so fertile its invention. A great deal is packed into every scene, as in *Kane:* of well-observed detail; of visual pleasure; of fine acting in minor roles (Guido Alberti's The Producer, Edra's La Saraghina, Madeleine Lebeau's Actress). And finally, like *Kane*, it deals with topics like art, society, sex, money, aging, pretense and hypocrisy—all that Trollope wrote about in *The Way We Live Now* —just the opposite of these cautious little (though not short) art films that lingeringly explore some tiny area of impingement between three undefined characters or, if the director feels in an epic mood, four.

The action, or Argument, is as simple as its development is complex. Guido (played by Marcello Mastroianni with style, humor and delicacy) is a famous director who has retreated to an Italian seaside health resort to avoid a breakdown and to finish the script of a spectacular of stupefying banality about the flight to another planet of the survivors of a nuclear war. The script is long overdue. A huge Canaveral-type launching tower has been erected on the beach—it cost a real $140,000 in the real film, we are told by the Joseph E. Levine handout which is also real, relatively. Cast, producer, technicians, everybody is waiting around while costs tick along like a taxi meter as Guido tries to break through his Creative Block, and meanwhile to placate and if possible evade their persistent demands. His mistress arrives (a full-bodied, empty-headed soubrette right out of a Franz Lehar operetta—really wonderful performance by Sandra Milo) and is presently followed by his wife (Anouk Aimée manages to look astringent and attractive simultaneously), necessitating another series of evasions and placations that are all the more difficult because his relation to each is unsatisfactory since he is still, in middle age, trying to square the sexual circle: to possess without being possessed, to take without giving. His personal and professional lives are thus speeding toward catastrophe on parallel tracks. It happens. Mistress and wife finally clash in a scene of irretrievable social horror. The movie comes to a smash at a huge publicity party the producer gives to force Guido's hand. Badgered by questions he can't answer, since the script is hardly begun, Guido crawls under a buffet table and shoots himself. He springs back to life at once and begins to solve all his problems, emotional as well as cinematic, in a happy ending that has been widely deplored.

There are three kinds of reality in *8½*, and the film proceeds with constant shifting of gears between them. (Like *Marienbad*, but a secular version of that hieratic mystery: quick, humorous, jazzy, direct—you always know what gear you're in.) There is Guido's real present, as outlined above. There are his memories of his boyhood and of his dead parents. And there are his Walter Mitty daydreams of a harmonious realm of *luxe, calme et volupté* in which all his problems are magically solved: the artist's world of creative fantasy. Its symbol is a beautiful young girl in white who keeps

D W I G H T   M A C D O N A L D

materializing and fading away throughout the film, and seems to be a kind of Muse. After his wife and his mistress have disastrously collided, Guido leans back in his café chair, closes his eyes (behind dark glasses), and revises the scene so that the wife compliments the mistress on her dress, and the two are presently waltzing together; since this works so well, Guido's editing goes all the way, and we have the lovely, and witty, harem fantasy, which poeticizes Freudian ideas about sex and libido even as it parodies them.

I hazard that *8½* is Fellini's masterpiece because it is about the two subjects he knows the most about: (a) himself and (b) the making of movies. He doesn't have to labor his points, he can move around freely with the ease of a man walking about his own home. And so much can be suggested in so little footage! That tall, aristocratic blonde, for instance, Guido glimpses several times in the hotel. She fascinates him because she looks like the heroine of an international spy thriller; he never meets her (the closest he comes is to put her into his dream harem), but he does overhear her end of a long-distance telephone conversation, which sounds like a bad movie script and which vastly intrigues him. Several kinds of parody are intertwined in this tiny episode: of movie clichés, of Guido's romantic eroticism and—a feedback—of a man whose job it is to fabricate these glamorous stereotypes himself falling for them. Successful parody is possible only when the parodist feels "at home with" (significant phrase) his subject. This familiarity also means that Fellini is able to keep *8½* right down to earth, so that what might have been one more labored exercise in fantasy—like De Sica's *Miracle in Milan*—is spontaneous, lifelike and often very funny. I think Fellini has become the greatest master of social comedy since Lubitsch.

8½ takes us further inside the peculiar world of moviemaking than any other film I know. I once asked the Argentine director, Torre Nilsson, why important movie directors seem to lose their creative powers so much more often—and completely—than major artists in other fields. (I was thinking of Welles and Hitchcock.) He replied: "In movies, once you make a success, you become public property; you are overwhelmed with fame, money, women, admirers, promoters, and you can never get away from it. A painter or writer or composer creates by himself, but directors have to have hundreds of other people around all the time. So they burn themselves out early." When I saw 8½, I saw what he meant. Guido is distracted in the literal sense: "to divide [the mind, attention, etc.] between objects." They're all here: the highbrow journalist who asks about his philosophy, and also the lowbrow one—"Couldn't you tell me something about your love life?"; the producer who bullies him about the production schedule and the accountants who nag him about costs; the property man who begs Guido to take on as extras his giggling teenage "nieces"; the playboy who wants him to sit up all night drinking; the man who waylays him in the lobby, waving a script: "It shows the necessity of universal disarmament; only a man of your courage and integrity could do it"; the press agents and tourists and mistresses. All there, and each wants a slice of him.

Because it is technically sophisticated, and because it deals with major areas of experience, these critics[7] look for philosophical depths in a movie which is superficial—I think deliberately—in every way except as a work of art. They call Fellini a phony for not delivering the goods, but I don't see his signature on their bill of lading. On the contrary, some of the best comedy in his film is provided by intellectuals: the affected young beauty who has written a treatise on "The Solitude of Modern Man in the Contemporary Theater"; the highbrow British reporter who pesters Guido with questions like, "Is it that you cannot communicate? Or is that merely a mask?" And above all the collaborator who has been assigned to help Guido complete his script—an eye-glassed, beak-nosed superintellectual whose lean face is fixed in lines of alert, sour suspicion. This personage—listed in the cast credits as The Writer, and played with waspish authority by Jean Rougeul—is endlessly articulate about the script; it's narcissistic ("Just another film about your childhood"), romantic, pretentious, tasteless, and mindless: "Your main problem is the film lacks ideas, it has no philosophical base. It's merely a series of senseless episodes . . . It has none of the merits of the avant-garde film and all the drawbacks." How can

[7] That is, the highbrow critics of *Hudson Review, The New Statesman, Sight and Sound*—and, alas, John Simon in *The New Leader*—as versus the midbrows in the daily and weekly press who shared my admiration of 8½.

DWIGHT MACDONALD

a director make more explicit his rationale? Life imitated art, as elsewhere in this strange film[8] and the actual highbrow critics reacted to *8½* much as The Writer did to Guido's script. For the "serious" critics have by now become habituated to profound, difficult films that must be "interpreted" from the language of art (what's on the screen) into the language of philosophy (what what's on the screen "really means"). It began with Bergman (whom I've always thought strongest at his shallowest) and reached a comic climax in the recent efforts of Franco-American *auteur* critics to read Hitchcock's *The Birds* as a morality play about Modern Civilization.

The off-putting quality of *8½* for all but the less intellectualized critics (and the public) is that it is nothing but a pleasurable work of art which might have been directed by Mozart—and there were no doubt pundits in his day who deplored the frivolous way he played around with Masonic symbolism in *The Magic Flute*. It is a worldly film, all on the surface: humorous, rhetorical, sensuous, lyrical, witty, satiric, full of sharply realistic detail and also of fantastic scenes like the great one in the steam bath. This is perhaps the difficulty; nothing for the interpretative tooth to mumble, no Antonionian *angst*, no Bergmanesque Godhead, no Truffaut-style existential Absurd to perplex us. Like baroque art, of which it is a belated golden ray, *8½* is complicated but not obscure. It is more Handel than Beethoven—objective and classical in spirit as against the romantic subjectivism we are accustomed to. It's all there, right on the surface, like a Veronese or a Tiepolo.

One could drop still another name, the greatest of all. Is there not something Shakespearean in this range of human experience expressed in every mode from high lyric to low comic, from the most formal rhetoric to the most personal impressionism? And don't the critics remind one of those all-too-serious students who

[8] "Fellini found himself embarked, with costly sets built and stars under contract, on a kind of explanatory sequel to *La Dolce Vita*," reports *The New Statesman*. When he found this didn't work, he did what Guido did—switched to a film about himself, that is, about a famous director who finds himself blocked on a film. Reality came as close to overwhelming Fellini as it did Guido. According to *Sight and Sound*: "Two weeks before *8½* opened in Rome he still hadn't made up his mind how to end it."

try to discover "Shakespeare's philosophy" and always fail because Shakespeare hadn't any; his "ideas" were all *ad hoc;* their function was to solve dramatic rather than philosophical problems.

Finally, in *8½* Fellini steals from everybody, just like Shakespeare. "Theft" on this scale becomes synthesis: *8½* is an epitome of the history of cinema. His thefts are creative because they are really borrowings, which are returned with his fingerprints all over them. The childhood episodes are Bergmanesque chiaroscuro, as the great scene on the beach when La Saraghina dances for the schoolboys, which echoes, right down to the brutal beat of the music, an even greater beach scene, that between the soldiers and the clown's wife at the beginning of *Naked Night:* but this is a Latin Bergman, sensuous and dramatic and in no way "profound." When Guido and his wife quarrel in the hotel bedroom, the bleak failure to make contact (and the austere photography) recall Antonioni, but *this* alienated couple don't suffer in silence, they yell at each other. The early scene in the rest-cure garden is full of heroic close-ups à la Eisenstein, but they are used (like "The Ride of the Valkyries" thundered out by the hotel band) for satiric counterpoint to the aging, prosaic faces of the invalids. The general structure—a montage of tenses, a mosaic of time blocks—recalls *Intolerance, Kane* and *Marienbad,* but in Fellini's hands it becomes clear, light, fluid and superficial. An obvious masterpiece.

APPENDIX: THE BRITISH FILM INSTITUTE POLLS OF CRITICS ON GREATEST MOVIES [9]

1952	1962	1972
De Sica: *The Bicycle Thief*	Welles: *Citizen Kane*	Welles: *Citizen Kane*
Chaplin: *City Lights*	Antonioni: *L'Avventura.*	Renoir: *Rules of the Game*
Chaplin: *The Gold Rush*	Renoir: *Rules of the Game*	Eisenstein: *Potemkin*
Eisenstein: *Potemkin*	Stroheim: *Greed*	Fellini: *8½*
Flaherty: *Louisiana Story*	Mizoguchi: *Ugetsu*	Antonioni: *L'Avventura*
Griffith: *Intolerance*	De Sica: *The Bicycle Thief*	Bergman: *Persona*
Stroheim: *Greed*	Eisenstein: *Potemkin*	Dreyer: *The Passion of Joan of Arc*
Carné: *Le Jour se Lève*	Eisenstein: *Ivan the*	Keaton: *The General*

[9] Films are listed in order of popularity.

DWIGHT MACDONALD

Dreyer: *The Passion of Joan of Arc*
Renoir: *Rules of the Game*
Lean: *Brief Encounter*
Clair: *Le Million*

Terrible
Visconti: *La Terra Trema*
Vigo: *L'Atalante*
Resnais: *Hiroshima, Mon Amour*
Vigo: *Zéro de Conduite*

Welles: *The Magnificent Ambersons*
Mizoguchi: *Ugetsu*
Bergman: *Wild Strawberries*

These lists reveal several things about the evanescence and trickiness of critical evaluation of cinematic art: (a) the changes in taste are rapid; (b) they show curious, and indeed inexplicable, time lags; and (c) they are often hard to justify by any reasonable standards. A general explanation might be that "problematical, raw, provisional, horseback" quality I've noted above, which makes for a trendy confusion in judgment.

1. *Rapidity of Change:* Of the 1952 dozen only three last through 1972 (twenty years): *Potemkin, The Passion of Joan of Arc* (ugh!) and *Rules of the Game*. Two last ten years: *Greed* and *The Bicycle Thief*. The other seven don't even make it to 1962. Of the 1962 list, three new titles are repeated in 1972: *Citizen Kane, L'Avventura* and *Ugetsu*, and five new titles are not. Of the twenty-four titles on the 1952 and 1962 lists, exactly half are one-shot pan flashes that don't last even a decade.

2. *Time Lag:* How come *Kane* (1941) didn't make it till 1962—and then was Number 1, as it was in 1972? And *Ambersons* (1942) only made it thirty years later. Some strange lemming migration must have set in belatedly—though with a benign outcome—but why? And why no Bergman until 1972, two decades after he began, and then *two* titles? True, *Persona* is recent, but *Wild Strawberries* dates from 1958. That Chaplin had two titles in 1952 and none afterwards, while Keaton first made it in 1972, shows a shift of opinion I've observed lately—and high time. But why did it take them forty years to catch up with Buster? And why does Vigo suddenly pop up with two titles in 1962—*Zéro de Conduite* (1933) and *L'Atalante* (1934)—and then pop down by 1972? Such changes in cinematic taste are as mysterious as the "Brownian movement" in physics: "the random motion of microscopic particles"—i.e., movie critics.

3. *Impenetrability:* It is hard for me, at least, and by now I suspect for most of us—to explain why, in the 1952 list, De Sica's charming but slight *Bicycle Thief* was Number 1—it had dropped to Number 6 by 1962 but still inexplicably clung on—while Rosselini's *Open City* and *Paisan,* the peaks of the Italian neorealist school, were passed over? (Rosselini has never made it, despite his important later films.) Or why they chose Carné's minor, and now forgotten, *Le Jour se Lève* over his masterpiece, *Children of Paradise*? Or why they chose Lean's *Brief Encounter* or Flaherty's *Louisiana Story* at all—or, in 1962, Visconti's *La Terra Trema*? By 1972 taste seems to be settling: there are no obvious duds, they've gotten onto Keaton and Bergman at last, and *8½* is Number 4.

4. My own "objective" choices as of 1972 for Twelve Greatest Movies of All Time would include four of theirs: *Kane, L'Avventura, 8½* and *Greed.* I would add: *Birth of a Nation, Caligari, Sherlock, Jr., Ten Days, Children of Paradise, Naked Night, Grande Illusion* and *Tokyo Story.*

2. Favorite Directors*

PETER BOGDANOVICH

A FEW MONTHS AGO, the British film quarterly, *Sight and Sound,* wrote me (and a hundred others), asking us to name our ten favorite movies. Caught in a perverse mood, I rattled off (in chronological order) the first ten that came to mind: *Young Mr. Lincoln* (John Ford), *Only Angels Have Wings* (Howard Hawks), *The Magnificent Ambersons* (Orson Welles), *Red River* (Hawks), *She Wore a Yellow Ribbon* (Ford), *The Searchers* (Ford), *Touch of Evil* (Welles), *Vertigo* (Alfred Hitchcock), *Rio Bravo* (Hawks), *North by Northwest* (Hitchcock). I acknowledged the absurdity of the list in an accompanying note which explained that on a different day, in another mood, the list might be altogether changed, though the four directors represented would no doubt remain constant.

But I've been thinking about it since then, and I'm a little ashamed of the list now just because it is so impulsive and such a lack of a sense of history is evident. How can one have a ten-favorite list—which automatically, no matter how loud one's protestations

* Reprinted by permission of *Esquire Magazine* © 1972 by Esquire, Inc.

to the contrary, translates into a "ten best" list—and ignore D. W. Griffith or Buster Keaton or Jean Renoir or Charlie Chaplin or Ernst Lubitsch or Fritz Lang? Not to mention Josef von Sternberg, Kenji Mizoguchi, Max Ophuls and F. W. Murnau. Picking one's ten favorite directors is hard enough, but then figuring out their best films is almost impossible. How to choose, for example, between Hawks in his *Bringing Up Baby* mood or Hawks in his *Only Angels Have Wings* mood? A dumb charade, at best. But like researchers for Guinness' *Book of Records,* people are always after superlatives.

Actually, I don't have favorite movies as much as favorite directors—men whose company I enjoy—and I can claim no consistency in these choices. Why does one feel like hearing Beethoven one day and Mozart the next, or Cole Porter in the afternoon and Hank Williams at night? I've seen about six thousand movies and I have a large fund of happy memories—many of which I like to recapture. Generally, my affection for a director goes through a very hot period, during which I try to see everything he's made—and, if I like the sum total, he joins a group of people to whom I return with affection.

I would admit a preference for English-language films. First of all, I hate reading subtitles; their intrusion makes it awfully hard to achieve the sort of direct impact with which movies are at their greatest. I also prefer talkies to silents (except the silent comedies) because of the intrusion of titles which usually only reduce the meaning of the images rather than enhance them. This may seem Philistine on my part, but it is a fact I'm afraid I have to live with. Nevertheless, since so much of everything in life is a contradiction, some of my most treasured memories are of silent films like *The Birth of a Nation* and Chaplin's *The Kid,* Keaton's *The Navigator* and *The General,* and Harold Lloyd's *The Freshman.* I remember seeing these and many others with my father, who took me often to the afternoon show at the Museum of Modern Art, where we sat with a wonderful feeling of seclusion—the subways that occasionally rattled by below us the only reminder of the outside world, which seemed so remote at those precious times. The world on the screen was more removed from reality than anything the talkies achieved —it was both more realistic and less too—a strange combination. I suppose the great silent films created a universe of their own that

PETER BOGDANOVICH

was more pervasive and haunting *because* of the missing element of talk.

They weren't really silent, since Mr. Arthur Kleiner supplied wonderful piano accompaniment—originally the films had had orchestras or organs to go with them—but the impact of the work relied on the power of the image, and this created a universal language which was wiped out by the addition of sound in the late twenties. I don't remember ever feeling as much at peace with pictures as when I saw those silents I grew to love. Perhaps it was with the sense of innocence they preserved, but I think it has something to do with the medium—which was less bombastic and more profoundly poetic than the talkies. Still today the great sound films are remembered, with few exceptions, for those elements that recall the almost mystical power of the silent screen—when the image was the beginning and the end.

I was not a child of the silents, though, which may explain my acquired fondness for them as well as my impatience with all but the best. On the contrary, as a kid I was more a fan of radio, though that medium died on me around the time I began my adolescence. But childhood memories are much more mixed up with "The Shadow" and "The Lone Ranger" and "Sky King" and Edgar Bergen and "Suspense" and Fred Allen and "The Great Gildersleeve" and "Gangbusters" than with the movies. Not that I didn't go to them a lot. In fact, I wanted very much to be movie star. I think I evolved from wanting to be either Douglas Fairbanks, Jr., or Errol Flynn when I was eight through Richard Widmark, William Holden, Gene Kelly, Jerry Lewis to Marlon Brando when I was thirteen. (I remember acting out at home, in strenuous detail, the essence of *Sinbad the Sailor,* and *The Adventures of Robin Hood* and *Kiss of Death* and *Take Me Out to the Ball Game.*) I know I always wanted to *look* like Holden, and wished my name were Jim—I don't think I could ever decide on a properly Anglo-Saxon last name, though I remember my dear father's distress when I announced around the age of twelve that I was going to shorten the one I've got to an ambiguous Bogdane. Can't recall whether it was to be James or Peter. That didn't really matter as much since in school everyone called me Bugs, because of a popular imitation I did of Bugs Bunny; as I grew older, the impersonations expanded and my nickname alternated between things like Dino, Jerry and Marlon. (My father's favorite name for me, when I was being particularly unpleasant, was Harry Fabian, a fairly scabrous character Widmark played in *Night and the City*.)

My favorite movies as a child had been *Red River, She Wore a Yellow Ribbon* and *The Ghost Goes West* (René Clair). I saw each of them numerous times, but never was really aware of who directed them, nor, in fact, that such a person was necessary. Orson Welles changed all that. I didn't see *Citizen Kane* until it was fourteen years old and I was sixteen, but it was the first time I remember consciously realizing that an overwhelming presence was possible to exist *behind* the camera. I'd thought vaguely about directing before that, but now it became a conscious ambition. I would guess Orson has been a similar inspiration to more people than any other director since D. W. Griffith.

Certainly he would have to be represented on any top-ten list of films, but I'd have a lot of trouble deciding which pictures. I like several of them even better than *Kane—The Magnificent Ambersons,* flawed as it is by the recutting of the studio, is an even more daring and imaginative work; it is also much less self-conscious and, I believe, truer to Orson's real personality. *Touch of Evil* is a terrifying, Goyaesque vision of corruption, and probably the greatest thriller ever made. His films of *Othello, Macbeth* and *Falstaff* (*Chimes at Midnight*) are, without question, the only original and valid pictures based on Shakespeare, and I am especially fond of them. One begins to see how hard it is to narrow the field within Welles's career in order to find the representative choice as "best." If Welles is difficult, with about fifteen movies to choose from, how impossible does it become with Ford's 140-odd pictures, at least twenty of which are magnificent; all the other great directors have had almost equally long careers and the possibilities become totally unmanageable. Allow me, therefore, to get out of this gracefully and say that the following directors are my choices for the greatest in movie history, and place in parentheses after their names the titles of several of their films that are among my favorites. But, to be perfectly honest, I would suggest seeing all the movies each of them has made, and picking out your own list. I like them all too much to choose.

PETER BOGDANOVICH

—Orson Welles (*Citizen Kane, The Magnificent Ambersons, Othello, Falstaff, Touch of Evil, The Lady from Shanghai, Mr. Arkadin, The Immortal Story*).

—John Ford (*Young Mr. Lincoln, How Green Was My Valley, They Were Expendable, My Darling Clementine, Fort Apache, She Wore a Yellow Ribbon, Rio Grande, Wagon Master, The Searchers, The Wings of Eagles, The Man Who Shot Liberty Valance*).

—Howard Hawks (*The Dawn Patrol, Scarface, Twentieth Century, Ceiling Zero, Bringing Up Baby, His Girl Friday, Only Angels Have Wings, To Have and Have Not, The Big Sleep, Air Force, I Was a Male War Bride, Red River, Rio Bravo*).

—Alfred Hitchcock (*The Thirty-nine Steps, Shadow of a Doubt, Notorious, Rear Window, Strangers on a Train, I Confess, The Wrong Man, Vertigo, North by Northwest*).

—Buster Keaton (*Sherlock Jr., The Navigator, The General, Our Hospitality, Seven Chances, College*).

—D. W. Griffith (*The Birth of a Nation, Intolerance, Broken Blossoms, Orphans of the Storm, Way Down East, True Heart Susie, Hearts of the World, Isn't Life Wonderful?, The Struggle*).

—Jean Renoir (*The Grand Illusion, Boudu Saved from Drowning, La Chienne, Rules of the Game, Swamp Water, The River, La Crime de M. Lange, Une Partie de Campagne, French Cancan, Diary of a Chambermaid, The Elusive Corporal*).

—Ernst Lubitsch (*The Student Prince, So This Is Paris, Monte Carlo, The Smiling Lieutenant, Trouble in Paradise, The Shop Around the Corner, Heaven Can Wait, Ninotchka, To Be or Not To Be*).

—Charles Chaplin (*The Kid, The Circus, The Gold Rush, City Lights, Shoulder Arms, A Dog's Life, The Pilgrim*).

My tenth choice is really too hard to narrow down between Fritz Lang, Josef von Sternberg and Max Ophuls, each of whom has made movies I couldn't be without. But then I wouldn't like to think of life without any number of others, from artists as diverse as George Cukor and King Vidor and Sam Fuller and Leo McCarey through men like Kenji Mizoguchi and F. W. Murnau and Erich Von Stroheim.

The list, let's face it, is endless.

3. On The Searchers

JAY COCKS

THE FIRST TIME I MET JOHN WAYNE, he grabbed me at the back of the neck, pulling the skin like a rein, and introduced me to a friend: "This is the fella who came from New York to stick a shiv in me."

I was reporting a cover story for *Time*. He was the subject. It was shortly after the appearance of *True Grit*, when a great many people were making the belated discovery that John Wayne was a fine actor. He was at last taken seriously because he did not seem to be serious about himself. Marshal Rooster Cogburn was a composite of the roles Wayne had played many times over for long years before. The performance was acknowledged self-parody, and Wayne did it with grace and humor and absolute assurance. I had liked the performance and laughed a good deal. Still, since I had always taken Wayne seriously, I wished the affectionate recognition had come sooner, and for something, not better necessarily, but closer to him; closer, anyway, to my idea of him and all he represented. *She Wore a Yellow Ribbon*, say, or *Red River. The Searchers* would have been best of all. But I settled for *True Grit*, and gladly. Besides everything else, it gave me the chance to meet him.

Wayne talked to me openly, as far as I could judge, but a little tentatively, too. He really did think the magazine was going to knife him, or at least he suspected there was a clear chance of that happening. What impressed me was, believing that, he went through with the interview anyway. It lasted, with interruptions, for the better part of a week, and he never tried to tough out or tease through a question. He hit them all square, and I don't think he cared, at the moment he was talking, how we used his answer or what treacherous Eastern context we might place it in.

He was being straight, even about his California frontier politics, as a matter of courtesy to me, and because he regarded the interview as part of his job, an ancillary chore that went along with being a movie actor and one that he was bound to do, as he was bound to act, always like a professional. It was the same strict adherence to an idea of form and obligation that he personified in films and that he used too with people who approached him from almost any direction at all. During one of our sometimes rambling talks in his house at Newport Beach, some kids—girls, I think, not older than thirteen—kept buzzing by the house in a motorboat, laughing and calling "Hi, Mr. Wayne, hi!" I doubt they even knew for sure he was home, but Wayne got up and walked out on his patio and waved right back at them and talked with them for a few moments over the distance and the sound of the motor.

I asked him whether, after so many years of that kind of attention, he didn't get a little irritated. "Why should I?" he asked me back. "They expect it. They deserve it. It isn't much." I had expected to like him, of course, but I wasn't quite prepared for this kind of directness—that, after all, is not part of the bargain in giving an interview, not even by the most professional Hollywood standards—nor could I have known that he would so closely and specifically resemble the staunch character he was on screen. It was not a case of a personality being shaped to an actor, but rather the direct opposite. He had become what he had often played. Like me, and many of my friends, for whom he was the incarnation of the romantic myth of a nonexistent West, he too believed the legend of John Wayne.

On The Searchers   35

He lived it, too, and lived it easily. Showing me around his house, he took me into a room crowded with souvenirs—blankets, rifles, bridles, saddles, hats, awards, medals—of a long career. He showed me a fine collection of kachina dolls ("Best private collection except for Barry Goldwater's") and a wooden cabinet standing on the floor which he took great care in opening. I expected a collection of pistols, but instead saw a set of books, packed tight, uniformly high and old. He took one out, placed it on the cabinet top, and started turning the pages, his large hands more tactful with the smooth pages than I would have thought possible.

The book was a collection of photographs. I think now it must have been one of the set of Edward F. Curtis's *The North American Indian*. Wayne talked about Curtis's pictures, which are splendid with the passion and dignity and romance of the Indian, the way I talk about *The Searchers*. He was lost in the legend, the record of the spirit of a people and a time, wondering over its richness, its vividness, talking about it with a mixture of awe and affection. I asked him about the Indians, how the whites had trampled them and beaten them out of hope, and he closed the book, still carefully, and said, "That's just the way things happen."

Ethan Edwards of *The Searchers* might have said the same. That was why the answer, which I regretted, did not surprise me. Even if I had been in a situation that would have allowed me to get angry about it—and the tactics of my profession discouraged that, for the moment—I doubt that I would have. I had come to know Wayne and liked him too well, over years of seeing him in movies and over the past few days talking to him, to be outraged and indignant. The answer was totally in character. I did not bother even to press him on it. I surely did not like what he said, but tolerated it anyway, out of a sense of familiarity. I had heard him say much the same thing, after all, in many movies. *The Searchers* I had come to think of as one of the best movies I had ever seen. Still it seemed to me there was much the same attitude of reflexive prejudice there.

The Searchers is John Ford's last great western. *The Man Who Shot Liberty Valance* had a complex and promising script, but it was shot too loosely and lazily, lit like a television show and staged on sets that were a disgrace even to the back lot. *The Searchers* is abundant in landscape and texture. It was shot mostly in Monument

36   JAY COCKS

Valley, Ford's territory. He alone made that blasted, monolithic terrain seem like the true scorched face of the West. *The Searchers* begins in Texas and spans, in the course of a narrative that encompasses a full decade, Canada and Mexico, as well as tentative niches of civilization all over the Southwest. Those places, in Frank Nugent's superb script, form a lovely litany: "Fort Richardson, Wingate, Cobb, the Anadarko Agency," as Ethan Edwards relates one night, resting on an old porch rocker, halfway through his obsessive quest for a niece captured by a band of maverick Indians. Yet as many miles as Ethan and his adoptive nephew Martin Pawley cover, Ford never really leaves the valley. There are a couple of brief, very beautiful winter scenes, photographed obviously in a different location at a different time, but they are used mostly for visual contrast and to denote the passage of time. It is the valley that dominates the film, stark and changeless and fearsomely grand.

Not long ago—and certainly in large part on account of Ford— I spent a little time in Monument Valley. I hiked in it, rode around through it, and woke in the morning with the sun shining into my eyes as it rose over the Mittens, the formidable natural rock sculptures that Ford has so often used as a backdrop behind a regiment of Seventh Cavalry or a lone rider. Staying in Monument Valley was like living for a time in the middle of Ford's imagination. His shade haunts the place. I had expected it might, but for me the whole valley was indivisible from my fantasies of it, all of which had been born of, and nurtured by, John Ford. The valley, and the breadth of myth it represented, reminded me of an old Western phrase I'd heard: "the only and original." They were definitive.

It doesn't matter at all that Ethan Edwards never really leaves the valley. It's a kind of limbo for him where he is forever fated to wander, to "ride away," in the words of the theme song. Ethan, like Wayne himself, is part of a West that never was but that has finally far more relevance for us than the West of hard fact. Ford, talking to Peter Bogdanovich, called *The Searchers* "the tragedy of a loner," but it is more even than this. Ethan himself is made of the stuff of legend. Standing outside the cabin in the last scene, silhouetted in the door frame, people pass all around him holding one another. Ethan stands apart and knows his place is not among them. He turns finally back out the door into the valley, to ride away from this new oncoming West of family and farms and settlement.

Edwards's decision to leave is not a matter of choice but of realization. Between the inside of the cabin and the valley outside is the gulf he cannot cross. It is not a decision between domesticity and being a saddle bum, but much more some small awareness that he belongs to the legendary West, not the historical one. The moment this becomes clear to him and he turns back toward the valley is for me far more moving than his search. The search not only ends here, but has led him over the long years to this crucial pass. That is its deepest meaning.

Wayne standing at the door, weight on his left heel, hands clasped at the wrist in front of him, hat brim blowing up in the wind, is an image that moves me as much as any I know, not only for its beauty, but for its melancholy and strong subtlety. Ford is a supremely intuitive artist, and I cannot be sure that he fully knew all that he was doing here. It doesn't matter, either, although relying so thoroughly on instinct does have its own traps, some of which *The Searchers* stumbles into and out of again like a stallion in a rut. Anyone who has working knowledge of Indian artifacts, for example, would know that jewelry worn by the film's Comanches is, in fact, Navajo, and of a design that would not be created for at least another twenty years after the period in which *The Searchers* is set. The home of Ethan's brother looks modest only by the standards of Saratoga Springs. It should properly have been made of adobe, and it should have been close and dark inside. Instead it is large and light, with beautifully beamed ceilings and a long fireplace with brittle blue china on the mantle and exquisite Navajo blankets (again, of anachronistic design) over parts of the smooth floors.

In any case, these would be quibbles, but they matter even less because the mistakes look right. The myth of the West, the movie myth, is Ford's creation more than any other man's, so whatever he chooses to show becomes acceptable almost beyond question. Such is the force and depth of his influence. It is very hard to break away. Only Sam Peckinpah has done it, yet his best movie—*The Wild Bunch,* another favorite—is about the same thing as *The Searchers,* the process of legend.

We are always conscious that John Ford's West is highly individualized and romanticized. There have been any number of recent attempts to show "the real West," which means in most cases that the characters are dishonorable, their lives hard and unenviable. Scrupulous as such a portrait may be about truth, it looks false and labored on screen, a clear measure of the impact Ford has had not only on our regard for verisimilitude, but our interest in it. We resist re-creation. Romance is the reality of the West we crave.

It was actually a boastful and romantic time, but Ford has added to it quantities of sentimentality and chest-thumping chauvinism and enticingly simple morality while letting slide any serious considerations of brutality, aggression or greed. When those elements are present, they are primitive. Ford's westerns are celebrations in which such things are necessarily given short shrift. One of the most touching things about *The Searchers* is Ethan Edwards's intimations of his own unheroic motives; the vengeance that compels him is without honor. He knows that somewhere, but does not recognize it until the moment he takes his frightened niece, now grown, in his arms and says, "Let's go home, Debbie."

Ford throughout shares Ethan's conflict over motive, and like Ethan, never seems sure until the last moment whether to kill Debbie or rescue her. At least this would explain the impossible change in Debbie, who in one scene is adamant about staying with the Indian Scar and his followers ("These are my people," she insists) and in her very next appearance is overjoyed to see her rescuer Martin and relieved to hear he has come to take her away. Practically, there would have been no cause for the film's final conflict and irony—once found, Debbie does not want to be taken away—if Debbie initially welcomed the sight of Ethan and Martin. Psychologically, no transition, however ingenious, could have convinced us that, once resisting, Debbie could be led away so eagerly.

This is a fault with the film that does matter. It is not a question of set decoration, like jewelry or beamed ceilings, but very basically of an unsettled moral account. With Ethan, Ford (and Frank Nugent too) believes that Debbie somehow deserves to be shot for "being with a buck." Earlier in the film, Ethan and Martin are confronted with two adolescent girls, recently recaptured from the Indians, who are gibbering and giggling insanely. "Hard to believe they're white," comments a cavalry sergeant as he tries to pacify them with a doll. Ford moves in for a—rare—close-up, showing Ethan turning away, not in sadness, but in anger and revulsion, thinking no doubt of Debbie and of similar horrors being visited on her pale flesh.

The Indians in *The Searchers,* as in most other Ford films, have strength and pride, but it is also always clear that Ford regards them as glorious savages. It is an idea he has never gotten rid of, one that rather destroyed the impact of his rueful pastoral of Indian humiliation, *Cheyenne Autumn.* Ford would understand Debbie's years with the Indians purely as an ordeal. He does not have Edwards really accept her at the end. Taking Debbie in his arms is much more a sign of forgiveness. But she has done nothing to be forgiven for. Implying that she has, portraying her almost as a repentant prodigal returned tearfully home, is a reconfirmation of the deepest kind of prejudice.

There are other similarly disquieting strains in Ford's work. He hymns the military with blind fervor, treats all manner of Irish blarney at too great length and with too much indulgence. If these things cannot be overlooked entirely, they are overcome by the full splendor of his feeling. *The Searchers* does not concern racial tolerance, after all, but the making of myth, the variant and irreconcilable processes of history and legend. It does not substantially diminish the film to recognize its flaws. The fact that *The Searchers* is strong enough to survive and surmont them is only an affirmation of its power.

Ford is a great deal like the photographer Edward Curtis, whose pictures John Wayne showed me that day. Certainly they both share certain stylistic similarities: a comparison of a Ford image of riders against one of the Monument Valley Mittens with a Curtis plate—say the one showing distant mounted Indians moving across the floor of the Cañon de Chelly—gives the same feeling of ritual and romance. Curtis and Ford share a deeper kinship too, I think. The critic A. D. Coleman has suggested that the romantic aspect of Curtis's photographs reflects the Indians' own romantic feelings about themselves and their world of grave beauty. In just the same way, Ford's veneration of the West seems both to embody and convey a very real kind of pioneer spirit, primitive and grand. So do all of Ford's fond embellishments, his indulgences and even his prejudices. The very roughness and even outrageousness of his concept of the West are qualities that return a kind of unembarrassed reality to the myth. It is the reason he can get away with so much.

Curtis's photographs caught and conveyed the same deep feeling of the legendary West to John Wayne as he and John Ford did to me in *The Searchers*. Both pictures and film set the tradition, both renew it. That is why I think I could not get angry over what John Wayne said that day about the Indians, or what Ford says about Indians in his movies. Those things are not unimportant, but they are secondary, and they form the dimensions of the legend. It is not necessary to like or agree with them to understand them or to love the whole of which they are an undeniable part.

Several years after I had spoken with Wayne, a friend, a journalist, met with him, and in the course of their conversation asked him about *The Searchers*. There was some problem with the distribution of the film, my friend had heard, something to do with the producer's not having done right by it and a confusion over rights that makes the film difficult to see. My friend asked Wayne if he wasn't disappointed that people might have missed some of his and of Ford's finest work.

"Well," Wayne shrugged, "I got paid for it." I can understand that answer, too. I wouldn't really have expected another. Hearing it, though, I remembered meeting Wayne's youngest son, born just a couple of years after *The Searchers* was made. His name is Ethan.

APPENDIX

I've been asked to supply a list of other favorite films. It's a little like being told to show your driver's license. For *Sight and Sound*, which made a similar request a while ago, I got up the following titles: *The Seven Samurai, The General, 2001: A Space Odyssey, The Third Man, The Magnificent Ambersons, Jules et Jim, Persona* and *Zero for Conduct*. Also included were *The Searchers* and *The Wild Bunch*, making a tidy ten.

Here are some more, in indiscriminate order: *Tokyo Olympiad* and *Across the Pacific* (both by Ichikawa), *Petulia*, and six of the too-few political films that seem to me worth caring about: *Open*

City, The Battle of Algiers, The Molly Maguires, The Organizer, Salvatore Giuliano, and *Medium Cool.*

Also, practically anything at all by Ingmar Bergman (excepting those early fifties' closet dramas like *Brink of Life*), Buster Keaton, Akira Kurosawa (especially *High and Low, Ikiru* and *Yojimbo*), John Ford (but not when the films are primarily about Irishmen, priests or true-life military careers), Howard Hawks and Alfred Hitchcock (most importantly *The Birds, Vertigo, Strangers on a Train, Psycho, North by Northwest* and *The Wrong Man*).

Olmi's first two films shown in America—*Il Posto* and *The Fiancés; Lola Montes; Shoot the Piano Player; City Lights; Ride the High Country* and *The Ballad of Cable Hogue* and *Pat Garrett and Billy the Kid* (the original cut); *Citizen Kane; The Lady from Shanghai; Touch of Evil; The Lady Eve* and *Sullivan's Travels,* the best of Preston Sturges's work.

And *Husbands; Who's That Knocking at My Door* and *Mean Streets,* Marty Scorsese's street autobiography; *The Big Heat* (and also *The Big Knife*); *Nightmare Alley; Kiss Me Deadly; Out of the Past; The Set-Up; Gun Crazy;* and good steamy Don Siegel movies like *Dirty Harry* and *Madigan.*

Any of an assortment of strong westerns by Anthony Mann or Budd Boetticher. Brando's *One-Eyed Jacks,* Henry King's The *Gunfighter,* Phil Kaufman's *The Great Northfield, Minnesota Raid.*

Lindsay Anderson's *O Lucky Man.* Max Ophuls's two remarkable essays *The Sorrow and the Pity* and *A Sense of Loss. The Godfather, Lawrence of Arabia, The Crimson Pirate.* For musicals: *Singin' in the Rain, Meet Me in St. Louis, Yankee Doodle Dandy, The Bandwagon.* For scares: Tourneur's *Curse of the Demon, Isle of the Dead, Curse of the Cat People*; and, by Tod Browning, *Freaks, The Devil Doll* and *Dracula*; and, by James Whale, *Frankenstein* and *The Bride of Frankenstein*; and Jack Clayton's *The Innocents;* and Corman's *The Tomb of Ligeia.*

Jim McBride's *Glen and Randa. The Producers. Where's Papa?* Michael Hodges's *Pulp. Alphaville.* And some of the odd, off-pitch movies that followed in the wake of *Easy Rider* and were immeasurably superior to it: Dennis Hopper's *The Last Movie,* Peter Fonda's *The Hired Hand,* Monte Hellman's *Two-Lane Blacktop,* Bob Rafelson's *The King of Marvin Gardens.* I like *Diary of a*

JAY COCKS

Country Priest, Ugetsu and *The Passion of Joan of Arc.* I've missed a lot of Renoir, although any list such as this would have to include *Rules of the Game* and *Grand Illusion.* I've seen all, I think, of Fellini, and would mention all his films up to, but not including, *Juliet of the Spirits*—most especially *Vitelloni, The White Sheik, La Dolce Vita* and *8½*—and *Toby Dammit* only after that.

Outcast of the Islands, Intolerance, Man of Aran and *Louisiana Story; To Be or Not to Be* (Lubitsch); Cukor's *Holiday, Adam's Rib* and *The Actress;* Vidor's *The Crowd;* Curtiz's *Casablanca* and *The Breaking Point;* Huston's *Maltese Falcon* and *Treasure of Sierra Madre;* Franju's *Judex;* Vigo's *L'Atalante.*

Point Blank and *Deliverance* (John Boorman); Walsh's *Roaring Twenties, Strawberry Blonde, High Sierra* and *White Heat;* Rossen's *Body and Soul* and *The Hustler;* Polonsky's *Force of Evil; The Manchurian Candidate* (Frankenheimer); Penn's *Mickey One* (forgetting about the Japanese artist), and *Alice's Restaurant.*

A Night at the Opera, Horse Feathers and *Duck Soup;* W. C. Fields's four Universal films.

Kubrick's *The Killing, Lolita, Dr. Strangelove* and the first forty minutes of *Spartacus;* the long "Be Black Baby" sequence in Brian De Palma's *Hi Mom;* the drive-in-theater climax of Peter Bogdanovich's *Targets;* the homecomings in *The Best Years of Our Lives.*

And there is the feeling I've left a lot out. Certainly there is a lot yet to see.

4. The Private World of Fahrenheit 451

JOSEPH McBRIDE

E VERY FILM CRITIC HAS, besides his "official" list of ten favorite movies, a private list filled with offbeat and often critically disreputable movies that he enjoys seeing over and over. Some of the entries on my private list are *Pilgrimage; The Ghost and Mrs. Muir; Japanese War Bride; The Shop Around the Corner; Targets; Three Godfathers; What's New, Pussycat?; On Dangerous Ground; Our Hospitality; Ace in the Hole; Support Your Local Sheriff; Merrill's Marauders; Blonde Venus; The Harder They Fall; The Bells of St. Mary's; Kiss Me, Stupid; Goodbye, Mr. Chips* (for Peter O'Toole's performance); *Compulsion* (for Orson Welles's speech); and anything with Jean Arthur. My "official" list is somewhat more orthodox, containing nothing which hasn't found at least a few published defenders: *The Searchers, Chimes at Midnight, City Lights, Trouble in Paradise;* Cukor's *A Star is Born; Psycho; La Ronde; The Quiet Man; The Magnificent Ambersons; True Heart Susie.* It's much easier to write about films on the official list, because one's esteem for them is more rational, but writing about the private list can be next to impossible, as I learned when I spent several weeks trying to justify my affection for *The Bells of St.*

Mary's and wound up concluding that if you don't cry when Bing Crosby tells Ingrid Bergman she has tuberculosis, I never want to meet you, and that's that.

Of all my "unofficial" favorites there is one which I've seen so often and defended so strenuously to my friends that it probably belongs on the proudly "official" list. But I'm aware that my regard for it is highly idiosyncratic and undoubtedly a little suspect, since not only the critics and the general audience, but also the maker of the film himself, are agreed that it is a failure. The movie is François Truffaut's *Fahrenheit 451*, based on the novel by Ray Bradbury. I would never claim it's one of the all-time greats, but I would like people to *like* it, because it's sort of my pet movie, the runt of my critical litter.

The college-town audience I first saw *Fahrenheit* with, shortly after its release in 1966, was, I suppose, representative of the reception the film was given around the world. Nervous laughter began with the spoken credits, became derisive with the shots of the toylike fire truck speeding through the countryside, and continued with mounting frenzy throughout the movie—not chuckles of amusement or complicity but antagonistic, boorish abuse directed at anyone in the audience who happened to be involved in the story. Particularly unnerving was the fact that the students and the townspeople in the crowd were taking turns endorsing their own favorite brand of fascism: cheers and whistles greeted the immolation of hated titles in the book-burning sequences, and a frightening round of applause followed the scene of a long-haired youth getting sheared by the Gestapolike authorities.

After that experience I began to develop an elitist attitude toward seeing movies in theaters and became an habitué of the private screening room. I think this is a feeling shared by most critics, and I'm sure it helps explain why there is such a gulf of taste between the critics and the public. Nowadays I'd much rather see a movie with a large crowd, even at the risk of occasional annoyance, because I've become convinced that a crowd can pick up the nuances of a movie much more quickly and accurately than any individual. Not that I believe the public is always right, but I think if a director is trying to deal with touchy material, he has to acquire the finess to *sneak* it across if necessary.

It's facile to say that the public's scorn for *Fahrenheit* could be attributed purely to the McLuhanite anti-intellectualism that was in vogue at the time the film was released. The big problem was that the public found Oskar Werner's book-burning fireman Montag a risible figure. As Truffaut recently admitted, "Every time my films have centered on a child, a young man, or a woman, they've been accepted by the public, whereas my failures always had adult men as heroes. Each time I show a man of thirty-five, he's refused: people say, 'No, his behavior is ridiculous, it's *childish.*'" For people expecting a strong political statement, Montag is impossibly naive in his satisfaction with the sylvan book paradise at the end of the film (a scene Jean Renoir told me was "one of the most beautiful things I've ever seen"). Montag is completely uninterested in any kind of violent resistance movement; his attack on his captain (Cyril Cusack) with the flamethrower is a solitary, individual deed which doesn't occur until his own home is invaded; and when he watches the dramatization of his "death" (by use of a double) on the state television system, his face registers the blank incomprehension of a child failing to cope with the chicaneries of the adult world. And for people who might accept Montag as a civil-libertarian hero keeping alive the principles of free thought, his meekness is embarrassing. Movie audiences will accept an intellectual hero only if he is a Byronic satyr (Ken Russell, *passim*) or if he is passionately involved in the public arena (Muni in *The Life of Emile Zola*, Montand in *La Guerre est Finie*). A man who just wants to read books in peace and quiet is unfortunately not the mass audience's idea of a hero.

In his candid, invaluable diary on the making of *Fahrenheit* published in *Cahiers du Cinéma*—the best account *ever* of the making of a film—Truffaut unfortunately gave the hostile critics plenty of ammunition to use against his film by frankly discussing his dissatisfaction with sets and special effects, his difficulties with the English language, and worst, his feud with Oskar Werner, which wound up with both men vowing never to work together again. First of all, no intelligent director is ever completely satisfied with a finished film; critics should know that. Truffaut once quoted with approval Abel Gance's suggestion that a director can only get 10 percent of his conception into the final result. And second, I don't

JOSEPH MCBRIDE

agree with Truffaut's disapproval of Werner's performance (being so close to the situation he was blinded), and I'm contemptuous of the critics' willingness to dump on Werner just because Truffaut gave them the cue. Truffaut claimed that Werner was constantly trying to overdramatize his role and make Montag into a more conventional hero. What really happened, I think, is a phenomenon which frequently occurs in moviemaking but is seldom remarked on by critics: the director's personal antagonism toward the actor tended in subtle ways to spill over onto the screen and make the *character* less likable.

Montag often displays a childish kind of narcissism and self-righteousness which Werner may very well have worked into the role by way of trying to make himself less child*like* and more "heroic." It's also possible to see Truffaut making creative use of this side of Werner/Montag as a way of defining the arrogant side of his intellectualism. Truffaut himself is a highly intelligent man who is congenitally unable to make high-sounding "statements"; like Montag, he expresses his rebelion by retreating into a more gentle, more civilized private world and sharing it with his friends (for Truffaut, the audience). If the childlike face of Montag watching his "death" is the original Truffaut conception of the character, the more complex Werner-Truffaut amalgam can be seen in, for example, Montag's bitter railing at his wife Linda (Julie Christie in half of a double role), who really doesn't deserve contempt so much as pity; as Truffaut directs *her,* we don't despise the character at all. In fact, when she walks out on Montag, she surprisingly packs a book in her suitcase—Truffaut's way of telling us that Montag's devotion to an ideal was so selfish that he didn't appreciate Linda's potential? When Montag waves a handful of paperbacks under her nose and snaps, "Behind each of these books there is a man—that's what interests me so," the humanism implicit in his statement is undercut by his lack of compassion for Linda. The "abstractly" allegorical nature of the character which some critics called a weakness of the film—that is, Montag's single-minded absorption in an idea—is actually an indication of a certain shallowness in *Montag,* not in *Fahrenheit 451.*

The other side of Montag, the poet, emerges effortlessly from Werner's diffident carriage, his shy dis-ease in society, his wide-eyed fascination with everything around him (except his wife), and, most beautifully, the sensitivity of his voice. The language the characters speak in *Fahrenheit* is not particularly rich in verisimilitude, and it often does sound strange and even (gulp) literary; rather like the language in Renoir's Hollywood films. I don't consider this a defect; science fiction films require a certain amount of verbal stylization in order to put us into their special "world"; if the characters sound like the guys in the corner bar, no art director can begin to convince us that we're in a different place and time.

The interesting thing about Werner's soft Viennese accent is that it serves the film better than the more indigenous tones of Julie Christie (who can sometimes be detected floundering for a correct line reading), and the flat, unstylized voices of some of the minor characters. For one thing, Werner's verbal distinction from other characters reinforces his loneliness and estrangement from them. And for another, it provides a neat irony: he sounds like a cultivated Nazi, and Montag's moral situation pointedly resembles that of the "good German" struggling with his conscience. (I was surprised when I read recently that Truffaut originally wanted Jean-Paul Belmondo for the role, and that he resented the way Werner made the character resemble a Nazi; why then did he cast Werner instead of some mild-mannered French or English actor?) Werner's elegant rhythms and fastidious phrasing make manifest the character's latent fascination with words—"Monday ve burn Miller, Tuesday Tolstoy, Wednesday Walt Whitman, Thursday Thoreau, Friday Faulkner, Saturday und Sunday Schopenhauer and Sartre; ve burn zem to ashes und zen burn ze ashes—zat's our official motto";—but the pedant in him also shows through his simplest utterance. I doubt that any other actor could have caught this blend of poet and prig so neatly.

Perhaps the most beautiful sequence in the film is that of Montag secretly sitting down in his rocking chair, by the light of the wall television, to begin reading *David Copperfield*. Pauline Kael has remarked: "One can visualize the scene . . . as it might have been done at Warners or MGM in the thirties, how his face would light up and change with the exaltation of the experience—the triumph of man's liberation from darkness . . . Truffaut is so cautious not to be obvious, the scene isn't dramatized at all. . . ." No, we don't see Montag's face "lighting up"; what we do see, first of all, is the light from the television tube slowly burgeoning from a pinpoint to a bright glare surrounded by a dark void on the wall screen. It looks like the explosion of light accompanying the birth of a nova, and it's a superb metaphor not only for "man's liberation from darkness" but also for the sense of creative energy liberated by Montag's simple act of turning on the switch—by his moral decision to turn on the switch of his mind. Truffaut doesn't dramatize Montag's excitement so much as he communicates it directly to us through the mise-en-scène.

Montag opens the book to the title page, the camera looking over his shoulder as he runs his finger under the words—*all* the words, down to the name of the publisher, the publisher's street address, etc.—speaking them slowly as he reads. When he turns the page, Truffaut fills the screen with the page, as Montag puzzles out the first words: "Chapter One. I Am Born. Whether I shall turn out to be the hero of my own life or whether that station shall be held by anybody else, these pages must show. To begin my life with the beginning of my life. . . ." The fittingness of the words to his own situation is most eloquent, and as Montag's excitement grows, ours increases through Truffaut's brilliant use of the camera. Truffaut cuts to an extreme close-up of a single line, panning from word to word and then making a whip-pan left downward as Montag's eyes jump to the next line. How sure is Truffaut's command of cinematic language! If he had merely cut to another close-up of the next line, he would have lost not only the visual exhilaration involved in the whip-pan, but he would also have falsified the physical experience of reading. The sequence ends as Montag finishes the line "It was recorded that the clock began to strike and I began to cry, simultaneously" by touching the word "simultaneously" again with his finger and repeating it wonderingly, as if the very concept of simultaneity, the identity of a thought and a word, had just reentered his mind.

One would think that, having conveyed so movingly the emotional and spiritual pleasure of reading, Truffaut would have won the praise of critics, whose métier, after all, is words. I can explain the critics' virulence on this point only by accusing them of lacking a sense of humor. Pauline Kael, whom one hates to perpetuate by quoting, outdid herself in obstinate point-missing, the kind of wrongheadedness which, as she once said of Bosley Crowther, leads us directly to the point: "The idea that one of the book people at the end might be devoting his life to preserving a text by Ray Bradbury (or *No Orchids for Miss Blandish,* which we also see in flames) is enough to turn the movie into comedy. The next step is to imagine all the jerks we've known and what they might give their lives to preserving—*Anthony Adverse? Magnificent Obsession? The Robe? The Adventurers? Valley of the Dolls?*" The logical extension of this argument would be that it was certainly bad of Hitler to burn Schopenhauer and Dostoevsky, but who'd give a damn if he'd burned trashy novels along with them? The point of the book-burning sequences is that words themselves are worthy of reverence, whether or not they are part of Great Books, because they are symbols for human thought. One hates to be crudely obvious, but the idea behind the film is that *all* thought is to be cherished. Besides *No Orchids for Miss Blandish* (a page of which is given the same huge close-up as is given to *Lolita* and *The Brothers Karamazov*), Truffaut's book burners also destroy a *Mad* magazine paperback anthology entitled *Greasy Mad Stuff,* a French treatise on billiards called *In Ze Pocket,* and a book of crossword puzzles in Spanish. I'm glad Truffaut didn't restrict himself to Mortimer Adler's list in choosing props—in fact, he didn't even *choose* many of the books but simply picked them up by chance, in batches—because that would have reduced the film to the level of a Stanley Kramer statement. The book people don't choose the books for their colleagues to memorize (wouldn't that be a bit fascistic?), but let them make their choices out of love or even simple crankiness. The book people are so broad-minded I'm sure they wouldn't even object to someone memorizing *Kiss Kiss Bang Bang.*

I may seem to be excessively defensive in discussing *Fahrenheit,* but one reason I like Truffaut so much is that I respond to his sense of irony. *Fahrenheit* is exciting precisely because it takes such an idiosyncratic attitude to a subject which in another man's hands might easily have degenerated into a standard liberal tract. Truffaut usually approaches a subject by indirection, working against the grain of audience expectation. When he's dealing with a sentimental subject, like *Jules et Jim* or *Baisers Volés,* the audience finds this

JOSEPH McBRIDE

approach invigorating because it takes the stickiness out of the romance and gives it the unsettling tone of real life; but when he ventured into social allegory, a genre people like to be Pure and Serious, the audience actually rebelled. It's revealing that in the introduction to his book on Hitchcock, Truffaut listed *Fahrenheit* among a group of Hitchcock-influenced films, surprising many readers who might have expected him to list *La Peau Douce,* his obsessive love story told as a suspense melodrama. *Fahrenheit* occupies roughly the same place in Truffaut's *oeuvre* that *The Trouble with Harry* does in Hitchcock's. Its wry approach to grim subject matter, its whimsical flaunting of contrivance, and its delight in teasing the audience, give it the air of a private amusement.

Which brings me round full circle to my "private list." What is it that connects *Fahrenheit 451* to *Japanese War Bride?* Why did I resent the audience's hooting at the book people and guffaw along with the audience at the slapstick gags in *Support Your Local Sheriff?* Most of the films on the list, I find, deal with individuals gravely on the outs with society, and many of them are comedies. The book-burnings in *Fahrenheit,* as Miss Kael notes, have their comic aspect. Most of the films on my private list (*especially* the comedies) take social pressures very seriously, and few of them uncritically exalt the individual over society. That's where the comedy comes in. *Targets* is about a sick boy who pleads for attention by shooting a score of people; *Japanese War Bride* is about a good-natured American G.I. who naively expects his small-town family to accept his Oriental wife with open arms. I enjoy the tension involved in seeing a naive hero, with the best intentions, coming up against the most odious reality and being forced to work out his own way of dealing with it.

What I don't enjoy are films like *Rebel Without a Cause* or *Easy Rider,* which make us feel that their heroes' naiveté is somehow a sign of moral superiority over the cynics and cretins who make up the rest of the cast. *Fahrenheit 451* is the story of an ordinary guy, nothing great, who becomes great through force of circumstances and through his own moral and intellectual honesty. The film shows how tough it is to come to a major decision, what struggle and courage it takes to be a lonely rebel; and the humor of Truffaut's treatment takes the solemnity and breast-beating out of the subject. Much of my pleasure in watching *Fahrenheit* is the appreciation of what Truffaut *avoids* doing—his disavowal of the easy jibe, the glib glorification and the quick solution. To avoid glibness and stupidity in today's world requires a special brand of genius.

Joseph McBride

5. On Not Playing Favorites

JOHN SIMON

THERE CANNOT, TO MY WAY OF THINKING, exist such a thing as "the best film," or even "the best film for me," which, for all practical purposes, is the same thing. There can be such a thing as "my favorite film," but there ought not to be, and I am pleased to be able to declare that I haven't got one. Not *one*, anyway.

First, about the "best." Every year *The New York Times* asks me to contribute my list of the year's ten best films. I comply, even though in my own publication, *The New Leader,* I wouldn't dream of setting up such a tabulation. The difference is that *The Times* pays a pittance for the list, and although one should never do for money something one disapproves of, there is no harm in doing something one feels indifferent about. The ten best films of a given year—that is still within the limits of the determinable, even if I usually cannot come up with more than eight. The single best film, however, even of one year—never mind all years—that is something else again.

Clearly the concept "best" must belong to a specific category: the best paper by a student in English 3b, the best figure among the girls out on the beach this afternoon, or the best riding boots. To try to nominate the best of all possible kinds of footgear seems to me already unreasonable, however. How can we evaluate on the same scale riding boots, gym shoes, sandals, opera pumps, ballet slippers, desert boots, overshoes, galoshes, and what have you? So, too, film is almost infinitely various, and eminently divisible into categories and subcategories. Then how can I compare on a single, basic scale a western, a musical, a thriller, a psychological drama, a historical spectacle, and so on?

When I was in high school, my friend Julian Beck—then still content to play roles like Lady Bracknell in *The Importance of Being Earnest* and very far from the concepts of The Living Theater —liked to amuse himself by loudly remarking at a production of *Hamlet*, "It's OK, but it's no *Oklahoma!*" Then he would go to *Oklahoma!* and be overheard exclaiming, "It's not bad, but it's no *Hamlet*." This would irritate the hell out of anyone within earshot (which is why Julian did it, so perhaps he was not all that far from The Living Theater even then), as well it might: there is nothing more otiose and fatuous than comparing incomparables.

Still I would go along with some sort of hierarchy of genres. I would insist that, by and large, a western is inferior to a searching analysis of souls or to an incisive investigation of social or political problems. In other words, a *Stagecoach* or a *Shane* is no *L'Avventura* or *La Règle du Jeu*. And yet, and yet! What is *The Seven Samurai* but a great Eastern western; yet it is surely no less a work of art than *The Rules of the Game*. Perhaps the answer is that any genre can be great in the hands of a supreme artist; in that case, we must make our division and comparative evaluation according to artists rather than genres—only to end up with just as many categories, or more. And so, with changed nomenclature, the problem remains the same: how can one compare a Fellini and a Bresson, or a Renoir and an Ichikawa?

I could, I suppose, go so far as to say that Bergman has made the greatest number of films that I find meaningful; but that does not mean that his best films (and he made some clinkers, too) are that much, or at all, better than the masterpieces of a few other filmmakers. The important distinction here is that, whereas I can choose the best among the films of a lesser director, say, a Hitchcock or a

JOHN SIMON

Cocteau, I could never conclusively pick the best Bergman. *The Naked Night, Smiles of a Summer Night, Winter Light* and *Persona* all seem to me masterworks, and I would no more be able to prefer one to the other three than I would expect a parent to be able to choose one among his several children. The reason one can select more readily among the works of lesser directors is, I suppose, that they either repeat themselves within a fairly narrow range, or that, their makers being hit-or-miss fellows, one can easily identify the one or two times they got lucky and hit the mark. In the presence of greatness, however, one cannot help being dazzled: when two spotlights are successively directed at one's eyes, it is hard to say which of them is brighter.

But to return to Bergman. Who could assert that his great comedy of manners and love is better or less good than his profound and bleak study of the role of humiliation in amatory relationships? Or that his relentless scrutiny of one arid day in the life of a sterile parson in a snowy, northern burg is more or less valuable than his paradigmatic dissection of two psyches—one complex, one simple —locked in an intense contest that subsumes virtually all the known emotions? Is the tragic better than the comic? Is the universalized better than the rigorously specific? No, we shall get nowhere with a term like "best" or even "better," once we have reached the true heights. Lower down, and within a delimited range, the terms may prove meaningful.

What about favorites, then? Picking favorites is no problem in a field where there are no bests—say, in desserts. In such areas one's private taste is the only possible arbiter, and there is no conceivable basis for arguing that chocolate pudding is better than pecan pie, or strawberry ice cream is better than butterscotch. When "bests" can, however, be presumed to exist, as within certain categories of film, the trouble begins. But what, you may ask, is the exact difference between a "best movie" and a "favorite movie"? "Best" is something we take to be superior to other movies according to various aesthetic criteria which, though far from absolute, have the authority of tradition, or are susceptible to some sort of comparative evaluation. "Favorite" is something that one likes best for possibly quite frivolous, idiosyncratic, personal and perhaps barely communicable reasons. And one is often aware of these conflicting scales. For example, I am conscious of the fact that *Vampyr* is Dreyer's most insignificant film, having little of the moral earnestness of his other works, little of their humanitarian zeal and religious fervor. But I find those films slow, heavy, tedious, even inept, and *Vampyr,* such as it is, more palatable. Clearly, then, "favorite Dreyer" and "best Dreyer" mean different things for me. Or, in the canon of Resnais's films, *Muriel* displays the filmmaker's techniques at their complex summit; yet I prefer, because it is less fragmented and more accessible, the relatively conventional *Hiroshima, Mon Amour.* So, when a favorite film is not the one that seems best in that category, one faces a moral dilemma: should one go with one's mind or with one's heart?

Naming the best film, then, may be an aesthetic impossibility; naming one's favorite film, an ethical one. Still, you wonder, are there no cases where my favorite and what I take to be the best coincide? Indeed there are, and from the ranks of these one can pick a number of favorites. But there are problems even with such plural choices. What one likes most at one age, one may subsequently outgrow; what seems to be marvelous in its day may look absurd some years later. As a boy, I wept over Charles Boyer and Irene Dunne in *Love Affair* at the Urania Theater in Belgrade, Yugoslavia; today the film's sentimentality might drive me out of my seat or even my mind. More recently, I was foolish enough to put *La Dolce Vita* above *L'Avventura* in an article that has since been reprinted and now makes me shudder with shame. A film like *Paths of Glory* looked pretty tough in its day; by today's standard in antiwar films it looks almost mushy. To pick a favorite, then, sounds like an unalterable commitment, but how can I be sure that my favorite today would still be my favorite tomorrow?

As I said, it is a moral issue. If you love a certain number of films dearly—have seen them many times and hope to see them many more before you die or go blind from looking at all those other movies—it would be unethical to pick one of them, more or less arbitrarily, and say, "That one is my favorite." The utmost one can do is name a handful of films and say, "These, as a group, are my favorites." Yet how do I arrive even at this conclusion? They are, to repeat, the films I have seen most frequently, and keep returning to. But why these and not some others? Some films, after all, aren't

J O H N   S I M O N

shown as often as they should be, or as one would wish them to be.

The great Hungarian humorist, Frigyes Karinthy, has a sketch about a man who wants a perfect, ideal beloved. He acquires a sequence from a film in which an ethereally lovely girl walks through a park, sits down on a bench, gets up and walks away. (I may have a detail or two wrong: it is some thirty years since I last read this little piece.) Over and over again the man screens this bit of film for himself, and enjoys the beauty, the ritual predictability, the faithful, dependable sameness of his ideal mistress. Then, one day, something dreadful happens: he notices a glance the girl shoots to one side while she is sitting on the bench. No doubt about it: she is flirting with someone else, or, indeed, she has espied her lover—her *other* lover! The horror of it: even this safe, foreknowable, unalterable beloved has betrayed him. All women are fickle!

The man, you say, is mad. Perhaps in Karinthy's little tale he is. In other films, though, in the truly great ones, this sort of discovery, on the n-th viewing, frequently occurs. On your sixth or seventh seeing of the film you notice something quite new—something much more startling, usually, than a sidelong glance. A whole new layer of meaning, perhaps. True, sometimes this is only because the film is somewhat elliptic, or even cryptic, and you are eager to come up with further interpretations. But up to a point the film deserves credit even for that, just as Sir John Falstaff does for being the source of wit in other men. In great films, however, as in great books, there is a rich ore of meaning that can be mined, perhaps not indefinitely, but for a good long time. Such films deserve to be favorites, but their number should no more be limited to ten, as it so often is, than to one, as the nature of this book would, apparently, have it.

Some years ago, when I compiled my first collection of film pieces for Macmillan under the title *Private Screenings,* I was asked to include a section of my favorite films in order to counterbalance the many harsh words I had for a large number of unfavorite films throughout the rest of the book. With some misgivings (because it all had to be done in limited time and space, and without a chance to resee the films), I sat down and wrote briefly—rather too briefly —about eleven films, whose titles I now repeat here, because they are still among my favorites: Bergman's *The Naked Night* and *Smiles of a Summer Night,* Fellini's *The White Sheik* and *I Vitel-*

loni, Antonioni's *L'Avventura,* Kurosawa's *The Seven Samurai,* Renoir's *The Rules of the Game,* Carné's (or, perhaps more accurately, the scenarist's, Jacques Prévert's) *The Children of Paradise,* Clément's *Forbidden Games,* Welles's *Citizen Kane,* and one film I am not quite so sure about any more, Wajda's *Kanal.*

But this list seems to me now too short. Some of my further favorites date from after the list was compiled; others I simply overlooked. I should now wish to add Bergman's *Winter Light* and *Persona,* and also, a notch or two below but still incomparably beautiful, *Shame* and *The Passion of Anna.* I think Antonioni's *Eclipse* should be up there, and Olmi's *Il Posto* (*The Sound of Trumpets*) and *The Fiancés.* Also Vittorio de Seta's *Bandits of Orgosolo* and Jan Troell's *This Is Your Life* (though the version we saw in New York was shamefully cut). It may be that some of the neorealist films of De Sica deserve to be included, though I haven't seen any of them recently and wonder how they hold up. I would now add another Carné-Prévert film, *Drôle de Drame* and Bresson's *Diary of a Country Priest* and *A Man Escaped,* though the Bressons with a certain reluctance, because I am not quite sure whether a sense of duty is not working on me here. (One tends to respect Bresson's intentions and integrity to the point where one loses sight of the actual achievement.) Buñuel should also be on the list, probably with *Los Olvidados* and *Viridiana.*

A number of films that may end up among my favorites haven't been around long or often enough for me to decide how pleasurable and necessary they are in the long run. Bellocchio's *China is Near* may yet qualify, as might some Czech films by Jaromil Jireš, Jiří Menzel, Ivan Passer, and the remarkable *Nobody Laughs Last* by Hynek Bočan, which so few people in this country have seen, alas. Andrzej Munk (whose untimely death was a great loss to film) should be represented by *Eroica,* especially if one could recover the film's missing episode, never shown here and hardly ever in Poland. I have seen some fine Hungarian films, notably those of Miklós Jancsó, but none that quite makes my list; there is one Yugoslav film, however, that probably should be there: Puriša Djordjević's *Morning,* but I would like to see it once more to make sure.

There is a number of Japanese films I now definitely want on my list, including several Kurosawas, Ichikawas and Ozus, as well as some by lesser masters—though none by the, for me, vastly over-rated Mizoguchi. The British film deserves to be represented at the very least by Reed's *Outcast of the Islands* and Lean's *Hobson's Choice*. From America, I should probably want to include *Dr. Strangelove*. You will notice that I am very chary of American nominations; the reason is that we have produced some of the world's liveliest cinematic entertainment, but extraordinarily little cinematic art. The New Wave makes its contribution to my list with Truffaut's *The 400 Blows, Shoot the Piano Player* and, despite its disappointing last part, *Jules et Jim*. If fractions are permissible, I might also include the first two thirds of Resnais's *Hiroshima, Mon Amour*. In the wake of this first wave come two more films I want on my list: Louis Malle's *Le Feu follet* (*The Fire Within*) and Alain Jessua's *La Vie à l'envers* (*Life Upside Down*).

Going back in time, there are some lovely French pictures that come to mind, for example, Julien Duvivier's *Poil de carotte* and, especially for their extraordinary performances, *Carnet de bal* and *La Fin du jour*. Jean Vigo should be on the list, at least for what he might have become. Among later French films, I'd include two by Claude Autant-Lara: *Devil in the Flesh* and *Le Blé en herbe* (*The Game of Love*). This line-up is far from complete; something of René Clair's should be included, and probably Clouzot's *The Wages of Fear,* but only in the uncut version, not shown, so far as I know, in this country. I do not, as you will notice, include silents, which, however impressive, do not speak to me in the way that a sound film does. That, presumably, accounts for my having respect rather than strong feelings for the great Russian masters; but I would dearly love to see again a film like Nikolai Ekk's *Road to Life*.

This, I repeat, is not an exhaustive selection, but to name more titles would surely exhaust the reader. And what if I were to include films that I love but would not consider absolute favorites—say, *M* and *The Blue Angel,* or some of those delightful or affecting Italian films like Luciano Salce's *Il Federale,* Dino Risi's *Il Sorpasso* (*The Easy Life*), Monicelli's *The Organizer,* Bolognini's *Il Bell' Antonio* and Zurlini's *Cronaca Familiale* (*Family Diary*), with its last sequences as moving as anything ever put on film. There would be no end to it.

What follows from all this? That one finds oneself having too many favorites for the term to have much significance, even if one could be absolutely sure that a favorite is a permanent one, that it is not guilt-induced, and that it is not merely a matter of that film's having been shown more often than others—or less often, if it is a case of nostalgic tricks memory plays on us.

Still, someone will insist, if you were stranded on a desert island with just one film, which one would you want it to be? Well, on a desert island one would want, I imagine, the film with the greatest masturbatory potential. Failing that, no single film would do; one would prefer one's memories of many films one loved. And that brings me to the screening room without walls, screen or projection booth of the mind, in which there are many screenings, but never of whole movies. Instead, there are single scenes, or performances, or shots that haunt one, that help bring some aspect of our experience or aspiration into sharper focus. But here the profusion is even greater, and playing favorites even more out of the question.

6. Ugetsu: A Meditation on Mizoguchi

ANDREW SARRIS

WHEN I WAS ASKED TO CONTRIBUTE to this anthology, I had two options: I could have said yes or I could have
said no. If I had said no, that would have been the end of the affair.
My integrity, my scruples, my sanctity, my aversion to the hysteria
of hyperbole would have remained inviolate. I could then scoff
at colleagues who participated in such blatantly promotional en-
terprises as a "favorite film anthology." Having said yes, however, I
would seem to be morally obligated to play by the rules of the game.
And these rules do not allow setting one's self up as a paragon of
critical virtue or as a being of supreme fastidiousness. In this, as
in many other matters, a simple yes or no will suffice. Nonetheless,
I am willing to bet that at least one contributor to this anthology
will take the opportunity to demean the others. In sports parlance
that would be called a cheap shot, since no one is more vulnerable
than a critic flushed with enthusiasm. And especially a film critic.
Indeed, mere superciliousness still masquerades as profundity in
the culturally insecure realm of cinema. And so I say in advance to
the nitpickers among us: Humbug! Play the game as it is sup-

posed to be played, or go stand on the sideline with the other kibitzers.

But as much as my participation in this anthology obliges me to accept its premises, I must make it clear at the outset that in my estimation, there is not a single film or a single director that towers over the rest. I have never been a desert-island man in the sense that I could make up a list of ten or a hundred or even a thousand films that could content me for the rest of my life. I need the constant challenge of rediscovery and renewal in a cosmopolitan, moviegoing life style. As Claude Chabrol once observed, there are no waves, new or otherwise, there is only the ocean. Similarly, there are no peaks in the cinema, only a series of plateaus, and on the highest of these (in my view) is Kenji Mizoguchi and a score or more directors from various places and periods. I could have written about a great many other films and about a great many other directors. It just so happens that of all the directors I admire most highly, Mizoguchi remains the most mysterious and inaccessible. I have never before made a sufficient effort to justify my admiration for Mizoguchi. Of the eighty or ninety films he directed in a thirty-five-year career, I have seen only a dozen, but I am finally satisfied that I have seen the bulk of his finest work. Perhaps I have nothing more substantial to go on than Mizoguchi's own self-appraisal in a 1950 interview with a Japanese film critic: "Born in 1898, I shall be fifty-two in May this year. For a Japanese film-maker, I am perhaps not quite so young any more. As you see, I am in excellent health. I still find myself greatly attracted to women. I admit to feeling very envious of Matisse when I read in an article the other day that, when he was seventy, he had a child by a young woman of twenty. In any case, I think the true work of an artist can only be accomplished after he is fifty, when he has enriched his life with accumulated experiences."

Mizoguchi's self-prophecy took form on the screen with *The Life of Oharu* (1952), *Ugetsu Monogatari* (1953), *Sansho the Bailiff*, *The Crucified Woman*, *Chikamatsu Monogatari* (1954), *The Empress Yang Kwei Fei* and *The Taira Clan* (1955). Mizoguchi died in Kyoto on August 24, 1956 at the height of his powers and popularity. He left behind a heritage of sublime achievement that his admirers in the West would ponder on for years and years

62   ANDREW SARRIS

to come. I am grateful to Peter Morris, Donald Richie and J. L. Anderson for all the material they have compiled in English on Mizoguchi's life and career.

Ugetsu Monogatari is but one of five "favorite" Mizoguchi films I might have chosen for this anthology. *The Empress Yang Kwei Fei* or *The Life of Oharu* or *The Taira Clan* or *Sansho the Bailiff* can be said to merit as extended and as ecstatic an appraisal as does *Ugetsu Monogatari,* which I have chosen partly because it is the most familiar of Mizoguchi's films, and partly because it is the most delicately balanced between the mystical and humanistic tendencies in the director's personality.

The title *Ugetsu Monogatari* has been translated as *Tales of the Pale and Silvery Moon After the Rain.* The film's official credits indicate that the scenario is by Mizoguchi, Yoda Yoshikata and Kawaguchi Matsutaro, and has been adapted from a novel by Veda Akinari. Not only am I totally unfamiliar with the novel, I am not even sure that the novel is the sole literary source of the screenplay. Peter Morris's invaluable monograph *Mizoguchi Kenji* (published by the Canadian Film Institute) is somewhat ambiguous on this point: "Inspired by the classic tale of the sixteenth century, the story is an amalgam of a Chinese legend often called 'The Lewdness of the Female Viper' (twenty times adapted to films in Japan and China) and a novel, *The House in the Broken Reeds.*"

Unfortunately, Morris never makes clear how much of the anecdotal material of the film is derived from the "classic tale of the sixteenth century," how much from "a Chinese legend," and how much from the novel. Or to what extent the various literary sources diverge or overlap as they flow to their ultimate destination on the screen. Perhaps it would have required another monograph merely to resolve this issue. No matter. The only point I wish to make is that my appreciation of *Ugetsu* is not based on the same proportion of overall cultural awareness as my appreciation of, say, *The Magnificent Ambersons.* As it happens, I neither read nor speak Japanese. Hence I cannot evaluate the readings of the dialogue in *Ugetsu.* I must either accept these readings on faith, or judge them deductively in terms of the parallel sensibility revealed in the supposedly universal language of the visual component.

"It is interesting to note," Morris tells us further on, "that the story on which *Ugetsu* was based was also used in a 1927 Japanese film, *The Obscenity of the Viper,* directed by Thomas Kurihara, who had been a cameraman for Thomas Ince in the U. S. A. By all accounts, this film showed considerable atmosphere. It would be interesting to know if Mizoguchi ever saw this earlier version."

It would, indeed; but again we are compelled to proceed with insufficient information. Beyond *Ugetsu* is a vast, shadowy configuration of cultural influences not only on Mizoguchi, but also on his collaborators and on his audiences. We must therefore defer any definitive appraisal of the literary origins of *Ugetsu* until some future unknown—if not, indeed, inconceivable—date. What is left to contemplate is a screen spectacle endowed with supposedly internationalizing and universalizing subtitles.

The two story lines that have been fashioned into the narrative fabric of *Ugetsu* may be said to be parallel but unequal. Involved in this rickety duplex structure are two obviously counterposed couples in a sixteenth-century Japanese village menaced by rampaging armies of one feudal lord or another. Genjuro (Mori Masayuki) is a potter so obsessed by his craft and the income it represents that he risks his own life and that of his wife (Tanaka Kinuyo) and little boy to keep his ceramics from being charcoaled in the untended kiln. Genjuro is assisted by a neighboring farmer (Ozawa Sakae) who dreams of becoming a great samurai warrior as an escape from both the drudgery of his work and the imprecations of his shrewish wife.

Successful in both rescuing his pots and evading the raping, recruiting and requisitioning soldiers, the two families set off for the city in a small boat to sell their wares and find their fortune. If I may pause at the bend of the river, it is to be noted that already Mizoguchi's contemplatively fluid camera work has cast a spell of stylistic conviction comparable to F. W. Murnau's in the boat trip of *Sunrise.* From the very first sustained traveling shot of villagers scurrying hither and yon across a brooding landscape, Mizoguchi establishes a tension between the essential wholeness of the world and the existential restlessness of its inhabitants.

By not cutting up visual reality into conceptual fragments à la Eisenstein and his devoted disciples, the nonmontage Mizoguchi,

ANDREW SARRIS

like Murnau before him, preserves the illusion that the world extends beyond the arbitrary frames of the screen. In this sense, a taste for Mizoguchi can be associated with a certain period of polemical aesthetics, a period in which the good guys of mise-en-scène were somewhat carelessly lumped together against the bad guys of montage. That is to say that if you liked Mizoguchi and Murnau, you were obliged to like also Ophuls and Renoir and Rossellini and Welles. It was a time in which deep focus contained hidden depths, and a camera movement could be construed as a moral statement. Indeed, the great aesthetic hero of that era was not a director at all, but that late great critic's critic, André Bazin, and it was Bazinian aesthetics as much as anything else that influenced many of us to turn irrevocably away from the more fashionable fierceness of Kurosawa to the relatively serene meditations of Mizoguchi. I once remarked (with more generosity toward Kurosawa than was expressed by fellow *cahierists* of that epoch) that Mizoguchi was to Kurosawa as Sophocles was to Euripides. Nowadays, among Mizoguchi's own country's filmmakers, it is Ozu who poses the most formidable aesthetic challenge to the West with an antithetical expression of existence as a waiting for death through rigidly static compositions photographed at the tatami level in contrast to Mizoguchi's dreamlike movement toward death through a stream of atmospheric adventure. Mizoguchi's is thus a cinema of perpetual anticipation, whereas Ozu's is a cinema of perpetual anticlimax.

Perhaps if Bazin were alive today, he could resolve the Mizoguchi-Ozu dialectic as charitably and as eloquently as he once resolved the Mizoguchi-Kurosawa dialectic in the days when *la politique des auteurs* prescribed an aesthetic Manicheanism. As Truffaut quotes from a personal letter from Bazin in that passionate period:

> I'm sorry I couldn't see Mizoguchi's film again with you at the Cinémathèque. I rate him as highly as you people do and I claim to love him more because I love Kurosawa too, who is the other side of the coin: would we know the day any better if there were no night? To dislike Kurosawa because one loves Mizoguchi is only the first step towards understanding. Unquestionably, anyone who prefers Kurosawa must be incurably blind, but anyone who loves only Miz-

oguchi is one-eyed. Throughout the arts there runs a vein of the contemplative and mystical as well as an expressionist vein.[1]

Returning to the bend of the river, we find our varied protagonists drifting in a sea of stylistic ambiguity. Through the mists of Mizoguchi's classical mise-en-scène another boat appears as in a dream of death, but it is nonetheless a real boat with a dying voyager, a victim of the violence lurking just beyond the arbitrary frames of the film. Whereas a similar encounter of the\living and the dead on the metaphorical waters is expressed merely on the single level of self-conscious symbolism in Ingmar Bergman's *Shame*, Mizoguchi operates on the additional level of wide-awake reality. Hence the flotsam and jetsam of dead bodies in *Shame* merely confirm that the ostensibly living characters are actually sleepwalking through the nightmare of a sensually senseless history. By contrast, the single corpse in *Ugetsu* galvanizes the living characters into decisive action. The potter decides to leave his wife and son behind on land, and the poignancy of parting is reinforced with the premonition of permanent separation by the expressive intensity of a sustained camera movement of the wife and child as they make their way along the shore to the outermost extremity of ground from which to wave their final good-byes.

We have now reached the first convulsive rupture in the narrative, and henceforth the emotional and spiritual inequality of the two parallel plots becomes increasingly apparent. We could actually detach the inferior plot from our discussion without appreciably affecting the ultimate implications of the work. The ambitious farmer and his nagging wife are a relatively sordid pair. What happens is that the farmer is granted his wish to become a samurai after a Grand Guignol episode with the severed head of an enemy chieftain. The risen samurai's abandoned wife wanders into the woods where she is raped by ubiquitously passing soldiers, after which she returns to the city to consolidate her new status in a house of prostitution. Who should then pop up at his wife's temple of shame but the preening peacock of a husband at the head of his band of warriors? The irony of the reunion of husband and wife is difficult enough to digest. What is worse is the husband's uncon-

[1] From the Foreword of André Bazin, *What Is Cinema?* Vol. II. Essays selected and translated by Hugh Gray (Berkeley: University of California Press, 1972).

ANDREW SARRIS

vincing abandonment of his lifelong ambition as an act of contrition. Mizoguchi himself complained of the facile resolution of the secondary plot: "The man played by Ozawa should not change his mind at the end, but continue, regardless, with his ambitious social climb. But Daiei didn't want this ending and forced me to change it. I don't like this brand of commercialism."

However, even if one could imagine Mizoguchi's implied ending, the rising samurai and his fallen wife would remain excessively schematic characterizations, existing not so much for their own sakes as for their ability to illustrate a rather elementary anti-militaristic thesis. They end up padding out the film with a spurious social significance without really expanding its more crucial concerns. That *Ugetsu* could become a landmark in film history with such a disabling subplot is itself something of a miracle.

Which means we must follow the path of Genjuro the potter and the two women who lead him beyond life itself before he finds his way back to the truth of his existence. But how does one describe an aesthetic experience in which meaning and mise-en-scène are fused together in one steady stream of luminosity? For example, the first entrance of the phantom princess Wasaka (Kyo Machiko) is effected not at night in her haunted habitat by the reeds and the marshes, but instead in broad daylight, amid the hustle and bustle of a crowded marketplace. Indeed, we do not yet know that she is a ghost, but there is something unsettling about her just the same. Mizoguchi's first shot of her is actually a rear-view shot of a very regally expansive sunhat making its way almost autonomously toward Genjuro's pottery stall. When we finally see a face emerging magically from this chrysalis of a hat, it is the face of the Japanese cinema's most beautiful actress (Kyo Machiko, often billed in the West as Machiko Kyo, and first recognized as the wife in Kurosawa's *Rashomon*), and the face also of one of the screen's most profoundly ambiguous temptresses. She ensnares Genjuro by treating him less as a man seeking diversion than as an artist seeking recognition. She lures him quite literally from the open marketplace of the humble craftsman to the closed palace of the coterie artist. Could Mizoguchi have seen in Genjuro just a little of himself, that strangely uprooted creature who became an annual apparition at the Venice Film Festival through the early fifties? No matter. The princess Wasaka initiates Genjuro into pleasures he never knew existed. His seduction is almost complete, but the spell is abruptly broken one day by a passing monk who sees death in Genjuro's face, and not only death, but evil decadence. Genjuro finally awakens from his morbid bewitchment, and thinks once more of his wife and son.

Meanwhile we have witnessed a harrowing scene with Genjuro's wife and a ravenously hungry straggler who stabs her for the food she is carrying for her child. Mizoguchi's intuitive flair for expressing spectacle in terms of integral space comes to the fore here as he shows us within one frame the parallel movements of the desperately wounded wife, with child in hand, and her demented attacker staggering along the wavering line of his own lunacy.

Genjuro returns to the village, peers into his hut through a dark window, sees nothing, cries out and hears no sound in response, and walks around the walls of his hut past other windows leading toward the door. And as the camera follows his movement, it captures almost in passing the suddenly luminous image of the wife sewing by a lamp. I have seen *Ugetsu* a dozen times or more, and this literally and figuratively moving shot of epic serenity never fails to shatter me emotionally. (That its scale of nobility is perhaps closer to Homer than to Joyce may be attributable to the greater affinity of Mizoguchi's narrative style with myth than with psychology.)

Genjuro awakens the next morning to learn that his wife, seemingly alive by lamplight the night before, has been dead for several weeks, having died only after bringing Genjuro's son safely home to the village. Thus Genjuro has awakened from two fantasies— one embracing the phantom princess Wasaka and her sensuous intimations to his vanity of fame, fortune and fashion; and the other a reverie of supernatural domesticity based on Genjuro's wish-fulfillment of his wife's physical indestructibility, a necessary illusion for his realization of her spiritual immortality. The film ends with Genjuro's speaking to his wife's spirit as he works at his craft, and his boy's placing flowers at her grave as the camera rises slowly to show the farmers in the fields beyond in a harmonic invocation of space and time as the stuff of community in nature and of humanity in history.

ANDREW SARRIS

I would never suggest that a critique, evaluation, description, appreciation or even synopsis of *Ugetsu* is in any way equivalent to the film itself. A film is one thing, and a piece of writing is another. Hence *Ugetsu* exists apart from my appraisal of it, and should not be compromised by my meager contribution to the body of criticism inspired by it. As I have noted, *Ugetsu* came before me at a time when I was especially susceptible to the mystical wholeness of its mise-en-scène, to the nobility of its central characters, and to the contemplative calm of its director's gaze. Even the deliberate slowness that seems to irritate many of my students nowadays worked in favor of the film as it did for the films of Dreyer, Bresson and Antonioni. Who needed Mickey-Mouse pacing when souls were at stake (and with Dreyer and Bresson even on the stake)? But *Ugetsu* (unlike *Odd Man Out* and *Citizen Kane*) has outlived and outgrown my more naive standards of aesthetic appraisal.

For example, the poetry that Mizoguchi fashions from the potter's wheel cannot be ascribed simply to the allegorical equation: Pottery equals Art. What I never knew until very recently but always vaguely sensed in *Ugetsu* was that Mizoguchi was as obsessed artistically with ceramics as with cinema. It is only when an urn, Asian or Grecian as the case may be, is incontestably itself that it can suggest anything else.

Another recent discovery I have made about Mizoguchi helps explain his inexhaustible fascination with the mystique of the female. An associate recalls that Mizoguchi was once grievously stabbed in the back by a former mistress, and that his films became darker and more reflective from that time on. This incident occurred years before *Ugetsu,* but somehow it helps me to understand the metaphysical helplessness Mizoguchi expresses in his confrontation with all forms of human passion. For Woman, especially, he shows his love, not by paternalistic understanding of her little secrets, but by passionate acceptance of her great mysteries.

7. These Are a Few of My Favorite Things

WILLIAM PECHTER

Do I HAVE a favorite movie? Do I have a favorite novel? (I have, I think, a favorite novella: Chekhov's *Three Years*.) Mcre important, *should* I have a favorite movie? The question provokes resistance in me even though I recognize it to be intellectually respectable in a way that a similar but (I assume) distinguishable question—What is the greatest movie ever made?—is not. And yet in some ways the silly question would be the easier to answer. If for greatness one requires breadth of compass, prodigious range of mood and style—in a word, richness—then it would be hard to think of a richer and, therefore, greater film than *The Rules of the Game*. Is it also my favorite film? Yes. Well, yes and no. That is to say, sometimes yes and sometimes no.

The argument that, in a general way, can be used to assert *The Rules of the Game*'s supremacy among films mirrors one which has been used to advance film's supremacy among the arts: that of its nature as a synthetic medium, one incorporating the resources of the other arts and transcending them by combining them. Why is it, though I might be inclined to a specific argument in behalf of *The*

Rules of the Game's supreme greatness, that I find the general case for it and for the film medium so uncompelling? Among films, *The Rules of the Game* may well be of incomparable richness, drawing not only on the resources of theater, music, painting and poetry, but on the muses of both tragedy and comedy as well. But do I really prefer it to films one might characterize as *narrow*, like Godard's *Le Petit Soldat* or Buñuel's *El?* And if by favorite film one means the film one is fondest of, do I prefer it even to such films as *Animal Crackers* or *The Fatal Glass of Beer,* which may not be describable as works of art at all?

There is a way in which film can be considered a synthetic (or, perhaps better, eclectic) medium that, for me, has greater meaning than theoretical speculations on aesthetic attributes. *The Rules of the Game* is a great work of art, and there are times when I want the experience of great works of art, but also times when I am drawn to films such as those of the Marx Brothers, which, in effect (and at their best), spit on art and culture. That I can gratify both impulses in seeing films—my impulse toward art and toward some different but related pleasure—is what most distinguishes my movie-going experience from my experience of reading and complicates any attempt to decide on my favorite movie. For how can one choose among incomparables? I may be unusual in this, but (apart from some occasional periodical reading) I no longer read with the motivation solely of being entertained, as I do go to some movies. (About as close as I now come to this is in reading Kingsley Amis, by whom I know I'll be entertained even when his novels fail artistically.) Of course, one may contend that Marx Brothers movies *are* works of art despite their aesthetic anarchy, and a film such as *Duck Soup* does seem to be (in part) a coherent satire of war and politics—which is one reason why the earlier *Animal Crackers* (at least in my fond memory of it), which satirizes nothing, seems to me a more perfect vehicle for the Marx Brothers's leveling nihilism: even the earlier film's technical primitivism seems felicitously to enhance its anarchic spirit.

The temptation to justify aesthetically one's pleasure in a Marx Brothers movie is, of course, understandable. One wants to celebrate what one likes, and film enthusiasts in particular have for so long been on the defensive vis-à-vis partisans of the other arts that such justification has been almost a polemical necessity. But the aesthetic justification of the Marx Brothers and of a great many other admirable films seems to me finally to falsify the nature of the pleasure to be found in them, as well as to misrepresent one's critical rectitude. Even now I feel faintly ashamed as a "highbrow" and a professional critic to admit to my fondness for a film such as *Shane*. I think one *can* defend *Shane* aesthetically, and I'd like to try someday to do this. But can any such justification completely explain why it is that I find *Shane*, of whose artistic defects I am fully aware, so *thrilling*? Isn't the appeal to me of *Shane* at least in part to something in me which is childish?

If there is a common denominator to the many and disparate films which at various times (at least during the times of my seeing them) are my favorite movie, it is the centrality in them of the human figure; the felt presence of a personality, whether that of the character, actor, star or even director (for certainly my onetime hero worship of such filmmakers as Huston and Welles was only a highbrow version of the ordinary fan's state of being star-struck, and so, I think, is much of the director-adulation of the *auteur* critics today). It seems to me, on reflection, no accident that the intensity of my moviegoing fluctuated; not so much the frequency of my attendance as the intensity of my concentration or fixation on the screen according to the fluctuations of social and sexual activity in my life. Though my attachment to films has managed to survive the assaults on solitude that becoming a husband and father entail, moviegoing remains, as it has always been for me, an essentially solitary occupation. This is in part, by choice, because I enjoy it more that way, but also, in part, because films were something gone to as an escape from solitude; and, in the latter aspect, what movies provided for me most of all was the company of another.

Given the complex intermingling of motives which brought me to movies, and the multiplicity of things which I found at them, can I really pretend to aesthetic rigor or avoid personal confession in attempting to choose a favorite among them? For one fairly long stretch of my life, I probably could have said *The Quiet Man* was my favorite movie, though I think now, no less than I did then, that it would be easy to make an aesthetic defense of the film, my admiration for it as an artistic achievement was at least equaled by my

WILLIAM PECHTER

absorption in the romance of the principal characters and my enchantment by the idyllic picture of a simple and beautiful way of life, far from the difficult and prosaic life of my own, into which I longed in fantasy to escape. (Though I love *The Quiet Man* still, I've grown a good deal less susceptible to basing fantasies on it; it remains one of my favorite films as do several others of John Ford, but probably it is no longer even my favorite Ford film.) Nor am I really always sure, as I was in the case of *The Quiet Man* (or in those of the several musicals, *The Band Wagon* chief among them, that I love, and from the elation of whose world I'm always somewhat reluctant to return to the nonsinging, nondancing world of my own), just where the artistic boundaries of a film end and my own fantasizing relation to it begins. On the simplest level, even after having published highbrow film criticism, I've sat raptly through abysmal movies whose plots and even titles I couldn't have related five minutes after leaving the theater, so single-mindedly was my attention focused on an adored actress (discretion forbids my naming the object of the last such infatuation as she's now the wife of another critic in a marriage any fantasist must find inspirational). On a more complex level, after having seen *Force of Evil* for the first time on a television program that consisted of the same movie being shown several times a day during the course of a week, and then seeing it again some eight or ten times during the course of that week, I hardly knew, by week's end, whether the characters in it existed only in the film and in my head, or whether they weren't real and were really enacting their recurring roles in a drama being played out, now and forever, somewhere in the unknowable reaches of New York City. I've since gone on to get some distance on *Force of Evil,* and after some false starts, even to write something that, I believe, does the film justice without scanting the qualities in it which made it, during that first week and thereafter, one of my favorite movies, But sometimes I feel that the immediate, "uncritical" response to certain films is really the most just criticism of them. At least, I've never come across any criticism of another of my favorite films, *Meet Me in St. Louis,* which improves on someone's saying to me after seeing it: "I'm so glad they didn't have to leave St. Louis."

Increasingly, however, as I sink into middle age, there is another figure whom I go to the movies in search of. Though my recollections of books I have read are no less vivid than those of films I've seen, it is rare that my memory of a book is situated in a memory of the experience of my having read it—of a particular time and place. Nor does my rereading of a book I read long before usually recapture for me the feelings I had when reading it the first time. Yet when I now see films I saw as a child in the forties, my memories of having seen them the first time—of a theater, a neighborhood, a kind of weather, a congeries of sights and smells, and most of all, the emotions of that person who once saw them—can flood back over me (I don't mean always, but sometimes) with an almost painful acuity. The experience, for me, is a recognition really of my own mortality, of aging and loss, and though I seek it out, I also fight it (I tend, for example, to think of all movies of the fifties on as "recent," and I'm always surprised when others don't regard them likewise). The "eternal return" of films has been often remarked on: there, for as long as the film stock itself is physically preserved, Bogart unwraps a parcel and Belmondo runs dying down a street, the Morgans and Ambersons go on a sleigh ride and Wyatt Earp sits lazily on the veranda, the tramp takes the flower from the now-sighted blind girl and Magnani steps before the curtain and replies to the director's asking her if she misses her three lovers, "A little." But preserved for me as well, for as long as my senses and memory survive, are all those past selves I left behind me, sitting and watching, rejecting and devouring, living parts of my life simultaneously with that life unfolding on the screen.

The question was asked: What is my favorite movie? My answer, if it is an answer, isn't the defense of any particular film or the elaboration of an aesthetic, but some discursive remarks on the nature of my moviegoing experience itself, though I hope they suggest why it is that I can't give the question any other kind of answer. Among my favorite films are those I can't defend aesthetically—films I love for extra-aesthetic reasons, and others which were once my favorites, and whose faults, though I now see them, I don't wish to speak of, preferring to be less the critic rather than unfaithful to those past enthusiasms for films which were once held dearly. We are all blind, whether blindly or willfully, to our loved ones, and to those we loved in our innocence most of all, and I don't

74   WILLIAM PECHTER

suppose my feelings in this are in any way unique. For example, Pauline Kael can't abide the sweetness of *Meet Me in St. Louis* yet is indulgent of the sweetness of Cukor's *Little Women* and D. W. Griffith. (I like much of Griffith's sweetness also; it's his bombast that turns me off.) If my becoming a film critic had been continuous with my adoption of an aesthetic or of a critical method, I might answer *The Rules of the Game* and be done with it. But my writing of film criticism has been continuous rather with my experience of moviegoing in all its aesthetic impurity. Relatively early it became clear to me that I was going to spend a large part of my life at the movies with or without benefit of any justifying profession. I've heard some film critics making impassioned defenses of their vocation and of film criticism as an art among the others and have no reason to doubt their sincerity. Probably such critics have their favorite movies and even nominations for the greatest film ever made. But, for me, from early on, becoming a film critic was less the pursuit of an exalted calling than a means of averting social disapproval by justifying unbreakable habit.

8. Lean and Lawrence: The Last Adventurers

STEPHEN FARBER

ACADEMY AWARDS, "ten best" lists, critics' polls of all-time greats—these are meaningless games but sometimes fun to play, and even useful if one doesn't take the results too seriously. The basic fallacy is the assumption that there are objective standards by which widely dissimilar works of art can be scored or graded, then classified on a precisely calibrated scale from the sublime to the ridiculous.

The question of favorite movies is slightly more manageable, for it involves only a personal, subjective judgment. Choosing favorites does not imply any presumption of absolute wisdom and truth. A number of movies have meant a great deal to me at the time I saw them, and this probably has only partly to do with their intrinsic merits. For example, Sidney Lumet's film of *The Group* may not be a great movie (though I think it is a very good one). But when I saw it, the year after I graduated from a small Eastern college, it intensified some of the questions I was asking about the insularity of my own college experience; its portrait of eight intelligent girls forced to acknowledge the shallowness and irrelevance of their youthful ideals moved me very much. On the·other hand, there are movies—some of Antonioni's, for example—that may be more lasting works of art, yet they have so little connection with my experience that they never fully engage me. A more open acknowledgment of the personal biases that inevitably affect criticism would probably be healthy.

I do not have one favorite movie, but *Lawrence of Arabia* for a long period seemed to me the most meaningful and compelling film I had seen, and I still have a special affection for it because it was one of the movies that helped me to see film as an art, as *the* great art of our time. I had always loved movies, but when I was in college in the early 1960s, American movies were not respectable, and art meant foreign films—which I went to see dutifully but without much real enthusiasm. *Lawrence of Arabia* seemed to reconcile the conflict I was facing; it was a Hollywood spectacular, yet prestigious enough to be reviewed seriously by the intellectual critics I was reading at the time. And it suggested to me how much movies might accomplish.

Lawrence of Arabia is not an innovative work, not an artistic breakthrough (in terms of style, anyway), though it was probably the first biographical film to treat its audience with complete respect. I think it represents one of the peaks of narrative cinema—traditional movie storytelling raised to its highest form. It contains many of the qualities that first drew me to the movies: narrative breadth and sweep, the re-creation of history on a grand scale, the interplay of larger-than-life characters, the use of seductive, exotic locales. These properties, so basic to the appeal of movies, are highly refined here, employed in the exploration of large, complex and challenging themes, strengthened with a rather astonishing psychological depth. *Lawrence of Arabia* combines the popular elements of cinema, pure visual poetry and the demands of a rigorous literary and intellectual tradition.

In the decade since I first saw *Lawrence of Arabia,* I have become more responsive to new kinds of films, films that expand the medium, ignoring genre formulas to offer fresh ways of perceiving the world —experiments in subjective and lyric and a more abstract, dreamlike cinema by directors like Fellini and Bergman, and even more recently, Bernardo Bertolucci, Ken Russell and Nicolas Roeg. I am not yet entirely certain how to respond to some of these movies, for they challenge the fundamental assumptions of narrative cinema that most of us have been bred on. But I suspect these are the experiments that point the way forward for films, and in another ten years they will seem even more important than they do now. These works have suggested some of the potentialities of film that a traditional narrative like *Lawrence of Arabia* does not tap.

Nevertheless, *Lawrence* seems to me one of the last great works in straight-line dramatic cinema. Although it is far from an innocent or simple film in implication, it represents a more innocent, less self-conscious mode of filmmaking, and one would think that the excitement of its subject matter and execution would guarantee it universal appeal. That is not the case, however. *Lawrence of Arabia* was a critical and commercial success at the time of its release, but since then its reputation has declined, and it is no longer very highly regarded by "serious" critics of film. In a recent international poll conducted by *Sight and Sound*, I was the only one of about eighty participating critics who listed *Lawrence of Arabia* in my "ten best," and only one other film by David Lean even appeared among the all-time favorites: one Japanese critic cited *Brief Encounter*. Lean, who won Academy Awards for *The Bridge on the River Kwai* and *Lawrence of Arabia,* and was once revered as one of the world's great directors, is now out of fashion even among many middlebrow American critics. One reason is the disappointing superficiality of his last two superproductions, *Dr. Zhivago* and *Ryan's Daughter*. But the main reason is the ascendance of *auteur* criticism, the tremendous influence of Andrew Sarris and his disciples on American film criticism. In Sarris's original pantheon Lean was consigned to the category of has-beens, "Less than Meets the Eye." And many critics despise Lean for refusing to bare his own soul for the camera.

The *auteurists* and other serious critics have been correct in focusing attention on the distinguishing characteristics of many directors' style, and more generally, in emphasizing the importance of personal commitment and authorship in film, as in any of the other arts. Where the *auteur* critics have often gone wrong is in building a cult around the "personal style" of some directors at the expense of reasoned evaluation of their films. Even assuming one can identify two films of the same director by certain quirks they have in common, does that make the films any better? Perhaps they only reveal the same sleazy and cynical kitsch sensibility—a "personal style" that is distinctly second-rate. The valuable idea of the importance of impersonality in art, clearly formulated by T. S. Eliot, has been largely forgotten. Eliot defined the creative process as the artist's "continual surrender of himself as he is at the moment to something which is more valuable. The progress of an artist is a continual self-sacrifice, a continual extinction of personality." And he elaborated with a famous rule: "The more perfect the artist, the more completely separate in him will be the man who suffers and the mind which creates."

This critical theory offers an approach to the art of David Lean, who constantly takes on new subjects—subjects of a certain magnitude—and surrenders himself to his work. His virtues are unfashionably classical virtues: discipline, clarity and control rather than passion and spontaneity. His films are finely wrought, perfectly crafted, and one takes pleasure in the skill with which Lean masters and controls complex, unwieldy material, not in identifying traces of private anguish or mannerisms which can easily be labeled a personal style.

To be sure, this kind of classical filmmaking has its dangers. Lean's greatest fault is a tendency toward the academic; at times everything seems overly studied, calculated with a mathematical precision that works against any sense of dynamic involvement. When the subject matter is not rich enough to validate Lean's classical approach—as in the rather thinly written *Ryan's Daughter*—his technical mastery can seem a chilly kind of perfectionism, over-disciplined and lifeless. Yet even in *Ryan's Daughter* there are passages of stunning filmmaking—the introduction of the shellshocked British major, the sequence in the pub where he momentarily makes contact with Ryan's daughter; through a purely cinematic language (which makes use of music and sound as well as visual imagery), Lean communicates a great deal of narrative information background with tremendous economy and imagination.

And although Lean's films do not immediately strike one as "personal films" in the way that Fellini's or even Hitchcock's might, they do have themes and concerns in common. Lean has social interests that may not be obvious to some American audiences. His films attempt to come to terms with the English character. While the very earliest films (*In Which We Serve, Brief Encounter*) idealized British culture (through characters who today seem more like caricatures of stiff-upper-lip Englishmen), the later films are devastating indictments of the deviousness, ruthlessness and psychotic unbalance of the English heroes more confidently celebrated in Lean's first war film. If distinctive qualities as a director are precision and self-control, it is interesting that again and again he has chosen to make films that bitterly question characters with those same traits. Perhaps his films are more personal studies than they first appear to be, though the burning personal obsessions are distanced and objectified. *The Bridge on the River Kwai* is Lean's most obvious and savage attack on British discipline, for the Alec Guinness character—strong-willed and tenacious though he is—is also rather frightening; his quiet determination slips into a blind, insane fanaticism. *Bridge on the River Kwai, Lawrence of Arabia* and *Ryan's Daughter* all contain studies of English military heroes in a state of breakdown, caught between cultures, struggling to reconcile their instinctual passion with their imposed British reserve—a struggle that eventually leads to complete disintegration and madness.

Lean's hero is most often an individual testing himself, trying to go beyond his world, beyond what he is—whether it is the airman involved in *Breaking the Sound Barrier,* the New England spinster abandoning herself to the luxuriousness of Venice in *Summertime*, or Lawrence of Arabia trying to obliterate his own identity by becoming a desert prince. Lean comes alive in foreign worlds, and his films make the exotic vivid and sensuous. Like the adventurers who searched for the source of the Nile in the nineteenth century, Lean wants to go beyond the limits of England, wants to shatter the restraints of English life; in *Lawrence of Arabia* he has a perfect surrogate hero for his own quest. But as Eliot indirectly suggests, to surrender oneself to "something which is more valuable" is to risk annihilating one's own personality. Self-transcendence can be very close to self-extinction; the search that Lawrence—and perhaps his director as well—is engaged in is a precarious one. The very opening of *Lawrence of Arabia* establishes this tension: a striking incongruity between the cultivated English countryside and the

STEPHEN FARBER

driven, obsessive quality of the motorcyclist who seems to want to violate the serenity of the landscape. In this setting the speed and intensity of the cyclist have a thrilling, dangerous quality. The frightening thing is that Lawrence's urge to break free of English domestic life is also demonic and self-destructive; in this scene it is quite literally suicidal.

The tensions boldly dramatized in this opening scene are then developed in much fuller detail throughout the rest of the film. Lawrence is in some ways a parody of the English gentleman—obsessively clean and fastidious, orderly and disciplined, quietly but relentlessly determined to accomplish the goals he has set for himself, and something of a colonialist in his slightly arrogant, patronizing attitude toward the Arabs. Yet he is ashamed of his illegitimacy, contemptuous of the immorality and lack of imagination of his fellow Englishmen, and he hopes to make himself over in the desert; in Arabia he can also become a god, can satisfy the heroic image of himself that England can never encompass. *Lawrence of Arabia* appears to be a traditional film, less "modern" than more intimate and *angst*-ridden films like Antonioni's or Bergman's, but it takes on one of the greatest modern themes—the confrontation of East and West, the eclipse of Western man in contact with a culture embodying fantastic dreams and primal terrors that his own society has suppressed. *Lawrence of Arabia* recalls Conrad; its subject is a man's discovery of his true self outside the stifling confines of civilized Europe.

Like other important modern works, *Lawrence of Arabia* concerns the question of personal identity. The great mystery in the film is not simply that of the desert, but of Lawrence's own character, of knowing what he is. And this mystery obsesses him, as it intrigues us. Lawrence finds in the desert an opportunity to plumb his own nature, to experiment with all the extremes of which he is capable. He tests his body, believing—and almost proving—that he is invulnerable to the elements. And the illegitimate Englishman can, in Arabia, reclaim his birthright as a natural prince, a leader of men, a national hero, a sun god, "El Aurens." After the capture of Aqaba, in an exquisite scene by the sea, Sherif Ali (Omar Sharif) brings flowers and throws them at Lawrence's feet: "Garlands for the conqueror, tribute for the prince, flowers for the man." "I'm none of those things," Lawrence replies with a genuine childlike innocence, awed by the possibility of what he may become. Yet the tragic irony is that in exposing himself and releasing the passion in his nature that England could not contain, he also releases a darker side of his personality—not simply an overweening pride but, associated with it, a thrill in the power of giving and taking life, a lust for violence and bestiality.

This is only the briefest introduction to the character of Lawrence. As written by Robert Bolt, and brilliantly enacted by Peter O'Toole, it is one of the richest, most complex and elusive characterizations in films. (I should note that I am writing of the original version of *Lawrence of Arabia,* before it was shortened for re-release in 1971. In the edited version crucial scenes have been eliminated from the second half of the film, and the character of Lawrence has become unintelligible.) A simple first viewing of the film might see Lawrence as essentially innocent and noble until his dreams for Arabia are betrayed by the machinations of English politicians, and his own sensitivity destroyed by the horror of war. That interpretation ignores the true complexity of Lawrence's motives for absorbing himself in the Arab revolt. What distinguishes him from the conventional movie war hero is that he is self-conscious about what he does, very deliberately *playing* the hero's role. This is established in a very early scene, when he extinguishes a match with his fingers; it is clear that he is trying to impress the other soldiers and also testing his capacity to withstand physical pain with a relish that seems slightly masochistic. As his gestures toward superhuman endurance become grander and more astonishing, his motives remain similarly ambivalent. His idealism is never "pure." When he rescues Gasim in the desert it is to prove that he is beyond the laws of men, subject only to the incredible demands he makes on himself. Ali says afterwards, "Truly, for some men nothing is written unless they write it." Later, riding across Sinai to inform the English of the Arab victory at Aqaba, he compares himself to Moses; later still, when entering Deraa without a single follower, he invokes the miracles of Christ. His pride does not exactly diminish his heroism, but it makes us uncomfortable and apprehensive. With his motives more tortured than in conventional melodramas, we understand the tremendous instability of the passion that drives him.

STEPHEN FARBER

But if Lawrence were no more than a victim of his own arrogance, his fate would not have the tragic quality that I believe it does have. Indeed, of all great modern films, *Lawrence of Arabia* is the one where comparison to classical tragedy might seem appropriate. What makes Lawrence's fate significant and moving is his intermittent *awareness* of the complexity of his own motives, his ability to distance himself, the furious and convoluted strategies he tries in order to maintain integrity, and his attempts—inevitably doomed— to escape what he is. At times he revels in his "extraordinary" stature; after one raid he walks unflinchingly toward a man who is shooting at him, then parades on top of the derailed train, flinging his robes behind him like a triumphant tribal king. At other moments he recoils from his own violence and from the reminders of his vulnerability, bitterly mocking himself and seeking refuge in an "ordinary," anonymous job which will not force him to confront extremes. After his humiliation at Deraa, he attempts to transform himself into a common British soldier, archly greeting the other officers in Jerusalem as if he were one of them—a desperate and hopeless charade. Finally, though, retreat is intolerable. His "destiny" tantalizes him and the vision of himself as god is too seductive to resist, so he constantly finds rationalizations for returning to the desert. He persuades himself of the vitality of the Arab movement, though secretly he knows that the British are merely manipulating the Arab revolt to secure their own holdings in Arabia. But by clinging to the dream that he alone can give the Arabs their freedom, he hopes to expiate his private guilt, somehow wash away all the blood and keep himself clean.

His dreams finally collapse in Damascus, in a Turkish military hospital, foul and unattended because the Arab takeover of the city has left everything in chaos. As he wanders among the dying and the dead, helpless to purge this vision of squalor and degradation, a British medical officer enters the hospital, and appalled by what he sees, throws Lawrence (still in his Arab robes) aside, crying, "Filthy little wog." The joke seems almost cosmic—the man who defied nature in his unsuccessful attempt to forge a new identity finally "accepted" as an Arab at this moment of humiliation—and Lawrence is too perceptive to resist it. His horribly twisted, uncontrolled but self-aware laughter brings his Arabian adventure to a shattering ironic conclusion. It is an image of utter disintegration and disorientation. Still bewildered about who he is, but stripped of all illusions, he is given the anonymity he. claims to want, and sent home broken.

The characterization of Lawrence holds the film together, but what makes it epic in scope is that it places an extraordinary character in a scrupulously defined historical milieu, surrounded by a gallery of only slightly less extraordinary figures, each of whom is drawn with a measure of complexity. The film gives a powerful sense of how political manipulation can exploit and pervert any personal, idealistic quest; the politicians and generals *use* Lawrence for their own ends, coldly playing on his noblest aspirations, as well as on his vulnerabilites, to achieve the goals that they consider expedient. Yet in a sense they are less dangerous than Lawrence—simpler, smaller people, more comprehensible and easier to deal with. As Prince Feisal, superbly played by Alec Guinness, wryly points out to the American correspondent: "With Major Lawrence, mercy is a passion. With me it is merely good manners. You may judge for yourself which motive is the more reliable." The ambivalence we feel toward Lawrence, and toward the more devious yet paradoxically more transparent people around him, is sustained throughout the film. Bolt's screenplay sketches in the political intrigues lucidly, crediting us with a good deal of intelligence, never filling in too much to make the ironies seem schematic. In addition, his dialogue is the rare screen dialogue (Bolt himself has not matched it in his other films) that, while completely utilitarian, can be savored for its beauty and elegance. It is not quite naturalistic dialogue; the characters are more articulate, more poetic, than we expect in "real life." The writing adds to the epic style of the film without sounding inflated or pseudobiblical.

Although *Lawrence of Arabia* has a literary grace rare in movies, it is also one of the most visually beautiful of modern films. The desert is a remarkably strong presence, and the images comment on the themes. The magnificence of the tableaux teases us with the promise of grand heroic action that Lawrence himself is not quite able to fulfill. The setting mocks his own vanity and insecurity, bringing his weakness into clearer focus and adding a fascinating ironic dimension to the film. At the same time the setting elevates

STEPHEN FARBER

and dignifies Lawrence's pride, for it can seem to validate his most extravagant aspirations; it is truly a setting for gods. Its emptiness attracts him too, for in the vastness of the desert he can lose himself and become as significant or insignificant as he chooses. The desert offers both dominion and death. In other words, the complexity in the film's attitude toward Lawrence is incomparably heightened by Lean's intelligent use of background as an integral component of the story.

There is one significant flaw—the evasion of the homosexual torture at Deraa—and this was no doubt a result of the censorship regulations in effect when the film was made. The episode in Deraa is given special emphasis by its placement in the film, but because homosexuality could not be explicitly treated, the significance of the experience is unclear. Lawrence's horrified reaction suggests that something more than a beating must have taken place, and there are oblique hints of homosexuality in the presentation of the Turkish bey; but unless we know the facts from outside sources, the sequence remains cryptic and unintelligible—and curiously portentous considering how little we see.

The other minor distortions of historical fact are not a problem. *Lawrence of Arabia* has a coherent vision of its own about the character, and while there are no major falsifications, liberties are taken for dramatic purposes. The satisfying thing about the film is that although it takes on a huge and demanding subject, it never reduces the subject; on the contrary, the people who made *Lawrence of Arabia* rise *to* the subject. Bolt and Lean are skeptical about the clichés of military heroism and uncover some of the psychological reasons for heroic action; but they never condescend to Lawrence, never turn him into a case study so that they can demonstrate a fashionably cynical theory of the warrior as psychopath. It is an observant and bitter film, but it is also one of the few modern works of any depth that takes the idea of heroism seriously. The film resists the simplifications of ideology. What is ultimately disturbing about Lawrence is that his greatest qualities—courage, passion, dissatisfaction with compromise—are inseparable from his most dangerous qualities—arrogance, barbarism, obsessiveness. The profound, unanswerable question is whether his truly breathtaking achievements can justify the horrible price that must be paid—by himself, and by those who get in his way. And that question will keep the film alive.

Lawrence of Arabia reminds us of some possibilities of the film medium that most modern directors are unwilling to explore. Its boldness and sweep make it one of the last great romantic, epic works of cinema. In a sense it represents the best of both worlds— a popular spectacle that is also abrasive and shattering art. Unlike the safe spectaculars produced in Hollywood over the years, Lawrence of Arabia invokes mysteries that continue to haunt the imagination.

9. Night World

DAVID DENBY

MOST OF US, I IMAGINE, would be willing to admit that our favorite novels, plays, movies, paintings, pieces of music, etc. aren't always among the greatest works of art; in fact, they may rarely be among the greatest. Works like the *Grosse Fugue* and the *Hammerklavier Sonata* and *The Brothers Karamazov* and *King Lear* and *Les Demoiselles d'Avignon*, if we refuse to protect ourselves against their full terrifying force, are more likely to inspire feelings of pain, exhilaration and exhaustion than feelings of simple pleasure. Great art, like a particularly intense love affair, can be nearly insupportable. (Certain comic masterpieces, like *Emma* or *The Marriage of Figaro*, provide obvious exceptions to such generalizations.) *Otello* is clearly Verdi's greatest tragic opera, and in the Toscanini recording one hears a frightening personal intensity being brought to bear on the orchestra, the singers, the chorus; the effect is literally overwhelming, a genuine cathartic experience, and I find that I can take the performance only one act at a time. *Otello,* performed with the ferocity it deserves, is almost "too much." I'm sure I turn more frequently to *Rigoletto,* a much lesser, but in its own way powerful and impressive, piece of musical theater. The conventional elements in *Rigoletto*—show-stopping arias like "Parmi veder le lagrime" and "La donna è mobile," the "curse" motif, the *cabalettas* at the end of several scenes—actually provide a certain comfort and refuge. We know these conventions are coming and when they arrive we take pleasure in their effectiveness and reliability. Perhaps only one scene in *Rigoletto* (the Sparfucile-Rigoletto exchange in Act I, Scene 2) is on the same level as *Otello*, yet the lower intensity of *Rigoletto* makes it for most occasions a more pleasurable experience. Our response to it alternates between moments of restfulness and edgy excitement, while with *Otello* we may never rest.

A favorite work of art, then, is one that we can relax with, one that we can repeatedly experience without risk of total involvement. We feel safe with it. It engages us without overwhelming us. Among the greatest movies, there are harrowing experiences of personal and social disintegration—*Greed, M, Umberto D, L'Avventura, Shame*—but I wouldn't include any of these, as much as I love and admire them, among my favorite movies. My favorites— the ones I watch most frequently—include the scewball comedies of the thirties, the Marx Brothers pictures, musicals like *Singin' in the Rain* and *The Band Wagon*, and, especially, fast-moving American melodramas like *Scarface, The Front Page, The Maltese Falcon, The Letter, Casablanca, The Big Sleep, All About Eve*, and *The Sweet Smell of Success. The Front Page* is shown rarely these days and *The Sweet Smell of Success* was a commercial failure when it came out, but this is still an extremely conventional list of films. It hardly seems a critic's list—it could be *anybody's* list. I don't particularly mind admitting that the popularity of these films enters into my experience of enjoying them the most personally. They are all good movies, and don't need critical defense, but it seems obvious that a good movie is defined as a favorite movie only when I can enjoy it repeatedly with friends—either old friends who come over to watch the movie on television or those spontaneous friends—the entire theater—that one discovers during a good night at a revival house. In such a case, the accumulated social experience of seeing the movie, with its associations of companions, lovers, wisecracks, arguments, etc. becomes as important as the movie itself. I can't im-

DAVID DENBY

agine wanting to see *Casablanca* by myself, nor can I dissociate *Casablanca* from the various people I've enjoyed it with. But I don't feel this way about many movies that are much better than *Casablanca*. I can remember my extreme annoyance after a showing of *Umberto D* when an acquaintance wanted to begin an immediate discussion and I only wanted to be alone. When we see a great movie, the experience is always silent, solitary and intensely personal; if we are deeply moved, even a stray, silly remark heard on the way out of the theater can be heartrending.

What are the qualities which turn a good movie into a favorite? With few exceptions my friends and I first saw the melodramas listed above on television in the middle fifties, when we were twelve or thirteen or fourteen. Obviously we were fascinated with these films because almost all take place in the corrupt night-world of crime, journalism, theater—the world that is a few years beyond the reach but not the imagination of an adolescent. The nervous, wisecracking men and women getting by on their courage and wit seemed so devastatingly in possession of that freedom and space which a fourteen-year-old allows as the sole superiority of adult life to his own. So we responded to the sophistication, the humor, the violence, and the American efficiency in storytelling (young people generally don't care about film technique, although, of course, they are extremely excited about actors and acting—probably more than adults are). Later on, as we saw these films again and again, we enjoyed them just as much—although we gradually began to regard their sophistication with increasing irony; perhaps *our* sophistication came to consist of a slight feeling of superiority to the movies we loved (a little backstairs snobbery being an essential element of true enjoyment).

One movie I have continued to enjoy with only the slightest change in attitude is Carol Reed's *The Third Man,* and I suppose it's my favorite film. This 1949 production from England lacked the exuberant energy of American melodrama; instead, it revealed what corruption looked like in a defeated and played-out civilization (postwar Vienna), after the party was over. Those good American melodramas I mentioned were tough-minded about sex and money, although they were often soft, in the end, on their heroes and heroines; moreover, engaging as criminality and extreme egotism might appear in the American films, these qualities were often firmly (sometimes bloodily) repudiated. *The Third Man* goes a lot further in its tough-mindedness—almost to the point of despair. Graham Greene's script sustains no illusions about anyone or anything, and although the villains are all punished, the hero is most decidedly not rewarded, and along the way the film offers about the most convincing rationale for nihilism and murder that I can recall hearing at the movies. Everyone who has seen *The Third Man* remembers the substance of what Orson Welles says to Joseph Cotten in the ferris-wheel scene, and nearly everyone, I imagine has been impressed and frightened by it.

It is of course, the supreme movie about the night-world, the ultimate example of that shining-streets-and-lurking-shadows "realism" that was so popular in the late forties. But in addition to its famous atmosphere—the knowing, world-weary people; the magnificent imperial ruins; the alternatingly menacing and ingratiating zither music—*The Third Man* sustains a mood of pessimistic irony which made an impression on me at fourteen and which seemed to reveal the nasty and permanent truth about adult experience, the truth that you could not feel superior to as you got older: life was not orderly and sane, but chaotic, sordid and dangerous; you didn't get what you wanted or possibly deserved; moral virtue, honesty and even courage might count for very little, and these qualities, as well as being useless, might make you unappealing to women and a general nuisance to everyone else. With its extravagant, almost voluptuous pessimism, *The Third Man* provides a pleasurable consolation in bad moments, a reassurance that nothing was ever meant to go right in the first place. It's so enjoyable, in part, because it gives the viewer the agreeable sensation of having confronted the worst.

Greene's characteristic pessimism and irony were reinforced in this case by producer Alexander Korda's choice of Vienna for a setting. *The Third Man* couldn't possibly have achieved the same effect if it had been set in Paris or London. In the postwar period the city of monuments and glory lies in rubble, is divided into quarters by the occupying powers, and is patrolled by military zombies in different uniforms who can't communicate with each other or the Viennese they are supposed to police. Reed and cinematographer

DAVID DENBY

Robert Krasker have framed the shots so that bits of rococo decoration appear in the corners of almost every composition, and Anton Karas's zither score is full of such café-repertory favorites as "Unter dem Lindenbaum" and "Alter Lied," but these traces of the imperial and gracious city are used in mocking contrast to its postwar dereliction. Perhaps the amenity of "Old Vienna" was always a bit over-elaborate, a bit sickly sweet, and with the authority of the city destroyed by war, its cultural style becomes the mere façade of decadence. The sinister "refined" manners, always such a cliché of villainy in American antifascist melodrama (as in *All Through the Night,* where the fifth columnists ran an art gallery), rings true in *The Third Man* as social description (it is also extremely entertaining). Dr. Winkel, with his collection of religious relics, and Baron von Kurtz, with his obscene little dog and his violin-playing at the "Casanova Club," are the clever survivors, the educated detritus of a cultured society bereft of economic stability or political power. Their style of ineffable weary cultivation is nothing more than a con man's charm—the false candor that hides the truth of their murderous racket in watered-down penicillin. And just as the economic center of a defeated city switches from legitimate business to black-market profiteering, the geographic center of Vienna has moved from its monuments, palaces and churches to its sewers (that most functional of visual metaphors).

Greene, the well-traveled minor novelist *par excellence,* is superb at creating characters living on the edge of desperation in some sordid or exotic milieu, and it's hard to think of a movie which has a better selection of such people than *The Third Man.* Holly Martins, the man who resists the sewer world, is the movie's nominal hero and its main source of irony. Martins is the author of pulp westerns, a well-meaning, ignorant and stupefyingly naive American. It's amusing to imagine him as Greene's nightmare image of himself —a writer who knows nothing, understands nothing and learns nothing; who is completely out of touch with the type of violent world that he writes about; who tries to live out an appropriate fantasy of solitary courage and rambunctious anti-authoritarianism, and winds up being rejected by everybody. At the very end Martins still hasn't gotten the point, he still doesn't understand that he cannot qualify as a replacement for Harry Lime—rotten bastard that he was—in the arms of Lime's mistress. Martin's courage and conscientiousness are dreadfully beside the point and at times destructive—his stumbling bravado gets an innocent man killed (Lime's porter). He's a hero who keeps searching for an appreciative audience, and everyone keeps telling him to go home. Finally he makes himself useful in the only way possible—by turning police informer and betraying his best friend.

Perhaps Martins is a warm-up for Alden Pyle, the murderously idealistic CIA man in *The Quiet American,* Greene's prescient 1955 novel about Vietnam. In this later work Greene has become extremely bitter about the stupid, well-meaning American. ("Innocence always calls mutely for our protection, when we would be so much wiser to guard ourselves against it; innocence is like a dumb leper who has lost his bell, wandering the world, meaning no harm.") Martins, of course, is far less dangerous than Pyle, even though he kills the man who fails to measure up to his ideals. We are invited to see him as a pathetic and comic figure, and Joseph Cotten makes him immensely likable. Not only do we feel protective toward him, we invariably root for him and suffer hideous embarrassment when he falls into the greedy hands of Crabbit (Wilfrid Hyde-White), the man who runs the culture racket and cons Martins into holding forth on "The Modern Novel." ("Mr. Martins, what author has chiefly influenced you?" "Grey." "Grey? what Grey? I do not know the name." "Zane Grey.")

A boy is often very confused about what makes one man attractive to women and not another; at the age of fourteen it seemed perverse to me that Anna (Alida Valli) would reject Martins at the end. Now it seems perfectly clear that if she hadn't rejected him the rest of the movie wouldn't have made much sense. For if Holly Martins has the virtue that repels, Harry Lime embodies the vileness that attracts. Harry, who knew how to "fix" things and how to get by in hard times; Harry, who made people laugh and knew where the fun was (and who also knew a quick way out—for himself—if the cops showed up); Harry, *who is an utter bastard,* gets all the love because his egotism is like an electric current—he makes things happen, he brings people alive. *The Third Man* renders homage to the dynamism of extreme self-love, and in Orson Welles it has the most famous and talented self-loving performer of the age. As

DAVID DENBY

written by Greene and played by Welles, Harry Lime is a man for whom all of humankind has faded into inconsequence; he has simply shut them out and found an essential gaiety in his loneliness. It is that gaiety, that American businessman's optimism, which makes him so attractive to the played-out Viennese. He may be rotten, but at least he isn't dead. In a single scene Welles takes this character through an'astonishing series of moods, starting out as hearty as an auto salesman at a convention, and passing through panic, cynicism, murderousness and back to geniality again. Since we don't see Harry until the movie is two-thirds over (although everyone is constantly talking about him), his appearance *had* to be dazzling or *The Third Man* would have collapsed.

Welles's entrance is a brilliant *coup de théâtre*: we know he's there, finally there, because that cat "who only liked Harry" is seen nestling against someone's feet in a darkened doorway. Then suddenly, after Cotten has roused the neighborhood with his drunken shouting, the light from an upstairs window hits Welles like a 2000-watt spotlight (Manny Farber has complained about the falsity of this shot, but I think it's hair-raising). Very quickly, in one of the few camera movements in the entire film, the camera dollies in (as if to say, *this* is what everyone has been talking about), and we see a self-amused and wickedly sardonic smile brilliantly emerging from black clothes and a black hat rakishly tilted—and that is all. A car comes between the two men and Welles is gone, leaving behind a clatter of footsteps and a strange, teasing shadow—it reveals a man running furiously but it doesn't change its position on the wall (an effect which is achieved, I suppose, by having Welles or someone else run directly toward the light source). Harry Lime is there, but he can't be reached.

Just how unreachable he is becomes clear in the famous scene on the ferris wheel. Greene has conceded that Welles himself devised the brilliant sophistry about the renaissance versus the cuckoo clock, but the best moment comes earlier in the scene, when Martins asks Harry if he's ever seen one of his victims. "Victims? Don't be melodramatic. Look down there. Would you really feel any pity if one of those dots stopped moving forever? If I said that you can have twenty thousand pounds for every dot that stops, would you really, old man, tell me to keep my money—or would you calculate how many dots you can afford to spare? Free of income tax, old man. Free of income tax." Greene is a Catholic writer and it's hard not to see this scene as a modern Temptation. And like all successful tempters, Harry is a psychologist of human weakness: two-thirds of human nature lies on his side of the argument. It's perfectly true, our feelings of pity lessen to nothing as we move further and further away from our victims. Harry's evil is insidious because he knows how to free himself from guilt (never look a victim in the face), and he offers the same freedom to others. Martins resists (perhaps because he lacks Harry's imagination), but he's the only one who does. Harry possesses the supreme nasty secret of the modern age which makes mass murder possible and even enjoyable, and he can't be reasoned with, he can only be killed.

The person who wants to kill him is Major Calloway, a character very much in the Conrad-Greene tradition of the man in authority whose moral passion consists of doing a rotten job as well as he can. In Trevor Howard's elegant and sardonic performance (Howard has always, *must* always, embody the bitterest truths about experience—his voice and face demand nothing less), Calloway stands between the cynical amorality of Lime and the useless idealism of Martins. He will manipulate people to get what he wants, but he's not unkind. Calloway, who knows the worst, is the pragmatic force, the professional, who tries to bring chaos under control. In the plot's final irony, Martins, rather than Calloway, finishes off Harry Lime; Martins has betrayed his best friend and finally killed him (as a last act of friendship, it is true), and although he is morally right to act as Harry's executioner, he loses the girl and possibly his soul. That cigarette he so carefully, so attentively smokes as Anna passes him by—is it not the final cigarette of someone condemned to the death of permanent isolation? It's a rather cruel punishment for his dullness and silliness, but it seems deserved; in a rotten world, no one has the right to remain an adolescent as long as he has.

Earlier I placed the word realism in quotation marks because that was the word used by some of the film's contemporary reviewers to describe its atmosphere. I think anyone can now see that in its overall design *The Third Man* is about as realistic as that eighteenth-century costume drama in which Alida Valli appears in the middle of the movie. To cite the most obvious (and overused) instance of expressive distortion, about half the shots in the movie are tilted off the horizontal axis by ten degrees or more, so that everything seems on the verge of sliding out of control. The stylization is insistent, from first to last; the term realism could only apply to the *moral* realism of Greene's story.

Possibly the critical confusion arose because *The Third Man* was one of the first British features to be shot almost entirely on location. But of course Carol Reed has turned Vienna into a vast stage set, and cinematographer Robert Krasker has abandoned naturalistic lighting in order to produce coal-dark, glossy blacks and harshly brilliant whites. (Color film, which requires hotter general lighting, was the death of "atmospheric" melodrama.) Much of the visual style of *The Third Man* was first worked out by Reed and Krasker in their previous collaboration, *Odd Man Out* (1946). As in the earlier film, much of *The Third Man* was shot at night; both films are very dark, very black, with only occasional shafts of brilliant light, so we get an impression of a constant struggle against nothingness, against extinction. But *The Third Man* goes further with certain mannerisms, and features one of the most aggressive and persistent uses of back-lighting in the history of the medium. The main source of light is almost always deep in the shot and *hidden*—glaring at us from around a corner or under an arch or at the end of a tunnel. Thus figures are often seen in silhouette or are preceded or followed by immense shadows (some of these shadows seem to have slipped off the walls of *Ivan the Terrible*), an effect of lurking menace that carries us along from scene to scene even if we are aware how portentous and repetitive it all is.

Moreover, Reed's stage-Vienna is almost as unpopulated as the set of an absurdist play. Where are all the people? The immense, alienating crowds of the modern city (often a presence in the German expressionist films which are the stylistic progenitors of this movie) have simply been swept out of sight; the individual in this bombed-out city is now *literally* isolated—alone in the vast squares, alone when scrambling down a pile of rubble, virtually alone in a large house. There are only two sizable groups of people in the film—the crowd that gathers after the porter has been murdered and that begins pursuing Martins by mistake, and the literary society that questions him so savagely on James Joyce and Zane Grey. Both of these crowds become obscenely aggressive; it's as if experience of war had turned the survivors into gangs of predators ready to be unleashed on random victims. Besides these two groups there are only shadows and echoes. And without the general city noise which we take for granted and whose absence is oddly frightening, every voice or footstep becomes a hideous intrusion on a void.

Echoes, like shadows, reveal duplicate selves—hollow, disembodied, unreal. Yet these duplicate selves dominate the movie. *The Third Man* remains the most haunting and insidious of all night-films because we realize that Martins, the plaintive ass with fantasies of glory, stands in for us, for all fantasy-ridden moviegoers, and that this representative of inadequate ordinary decency has less personal force than the loathsome disembodied presences lurking about in the shadows of the ruined and powerless city.

10. The Rules of the Game

RICHARD ROUD

I T MAY SOUND SNOBBISH to choose *The Rules of the Game* as one's favorite film, for it is generally considered one of the world's greatest films; to say that it is one's favorite seems like showing-off—only the best is good enough for *me*.

Choosing a film as one's favorite implies that one has personal reasons for liking it; that is, in fact, the case. For some, like Leo Braudy, the main subject of *The Rules of the Game* is "the retreat into theater." For Bazin, it was probably the most total expression of depth of field used to present the ambiguities of reality. For me, it was something much simpler and, to me, more important: it was the discovery that life, and particularly love, was not as simple as I had been brought up to believe.

I first saw the film in January 1951 in Paris. I was twenty-one years old; I had been in France on a Fulbright for several months; and I was troubled.

Of course, Europe had been a very enriching experience; like Henry James's Chad Newsome (in *The Ambassadors,* which I was only to read the following year) I had had a vision of another

97

world, a richer reality. But also a disturbing one—not because, like Chad, I suddenly discovered that these charming, witty Europeans were all evil. I was too sophisticated for that; lots had happened since James's hero had sailed forth out of New England.

No, it was the discovery, which the film crystallized, that there was in fact a Game which everyone was playing, and that it had its Rules, and that I didn't know them.

I think what shocked me most in the film was one character saying about another that he was "too sincere." I had never heard anyone talk that way in an American film—to make it worse, the character who said it was no Benedict Arnold, but a reasonably sympathetic person.

How could you be *too* sincere? I puzzled. Hadn't we all been brought up on the notion that sincerity was the highest virtue? I even remember people saying during the war, "Well, I think Hitler is *sincere*," as though that were somehow an attenuating factor.

Now, of course, looking back, I see that although American society pretended to believe this, it did not practice it. But I was too young to realize that; I had left home too soon. Something else became clear at that moment: although I had majored in English, minored in French, and read a large number of the classics, my notions about love and personal relations corresponded much more to Hollywood movies than it did to Dostoevsky, Flaubert, or George Eliot. What was the point of reading Proust if one expected one's love affairs to follow the lines laid down by Lenore Coffee or any of the hundred Hollywood scriptwriters who, I suddenly realized, had given me my notions as to how people behaved when they were having an affair.

But if I was shocked by "too sincere," I recognized myself all too well in another statement made in the film: Dalio, at the end, saying "I am suffering, and I hate that." I still naively thought that if one person loved another, then it was bound, somehow, to come out all right. Tragedy was something awe-inspiring and noble; the notion that tragedy could pop up into everyday life without any flashes of lightning or clashes of cymbals was a new idea—one which I have since, like everyone else, learned to live with.

Then too, André Jurieux, the aviator, was there for me to identify with. Hadn't he, after all, come from America, as I had? He was sim-

RICHARD ROUD

ple and sincere, and here he was mixed up with all these people who managed somehow to be in love with several people at once. His bewilderment was mine, but not quite, for I had been there long enough to realize that although he and I were obviously in the right, there were an awful lot of other people—nice people—who felt differently about the matter.

Or perhaps I was already corrupt: I still know dozens of people who firmly maintain that marriage means fidelity, that it is *impossible* that a man can love his wife and also be carrying on an affair. Either he *really* loves his wife or he doesn't, and if he does, then he can't have an affair with anyone else. And what *The Rules of the Game* confirmed (for nothing can teach you something you don't already know, however obscurely) is that it all depends on what is meant by *really,* and that anyhow people's needs are much more complex than we had been led to believe. The Marquis de la Chesnaye *does* love his wife Christine; he also loves Geneviève. Christine *does* love her husband, but she also loves André; and it is also possible for her to contemplate an affair with Octave. Pretty strong stuff for someone who had been brought up on *Now, Voyager!*

But there is another reason why I was struck by the film: the way it brought absurdity, which I was beginning to realize was inherent in human life, into art. The previous year saw the first productions of the plays of Ionesco, and a year after that we had *Waiting for Godot.* But obviously the "theater of the absurd" was in the air, and in January 1951 I was very aware of it in *The Rules of the Game.* It was the first film I had ever seen that was neither comedy nor tragedy, melodrama nor social realism, but rather an insane combination of them all.

And what had me on the edge of my seat was the central Walpurgis Night sequence: the after-dinner "entertainment" in which everything comes to a head, and which is treated like a Marx Brothers film scripted, not by S. J. Perelman, but by Feydeau (whose bedroom farces had just begun to be revived in France at that time). But more exciting than the farcical treatment of serious things was the feeling that, underneath, the farce was more truly tragic than any I had heretofore experienced. The phrase "tragic farce" is well established nowadays, but at the time it was new and daring. (Of course, when the film originally came out in 1939, it was totally unacceptable, as witness the disastrous first-run career of the film. By 1951, however, we were ready for it.)

And this mixing up of the genres seemed to correspond to the content of the film. Just as love and life were not so simple as one had thought, so a film that was to express this new vision had to be different from those made before. And the mixture of farce and tragedy corresponded, in my mind, to the ambiguities of the characters.

What I was not aware of at the time was that Renoir's mise-en-scène brought this out all the more. I probably noticed that the camera moved around a lot, but I was certainly not aware that his emphasis on long-ish sequence shots created an effect of simultaneity which only reinforced the themes of the film. But I dare say this had its effect on me; I didn't notice, for example, that the whole Walpurgis Night sequence—from the beginning of the show to that fantastic moment when Dalio says to his maitre d'hotel, *"Faites cesser cette comédie!"* ("Stop this farce!") and the answer comes: "Which one?"—was done in an incredibly small number of shots— about fifty in all. But it had its effect, nonetheless.

All this is ancient history now. But seeing the film over and over again through the years, it is still as fresh as ever. Naturally, one is impressed with different things now, its encyclopedic quality, for example. The French have always gone in for the big novel—or rather sequence of novels—which portray a whole society. They were the first nation to produce an encyclopedia, and their novelists have gone on producing them—Balzac with his *Human Comedy*, Zola with the *Rougon-Macquart* series, Proust, Roger Martin du Gard with his pre-1914 saga *The Thibaults*, even Jules Romains's endless *Men of Good Will*.

If France were destroyed tomorrow, and nothing remained behind except *The Rules of the Game*, the whole country and its civilization could be reconstructed from it. We have nothing like it here in America—not *Citizen Kane*, not *Birth of a Nation*, not anything. The only Great American Novel which even tried to bring it off was Dos Passos's *U.S.A.*, and although I persist unfashionably in thinking it a remarkable achievement, it seems, next to *The Rules of the Game*, overly fabricated.

100   RICHARD ROUD

Everything is in *The Rules of the Game*, every strata of society—with the possible exception of industrial workers and peasants, but even here there are glancing references to M. et Mme de la Bruyères's factory in Tourcoing, and a glimpse of the peasant class in the character of the poacher Marceau.

But it is not just twentieth-century France that is present in the film: we know that Renoir was inspired by Musset's *Les Caprices de Marianne*, and that he carefully reread Marivaux before writing the script. It is France itself which the film explores, and this gives the film an incredible richness and takes it beyond a simple tableau or portrait of 1930s France.

Nevertheless, it is also very much of its own time, as a double bill consisting of this film and *The Sorrow and the Pity* would clearly reveal: one could almost predict how each of the characters would react in Vichy France (Schumacher joining the French SS, and Marceau joining the Resistance, for example).

But no matter how important a film's themes may be, and how revolutionary its technique, it stands or falls in the long run on its material qualities, and in the case of this film that means, above all, the performances, the direction of the actors—who are after all what we *see* and *hear* in the film: the raw material. And one is amazed at just what Renoir has done. It is an open secret, for example, that he chose Nora Gregor for the part of Christine because he had fallen in love with her, and only as he began to make the film did he realize her inadequacies—her physical awkwardness, her difficulties with the French language. What he did was to modify not only her role, but the whole film: Mila Parely's role (as Geneviève, La Chesnaye's mistress) was built up so as to compensate for whatever Mme Gregor could not bring to the film. His use of Dalio to play the marquis raised a lot of eyebrows, for he was not exactly the most aristocratic of types; it works because Renoir convincingly changed him from a patron of the arts into a half-Jewish collector of musical toys.

What he did was to bring the documentary method into fiction filmmaking. Long before the term was invented, Renoir was creating his own kind of *cinéma verité,* in which the film is almost as much a documentary on the actors as it is a story. Improvisation plays a large part in Renoir's technique, and it helped to enrich his treatment of the characters. Because he had got the marvelous trio of Carette, Gaston Modot, and Paulette Dubost, for example, he decided to develop the "servant" part of the story while downplaying the Nora Gregor role.

And then there is the role played in the film by Renoir himself. It is as though he included himself through a kind of scrupulous honesty: he could not except himself from his portrait of society; he did not wish to stand outside. Renoir's character, Octave, is more than a little ridiculous, and I feel sure that Renoir knew this and did not shrink from it. (A friend has suggested that the *real* reason I like the film so much is that I identify with Renoir/Octave, and I must admit there is a certain resemblance in face and physique, and in his bumbling gesticulations; Octave is always clumsily throwing himself around.) The film would not be the same without Renoir/Octave; he serves as the standard against which reality and fiction can be measured. And as in a Pirandello play, the two become ultimately confused; that would seem to be Renoir's point, even if he did not grasp it fully at the time.

It seems that Renoir did not "know" what he was doing—when the film had its catastrophic premiere, he was amazed by people's reactions. He may not have been intellectually aware of his audacity, but the film is no accident. Everything in his career leads up to it, just as everything since is a development of elements that are already present—however unconsciously or inarticulately—in this watershed film.

There is yet another reason why this is my favorite film: I have emphasized its riches, but the spectator has to dig for them. He has to contribute, and in so doing, he becomes a part of the film, in much the same way as the director became a part of it by playing Octave.

And this may be why, ultimately, I prefer it to another of my favorite films—Bresson's *Les Dames du Bois de Boulogne*—an almost perfect film, but one which hardly needs the viewer to complete it. It is a much more conscious work of art; everything has been planned, nothing left to chance. Rather than *use* the actors as Renoir has, Bresson has obliterated them. They become Bresson's puppets, whereas the opposite is the case with Renoir. And here again one

RICHARD ROUD

sees the significance of his acting in the film. Bresson's films are Bresson. Renoir is saying, this is me, these are the others; put them all together and, to misuse Carson McCullers's phrase, you get the we of me.

The Rules of the Game is an open work, from which no one is excluded, either in the making of the film or in the experiencing of it now. I love Vigo's *L'Atalante:* it is perhaps the most purely "poetic" film ever made, but it is not my favorite film because—because Vigo didn't *want* it to be. It is his film, his vision, and we are kept a little outside of it.

In *Citizen Kane,* another favorite, Welles does indeed play a role in his film, as Renoir did, but the difference is monumental: Welles plays Kane in such a way as to keep Welles *out* of the film, to keep us at our distance from him. It is, of course, a much finer performance than Renoir gives; but it is also a much less personal one. Welles hides behind Kane, whereas Renoir, almost indecently, exposes himself as Octave.

Oddly enough, a film that much resembles *The Rules of the Game* is Resnais's *Muriel,* another favorite of mine. Like the Renoir, it is a panorama of French life, this time postwar. And Delphine Seyrig, although a much greater actress than Nora Gregor, also gives a performance which is against the grain for her; Renoir made a "mistake" in casting Gregor for the part, and that is paradoxically why she is so moving. Resnais chose Seyrig purposely to play a part for which she must have seemed—and is—oddly suited. And paradoxically she is great in the role just because the Seyrig of *Marienbad* was all wrong for the Hélène of *Muriel.* And while Resnais did not go so far as to appear in his own film, the actor he chose for Alphonse is in fact playing a version of Resnais himself—an unsympathetic, unflattering version, showing himself at his vacillating, temporizing worst, just as Renoir showed himself at his worst as Octave. Masochism, objectivity, or humility? A mixture of all three.

One admires some people and some things because they are different from oneself. And one admires others because they are the same. I like Bresson's, Godard's and Straub's sensibilities because they are totally unlike mine. I go all gooey at Demy's *Lola* and Ophuls's *La Signora di Tutti* because their sensibilities are all too much like my own. But I think what I like most is a mixture of my own temperament with something a little different; or, shall we say, my view of myself on one of my better days. That is why I like Bertolucci, and that is why *The Rules of the Game* remains my favorite film.

11. French Cancan

ROGER GREENSPUN

THERE IS SOMETHING fundamentally suspect about
the mere idea of a favorite movie. It is not quite an offensive idea—
like the yearly insult of the ten-best list or the various film critics'
choices, which are intellectually unimaginable at best and intellectually scandalous at worst—but there is still something very wrong
with it. I assume that "favorite movie" isn't necessarily "best movie,"
but merely the one you like the best for any dumb reason or for no
reason. And though I approve the informality, I'm annoyed by the
idea—partly because it seems so childish.

In one area or another, I've had a number of favorites in my time.
But there have been fewer as I've grown older, and loyalties to my
own preferences have grown less significant—perhaps because there
are more preferences, and because the loyalties are now easier to
maintain. I doubt that I could even begin to reconstruct the intensity
of my taste for French vanilla ice cream when I was ten years old,
though I've kept the taste despite everything that rum-raisin, choco-
late-ripple and sagging stomach have done to lure me out of it.
Later, classier enthusiasms—Frederick Delius in music, Edgar Allan

Poe in prose (for the landscape sketches!)—surely have more to do with pose than with feeling, and I think that passing out of them is less a matter of growing older than of growing up.

Some years ago, at a time when anything else seemed better than whatever was going on in my life, I began playing a kind of favorites-by-elimination game, in which I decided not what I liked the best but rather what I would most dislike to have forever to do without. Though most of my semiconscious time then as well as now was given to fantasizing about women and sailboats, my selections by deprivation never got beyond food. That may have been all to the best, because the results were pretty weird. I imagined the traditional desert island on which I would be stranded, probably for life, and I tried to come up with the one thing that I should most hate not ever being able to have. I came up with two—one to eat and one to drink. They were grapefruit and dry martinis. And that takes me as far along the road to essentials as I care to go. My desert island didn't include a movie theater.

"Favorite" is really a matter of simplistic autobiography. Food may properly be a favorite, or a Raggedy Ann doll, or a teddy bear, or a shady hideaway under the old oak in the garden, if that's the kind of life you've led. But not novels or poems (except to the foolishly romantic) and not movies either—because they all represent a much more complex experience than any that can lead to the picking of favorites, and they all come equipped with the kind of self-sufficiency that must be part of what we like to call "aesthetic distance," which is surely as much an attribute of *The Horse Soldiers* as it is of, say, *Remembrance of Things Past*.

But now that I have established my virtue, I had better admit that I do have a favorite decade for movies—the 1950s—and that I do, in a sense, have a favorite moviemaker—Jean Renoir. I pick the 1950s partly because it was late in the 1950s and very much in terms of the 1950s that I first became really conscious of movies, but mostly because movies themselves came to a flowering of consciousness (just before self-consciousness) roughly in the same few years. I think there were more good movies made in the 1950s than at any other time (not more passably good ones; more very good ones), and if you were mining for masterpieces, that would be your

ROGER GREENSPUN

richest lode. And I pick Renoir because, given the history of movies so far, he seems to me incontestably the greatest artist. Indeed, saying that Jean Renoir is my favorite filmmaker seems, for its inevitability, a little like confessing that Shakespeare is my favorite English playwright.

The usual view of Renoir's career finds him rising during the 1930s with the kind of socially sophisticated humanism that reached its peak either in *The Grand Illusion* (1937) or *The Rules of the Game* (1939), depending upon how knowledgeable a usual view you happen to follow. Then comes exile to America during the war years, the inevitable decline of good things European, and in the 1950s an international hodgepodge of movies, distressing to the critics partly because those movies in their freewheeling theatricality seem a deliberate affront to the qualities, specifically the humanistic realism, for which the critics valued Renoir. There were certain exceptions—*The River* (1950) for its gentle Anglo-Indian universalism; perhaps *The Golden Coach* (1952) for the very classicism of its theater (commedia dell'arte rather than musical comedy)—but nothing really to reverse the downhill slide of an artist who had committed the cardinal sin of advancing beyond his admirers' ancient preconceptions.

All this has given Renoir a fairly minor place in many film histories, with a couple of classics now thirty years old, the unavailability of everything that came before and the perverse artificiality of almost everything that came later—with no fancy camera tricks and no promulgation of an aesthetic or a school of the sort that provides the people who write articles something to write articles about.

If you look up the popular press reviews of Renoir in sequence since 1937, you will generally find that each new film is referred back to *The Grand Illusion*, from which each new film tends downward. A more stupid view of artistic development would be hard to find—though as stupid a view is easy enough to find duplicated for Ford or Hawks or Hitchcock or Dreyer, or any of those movie masters whose misfortune it has been to live brilliantly out of their time. In this respect, the history of all reputations in the arts usually suffer. But reputations in the popular arts suffer most, because their audience places the least value on individualistic insight—and no

French Cancan   107 value at all on the perpetually unfashionable clarity of vision that sometimes attends exceptional old age.

But if you grant Renoir his clarity of vision, you will have to admit that he is using it to look in some unusual places, especially if your ideas about movie greatness include a certain weighting toward naturalism (read, lower-middle-class naturalism), as the ideas of most published theoreticians generally do. Renoir in the 1950s seems to choose a kind of farcical frivolity, the very last vehicle you'd expect for high seriousness or even for the low seriousness that for so many people is the only proper excuse for going to the movies. Except for *The River* the films are either about theater or they *are* theater (*Golden Coach* even begins with the traditional three blows of the French classical stage and ends with the closing of the curtain) in the sense that they work with a fairly magnificent perversity to emphasize the artificiality rather than the reality of their actions. *Picnic on the Grass* (1959) and *Elena et les Hommes* (1956—until recently, available here only in an edited English-language version called *Paris Does Strange Things*) are both farcical comedies—the former out of pastoral and the latter out of comedy of manners, though those distinctions blur, and both films become comedy of manners in vastly different pastoral settings, while (as is traditional for pastoral) both have very profoundly to do with the artifice of politics.

This highly complex respect for literary or dramatic types is a clue to the later Renoir, a clue that people are willing enough to follow when it is adequately framed and made sufficiently obvious —as in *The Golden Coach*. It is a clue that is more difficult to follow in the possibly more brilliant *Elena et les Hommes*, and it is a clue that can positively get you lost in the thickets (quite profitably lost) when you try to apply it to *French Cancan*.

French Cancan, for anyone who has read this far, is what, if I believed in such nonsense, I should offer as my favorite movie.

I don't think it is the greatest movie. I don't think it is the greatest Renoir. Nobody else does, either. It is a musical, made in 1954, and it deals with the opening of the Moulin Rouge near the turn of the century. When Renoir's movie came out it was of course compared unfavorably with John Huston's *Moulin Rouge*. And now that

ROGER GREENSPUN

enough time has passed so that things should begin assuming their proper perspective, it is still so little esteemed that recently, when I wanted to show it to a class of film students, I found that it wasn't even available on 16mm—in a period when virtually everything has been put on 16mm. But in spite of this neglect it doesn't qualify for, say, "favorite forgotten film" either, because that is altogether too trivial a category (better for such movies as Allan Dwan's *Slightly Scarlet* or Delmar Daves's *A Summer Place,* two minor glories of the 1950s). And if *French Cancan* isn't the greatest Renoir, it may just possibly be the second greatest Renoir. In any case, it belongs with the supreme and, especially, supremely *intelligent* achievements of twentieth-century artistic imagination.

As I have said, it is a music-hall story. Not a romance, though there are a few romances involved, and not a real-life history, though its sense of time is at least in some measure historical. The story is very trivial. A Parisian impresario named Danglard (Jean Gabin), down on his luck and slightly bored with his love life—his star entertainer, known as the Belle Abesse (Maria Félix)—takes a recuperative night on the town. His party goes slumming and visits a bar in Montmartre, where Danglard meets and dances with a poor laundress named Nini (Françoise Arnoul). Moved by the spirit of the people (mostly whores and pimps) and by the vitality of their dancing, and intrigued by the lovely and limber Nini, he is inspired to open a new club on that very Montmartre site. To be called the Moulin Rouge, it will cater to the common people and will revive the old popular style of dancing, the cancan.

Everything goes well enough until the day of the dedication ceremonies, when Nini's boyfriend, a baker's assistant, jealous of Danglard's attentions to the girl and furious that he has made her a principal dancer, attacks the impresario and injures him seriously enough to put him in bed and bring the construction of the Moulin Rouge to a halt. Financing fails, morale collapses and everything looks completely black until a *deus ex machina* in the person of a foreigner, a young prince (Gianni Esposito), who falls in love with Nini, comes to the aid of the project so that the now-recovered Danglard can bring the Moulin Rouge to its opening night and the performance that climaxes and closes the film.

I've left out a good deal, all of it important, and much of it almost equally conventional: the pathetic love of Prince Alexandre for Nini (she doesn't love him, she loves dancing; he tries to shoot himself but only manages a flesh wound); the comic love of everybody for the Belle Abesse (she will eventually marry, but wisely, for money); the local color of Montmartre; the street singer Esther Georges (Anna Amendola) who, before the end of the film, replaces Nini in Danglard's parade of stageworthy mistresses and who comes to mean almost as much to the Moulin Rouge as does the whirling tide of cancan dancers.

You won't appreciate *French Cancan* by learning the plot, though the plot seems more and more useful and more intricately meaningful the better you get to know the movie. The whole matter of Prince Alexandre, for example, a fool of love among people who cannot tolerate such foolishness; heir to a kingdom that is, by his own account, full of nothing but tobacco, sheep and roses; unfailingly "nice" (everybody calls him that), he comes offering a happy ending, wealth and marriage in another country—a fairy-tale world that is not the fairy-tale world of the film. Though wholly likable (indeed, the movie is quite without ordinary antagonists), he is for Nini morally wrong—in the way that certain solutions in great literature, though apparently good, are morally wrong (as, say, Nausicaa for Odysseus) because they conform to wishes rather than to realities and because it is the part of wisdom to reject them. But he is also aesthetically wrong for Nini because he promises her rest and retirement, a happily-ever-after ending which is necessarily an escape from time—whereas the whole movement of the film, and of Nini's career, is toward a total commitment to time as furnishing the only terms in which life is worth living. Dreamy Prince Alexandre epitomizes one extreme of romantic agony; the violent but practical baker's boy epitomizes another (he is willing to kill for his love so long as he thinks he can get her, but settles easily for another girl when that love proves ultimately unattainable); the Belle Abesse with her assorted grand affairs epitomizes a third—but her position is already defined and accepted, and her role outside the theater is essentially to parody passion.

Of course *French Cancan* never ventures too far outside the theater. In some respects it serves as a tribute to the theatricalism of movies, and even its exteriors are obviously, and charmingly, sound-

ROGER GREENSPUN

stage constructions. The streets of Montmartre, the little hill where, under some drying laundry and one forlorn dogwood tree, the prince offers his kingdom to the pauper, the façade of the Moulin Rouge itself—all have more to do with the art of the scene painter than with physical reality. And yet all feed a reality that is no less responsible for being so loyally theatrical.

For it is in terms of theater that Alexandre is proven virtually a paradigm of *irresponsibility*. In rejecting him and choosing the theater, Nini chooses not for personal happiness (she is immediately made unhappy by Danglard's dalliance with Esther Georges, and her first lesson in the Moulin Rouge is that there is no undying anything and that she too will pass), but for a kind of generalized necessity that for a while she may participate in, that that pre-exists her and will continue after her, and is cruel and exhilarating and leaves no time for tears. At its most trivial the sentiment involved reads something like "the show must go on." At its most profound it reads something like "the show *will* go on," and this at one level or another is the burden of all the great Renoir films of the 1950s, when theater as a metaphor for life comes for a time to supplant the road and the river, the great ultimate images of almost all his earlier films.

A good many of the impulses behind *French Cancan* point toward the desirability of making a virtue of necessity. In this connection, Renoir's great quality is his understanding of which necessities seem particularly virtuous—for there is always a choice—and in his further appreciation that the liveliest necessities are also the hardest and the most painfully indifferent to whatever does not feed their liveliness. *French Cancan* is an unusually tough and tough-minded movie, and as it proceeds, it leaves behind a trail of hurt feelings that range from picturesque pathos to something very like homicidal rage. These feelings are never reconciled. They are noticed, appreciated, given a certain passionate play (and an equally certain dose of parody) and then dismissed as distracting from the real end of life—which, in this case, is of course to sing and dance. Anyone with enough sense will accept the inevitable, as Nini does when she gives up her pique at Danglard and agrees to star in his cancan, or as the baker's boy does when denied the chance to marry

French Cancan   111

Nini. He seems tacitly to realize that his aim is really the estate and not the woman, and he prepares to marry Nini's best girl friend instead.

Renoir is an artist concerned with the vital continuity of things. That is why the road and the river, which go on, are his most persistent major images. It is one reason why his last great movie, *The Elusive Corporal* (1962), a prison-camp escape film, which begins with the a declaration of peace (the French capitulation to the Nazis), ends with an agreement between the corporal and his friend that in a rather special sense war is their métier, and for them, even free and in Paris, it is essential that the fighting continue. That is also why individual tragedy in Renoir's hands, as in the much-admired *Toni* of 1934, can seem just a bit forced and trivial when balanced against everything else in the world—even when balanced with everything else in the world that surrounds the personal tragedy.

And finally, that is why the most profound Renoir films play (I mean, literally, play) with ideology and science, with war and political history, with art and entertainment—to the end that they may discover new combinations, as in the image of the bridal bouquet that closes *Picnic on the Grass* (1959) and combines the conventions of society with the forces of nature in order to save modern Europe, restore to life some of its ah-sweet-mystery, and assure the continuity of at least one more generation for Western civilization. Such an image in such a movie with such import may seem like an insufferable affront, redeemed only by its innocence. But in fact it is really not so innocent, and it is richly and honestly earned, and its audacity is no less than the ultimate clarity of the best mind and the most thoughtful style in the history of movies. To accept all this will take a lot of looking, for nothing in Renoir's later work seems especially remarkable at first glance, but rather deepens and grows mysterious with familiarity. The magnificent entertainment that closes *French Cancan* is of this order: an elaborately staged number featuring the Belle Abesse; a barrel-organ tune sung by Esther Georges as she strolls in through the street doors of the Moulin Rouge as if to serenade from the heart as well as to the ears of her audience; the cataclysmic eruption of the cancan dancers, who enter from before, behind, above and virtually between the legs of the audience. Their purpose is to obliterate the space between audience

ROGER GREENSPUN

and performers; in their own small way, to introduce chaos, and, together with it, the premonitions of a new order based on their vitality, their skill, their exuberance, their direct assault on the emotions. Their appeal is irresistible, being made up equally of an outspoken theatrical corniness (the cancan is an old dance, a common people's dance, recalling a mass public to its power) and, in their mode of dress, their life style, and the glorious splits they do on the floor, an open invitation to sex.

To their call, not even weary old Danglard, who imagined them into being in the first place, is immune. Sitting alone backstage at the Moulin Rouge, his feet respond to the music and he is drawn back into the dance in his own way—to find, in the audience this time, a new girl, who surely will replace Esther Georges, who has replaced Nini, who replaced the Belle Abesse, so long as it takes him to prepare her for the theater. All this is very close to the conventions of the show-biz musical comedy—as it clearly means to be. Renoir has never tried to make his movies unlike whatever generic type they happen to be—and least of all the 1950s comedies. But it is also very close to the kind of half-mystical understanding that is granted only to the greatest art. For even among the magnificent films of Jean Renoir, only *French Cancan*—by its energy, its clarity, its sometimes terrifying submergence of the part in the whole—is able, not to observe or to report upon or try to re-create, but rather to participate in ecstasy.

12. Some Nights in Casablanca

RICHARD SCHICKEL

IT IS REMEMBERED mainly for its dialogue, which admittedly loses something in translation to the printed page:

CAPT. RENAULT: What in heaven's name brought you to Casablanca?
RICK: My health. I came to Casablanca for the waters.
RENAULT: The waters? What waters? We're in the desert.
RICK: I was misinformed.

And:

UGARTE: You despise me, Rick, don't you?
RICK: Oh, if I gave you any thought I probably would.

And: "Here's looking at *you,* kid." And: "Round up the usual suspects." And: "I'm only a poor corrupt official." And, most famous, and most often misquoted: "You played it for her. You can play it for me. If she can stand it, I can. Play it."

The film, of course, is *Casablanca.* It won an Academy Award in 1943 as best picture, and its director Michael Curtiz and its writers Julius and Philip Epstein and Howard Koch also won Oscars for their work on it, which is no guarantee of anything, except that the picture was commercially successful and inoffensive to what in those days was generally referred to as "the movie colony." Later, in the 1960s it became the centerpiece of the collegiate Bogart cult, a harmless enough fad (especially when you consider some of the other fads that generation embraced). Still, objectively speaking, the film is probably entitled to no greater celebrity than any other work that happens accidentally to be entitled to footnotes in two disparate volumes—one the history of Hollywood in its highest moments of power, the other a social history of a time when both American movies and American society were in much deeper trouble. Setting those matters aside, the film as film remains what it always was—a somewhat better-than-average example of what the American studio system could do when it was at its most stable and powerful, with the anxieties occasioned by consolidation, the coming of sound and the depression behind it; and with the cataclysm compounded of television's arrival, political witch-hunts and the enforced separation of studios and theater chains still all but imperceptible, hull-down on the horizon of the future.

But if the claims for *Casablanca* are so modest, what is it doing here, surrounded by essays on more distinguished, or at least more historically significant, films? In part it's because the editor required his contributors to name favorite movies, not best movies. In part, it's a matter of perversity. Who wants to name *Citizen Kane* or *Intolerance* or *8½* as one's favorite movie? *Anybody* can do that. But mostly one puts down *Casablanca* because it is a representative— and a very fair one—of a period in American movie history that, if not great, was certainly interesting—especially to me, whose concern for the medium and sense of the world outside my own provincial, middle-class neigborhood was formed during it.

Nostalgia, of course, colors our view of the movies that impressed us in childhood and adolescence. It is very hard, even for a critic who has steeled himself against sneak attacks on his emotions by this trickiest of mediums, to resist the pull of his first favorites, those films that initially suggested to him the possibility that film was something he might care about seriously, thoughtfully. On the other hand, one has to guard against reaction. I've seen for a second or third time a large number of movies I thought I loved best as a kid and I find I have a tendency to turn rather violently against them, as if, somehow, their makers had deliberately set out to betray me, to cast a shadow on my youth. I find, on reexamination, that *Casablanca* is not as perfectly wonderful as I once thought it was. Yet it remains, as so many of its contemporaries do not, enjoyable, a suitable object for affection.

To me this is remarkable because so very few "serious" films of *Casablanca's* time hold up at all. On the whole it seems to me that it is only in the middle range that the films of the forties continue to exert a defensible claim on us. Obviously, the "B" pictures and the routine program features, designed to soak up studio overhead charges and to provide a reliable flow of "product" to the theater chains controlled by the studios, were built to self-destruct in a few months, the more easily to make room for other films exactly like them in appeal. A lot of this stuff remains eminently watchable in a mindless sort of way, but it requires an unregenerate film buff (or an *auteur* critic) to find any lasting merit in it. On the other hand, the films that Hollywood at the time regarded as important and prestigious, fare, as a whole, even worse when viewed with the perspective of twenty-five or thirty years. For one thing, the big pictures were junked up with "production values" by a Hollywood made suddenly prosperous by wartime economy, and directors were encouraged to linger over these irrelevancies by producers who liked to see what they'd paid for up on the screen. Also, the moving camera was coming into vogue just then, and the long crane and dolly shots were, of necessity, rather stately in pace. This, too, contributed to a slowing of the rhythm of important films (these shots were too expensive to set up for cheap films) and one misses, in the major films of the forties, the energy and driving pace of the good films of the thirties, which derived from an entirely different set of editing and shooting conventions (takes were shorter and scenes tended to be broken down into more shots, so that fluidity was sacrificed but a certain nervous rhythm was gained).

One even misses the high key lighting of the earlier films. Charles Higham and Joel Greenberg, in their little book, *Hollywood in the Forties,* devote a key chapter to the "black cinema," and they use the term quite literally. The European directors who had been arriving in the United States in increasing numbers over the previous decade had gained considerable influence in Hollywood by the

RICHARD SCHICKEL

forties. For understandable reasons their vision was darker than that of their American colleagues and their style, with its emphasis on picturesque menace (dimly lit night streets, a photogenic fog rolling in, lots of shadows and silhouettes) was very useful at a time when stories of spies and underground activities on the continent were good box office.

At the time, of course, no one mentioned the *film noir* and, largely ignorant of other styles of filming, I simply accepted its stylistic conventions as the way movies should look, perhaps had to look. I was similarly acceptant of Hollywood's discovery of the Freudian explanations of human motivation and of the long pauses required to work these into the action. Nor, in my innocence, was I in the least bothered by the political speeches that turned up in the strangest places—in the mess room of a submarine in *Destination Tokyo*, for example, or in the middle of a jungle in *Objective Burma* or, for that matter, in a suburban living room in *Since You Went Away*. I'm not certain I even understood that these were, in fact, political speeches, As a rule they were couched in very general terms and simply outlined the pleasant prospect of a peaceful, prosperous future dominated by the spirit of international cooperation between a list of democratic nations that carelessly included such countries as China and Russia. If these expressions of optimism seem impossibly naive in retrospect (and dramaturgically ridiculous) they seemed perfectly sensible to a pre-adolescent child, who did occasionally wonder what we were fighting *for*, since what we were fighting *against* was made abundantly clear not only in these movies but throughout popular culture.

Nor at the time could one possibly object to the indirect method of portraying American values—the small military unit, composed of men drawn from diverse backgrounds, yet marvelously cooperative and mutually supportive under the impress of danger. Restudying these films, this conceit seems awkward and unrealistic, but then it seemed just exactly right—a logical extension of the boyish gangs to which we all belonged and proof that our own youthful values might have some useful function in the adult world.

I have gone into all these matters here mostly to demonstrate that part of the enduring appeal of *Casablanca* lies in its avoidance of the most common conventions of its time. To be sure, it can be regarded as a *film noir* (and at the time James Agee objected to Curtiz's camera moving like "a nautch dancer"). In fact, however, its movements are not as tortuous as Fritz Lang's were and Curtiz's setups and lighting are almost never as self-conscious as those of his competitors who clung more rigidly to the Ufa style. Indeed, it seems to me that at his best Curtiz struck a rather felicitous balance between the European style and the determined plainness of Hawks and Walsh, whose preferred shot was the medium shot with the camera waist-high and stationary. The advantage of balance is also apparent in the film's lighting. The ending at the airfield on a foggy night is, of course, a classic *film noir* sequence. And there are one or two other shadowy sequences as well. But the greater portion of the movie is set in Rick's brightly lit nightclub and there is more daylight in the film than I had, in fact, remembered.

The virtues of balance are apparent throughout the film. Originally the studio announced an all-American cast of players who rarely rose out of the most routine kind of program features—Ann Sheridan, Ronald Reagan, Dennis Morgan—indicating an executive judgment that the property (an unproduced play) was not a very strong one. I don't know what happened to change the corporate mind, but the notion of having the dark, saturnine Bogart play opposite the sober, almost antisexual Ingrid Bergman was a brilliant one. One understood that Miss Bergman's film *persona,* unlike Miss Sheridan's, did not undertake affairs lightly, that her previous relationship with Bogart in Paris ("You wore blue, the Germans wore gray") was, indeed, a once-in-a-lifetime thing, sufficiently intense to break through her reserve (and her loyalty to her imprisoned husband) and his cynicism. Simply by being present these opposites created a depth, an ambiguity, in the film's central relationship that no writers could have created. Then, too, Paul Henreid, as Victor Laszlo the underground leader, is believable as no American actor could have been. And that is no small matter in the overall scheme of the film, since he is required to make us accept the unlikely possibility that (a) he is the head of *all* such subversive activity in German-occupied Europe and (b) so valuable a figure would surface and disport himself in public as he does here—even to the point of conducting the crowd in Rick's in the singing of "The

RICHARD SCHICKEL

Marseillaise" under the eyes of a tableful of German officers whose own Nazi song is drowned out. Corny as it is, the scene is the movie's emotional high point and it works, I think, because Henreid effectively underplays throughout with such dignity and intelligence. Only Paul Lukas, in *Watch on the Rhine,* gave us a comparably believable portrait of a character then strange to the mass sensibility —the committed intellectual.

Henreid's presence, in turn, is balanced by Conrad Veidt's cannily understated performance as Major Strasser, the Gestapo officer drawn to Free French territory in part by the murder of the couriers who carried the letters of transit which are, to borrow Hitchcock's term, the "MacGuffin" (the device that sets the plot awhirl), in part in pursuit of Laszlo. This character is in many respects Henreid's exact opposite. Unlike so many movie Nazis he is not, apparently, a sadist. Rather, he is an ideologue, a man of action and a fanatic—all qualities present in Laszlo as well. One likes the way he is written and played precisely because he is not seen as a monstrous sport of nature but as a recognizable human being reasonably serving a doctrine that is, to him, a realistic reading of history and of human need. The worst he can say about his opponents in the film is that they lack his prescience about the inevitable triumph of fascism—and that they are romantics, which is, God knows, true enough.

But sharply and economically etched as all these characters are, artfully set as they are in the total composition, it is Claude Rains as the Vichy police chief, Louis Renault, whose performance holds our deepest continuing interest. It is inconceivable that he did not win an Academy Award for it (Charles Coburn took the Oscar that year, for his work in *The More the Merrier*), since the American screen of that time offered few such energetically duplicitous bits of acting. In the scheme of the film, the role performs two functions. He balances Bogart, of course, making his progress from opportunistic cynicism to idealism at the same time Rick proceeds from his rueful cynicism to idealism. More important, however, he stands as the ambiguous emotional center of the film, the human embodiment of Casablanca's mystery and corruption. It is, finally, on his behavior that a satisfactory working out of the plot depends, on his refusal to stop the plane on which Bergman and Henreid make their escape, on his refusal to arrest Bogart for the murder of Major Strasser, that our pleasure rests.

But that is perhaps too dry an analysis. For the fact that whenever Rains is on screen the movie is charged with the excitement that only a good actor enjoying himself in a good role can create. Rains's gifts seemed to me often underutilized in rather stodgy parts, but here, for once, he was permitted to run free. He was given most of the really good lines in the film and he handled them with a cool panache that he was seldom to achieve elsewhere. My own favorite moment occurs when he announces that he is "shocked, shocked" to discover gambling going on in Rick's back room, while pocketing his winnings without missing a beat. In short, he picks up, brightens the tone of a movie whenever its essential romanticism threatens to go soggy. Balance again.

Obviously this balance is built into the structure of the film. But it is no less apparent in the dialogue. And it is something of a miracle. For the project had quite a checkered history. It began as yet another job of adaptation by the Epsteins, who were twin brothers and very efficient adapters of plays when they weren't doing originals that were mostly light, charming romances (for example, *Strawberry Blonde*). It was, in fact, the urbane Julius Epstein who was dispatched to David O. Selznick to tell him the story line of the film and thereby win his consent to lend Ingrid Bergman to Warners for the lead. His task was not lightened by the fact that, at the time, the Epsteins had not, as the phrase then went, "licked" the story, and that during the interview the producer was preoccupied with a huge bowl of chicken soup that he was noisily consuming. Epstein prevailed, mainly by reassuring the producer that his valuable property would be handsomely costumed and that her vehicle would put the public in mind of a previous hit that had taken its title from another North African city, *Algiers*. The trouble was that the Epsteins, who had lately worked with Frank Capra on *Arsenic and Old Lace*, were recruited by him to come to Washington and work on his *Why We Fight* series—a brilliantly edited series of domestic propaganda shorts. So they had to abandon the script in mid-passage, though they continued to send pages from Washington.

Meantime, Howard Koch, who had been responsible for the script of Orson Welles's famous *War of the Worlds* radio broadcast, and who was now a screenwriter of no fixed intellectual abode, was set to work on the film. He was a different sort of romantic from the Epsteins. The year before he had adapted Somerset Maugham's *The Letter,* an entirely apolitical and dull Bette Davis vehicle. His next assignment would be *Mission to Moscow,* one of the most remarkable films produced in America during the war, in that it offered audiences nearly two hours of unrelieved Stalinist propaganda (including the recitation of the party line on the purge trials, the Hitler-Stalin pact and the invasion of Finland) as well as a portrait of the dictator as a sort of Judge Hardy in the Kremlin. What, exactly, he contributed is difficult to determine, though certainly he was a more political creature than the Epsteins and may have given the film its world view, such as it was. Anyway, the brothers returned to the studio after a couple of months and it is confirmed by them and by Miss Bergman that the script was not finished when shooting began. In particular, no one could decide how the film should end—should she stay in Casablanca with Rick or leave on that plane with Victor Laszlo? "Play it in between," she was instructed, "and we'll shoot both endings." Happily, they shot the one in which she and Bogart renounce one another, the one in which the problems of two people are compared unfavorably to "a hill of beans," given the great struggle against fascism going on around them. It was, by the standards of the time, politically correct. But more importantly, it was romantically correct. When the dailies were viewed, it was agreed that there was no need to shoot the alternative ending, that this one was right and true and beautiful.

Perhaps it is fair to say that the essentially apolitical Epsteins balanced the more leftishly committed Koch. Or that everyone was fortunate to catch the latter at mid-point between *The Letter* and *Mission.* For politics here form only the basis for a personal drama of a quite believable sort, are just another element in a well-proportioned and fairly complex plot. Nor can it be said that the issue explored—a man trying to strike a suitable balance between selfish interest and commitment to political ideals—was (or is) uninteresting. Indeed, it seems to me to form one of the very few valid bases for political (or, more properly perhaps, politicized) drama. At any rate, it is established through a few throwaway lines that Bogart's Rick has, in the past, served as a soldier of fortune (gun-running division) for Ethiopia and Loyalist Spain, and although he insists that he was well paid for these activities, Major Strasser observes that he might have been even better paid had he chosen to work for the fascists. To which Rick has no ready reply. It is also established that even this slightly ambiguous idealism has been shattered by Ingrid Bergman's mysterious desertion in Paris and that, as a result of this personal betrayal, he will "stick my neck out for nobody" now. If even so ideal a thing as their love can be betrayed, rather obviously political idealism—so much more complex and ambiguous —represents a worse peril. The film's chief drama consists, quite simply, of rekindling in Rick his willingness, at the very least, to stick his neck out for others.

We are convinced, of course, that he will, and such suspense as we derive from this line of the plot consists largely in wondering exactly how long it will take him to do so. (After all, he rigs his roulette wheel to allow a young refugee couple to win passage money out of Casablanca so the wife will not have to earn it in Renault's bed. If he will make such a *beau geste* for strangers, how can we imagine that he will not act similarly on behalf of the woman he once loved, the cause of his current anguish—especially when it is obvious that the man for whom she has deserted him is such a worthy and valuable citizen of the world?)

Still, in the end, the script makes it clear that something more than mere human decency motivates his renunciation. As Rick tells Ilsa while putting her on the plane for Lisbon: "It doesn't take much to see that the problems of three little people don't amount to a hill of beans in this crazy world. . . . Here's looking at *you*, kid." It is a measure of this film's grace, I think, that Bogart speeds unemphatically through this speech and that the words themselves are flat, without the ring of preachment. In an era when every film that touched upon the war seemed to end in an explosion of rhetoric, *Casablanca* went against the grain at the end as it had throughout.

I don't want to make too much of this. Damage has already been done to Bogart posthumously by trying to make an existential hero out of the screen character he created when nothing so fancy— or self-conscious—had been intended. Nor do I imagine that the other people involved in *Casablanca* were aware of just how well their work would turn out. Quite the opposite, apparently. None of

RICHARD SCHICKEL

them thought very highly of the thing and the initial critical response was no more than respectable, even with Agee, who had a rare gift for finding silver threads among the dross, wondering why it was "working up a rather serious reputation as a fine melodrama." He quite correctly observed that the small-part players and the atmospheric scenes were "not even alien corn" (Peter Lorre and Sidney Greenstreet in particular, were wasted). He also cited a couple of whoppers in the dialogue that one would prefer to forget: "Oh, Victor, please don't go to the underground meeting tonight." And, also from Miss Bergman's lips, "From now on you'll have to do the thinking for both of us, dear" as she swoons onto a lover's couch with Bogart, who quite clearly is not about to do much thinking—not for the moment, anyhow.

It does no good to respond to this perfectly justifiable criticism by inflating the claims for *Casablanca*. The fact is that the film came to seem better and better as more movies sought to deal with the issues of war—and the characters of the men who fought them —and came up lame. When they essayed humor it was of the locker-room sort—and the men who wrote the stuff were, by this time, far, far away from the sound of real proletarian voices, so it seemed false at that time and has not improved at all with age. Worse, everyone was so anxious to stir the home front to greater efforts with its rivet guns by promising a brave new world after the war that they would bust a character wide open, the more conveniently to insert an agit-prop speech in his mouth. Or to let him rant on about the natural bestiality of the Japanese or German national character. Or else to refer in the most embarrassing terms to the simple values for which he fought—like his right to boo the Dodgers, as the famous magazine ad put it. In contrast, *Casablanca* berated nothing and promised nothing. And as time goes by that begins to look awfully good in contrast to its contemporary competition.

What it did instead was work up a highly stylized atmosphere— one which supported both its deliciously rueful romanticism and the convention that even Gestapo officers assigned to this exotic locale must have been chosen, in part, because of their ability to engage in worldly cross talk with the native population. High art—whatever that is—it certainly was not. An accident it certainly was, for most successful American movies are that—a congeries of disparate talents who somehow, for one special moment in time, strike sparks in a way that only happens to them, as individuals, three or four times in a career.

But most of what I have written here is *ex post facto*. When I first saw and fell in love with *Casablanca*, I was all of ten years old. I was very much a child of the provinces. I had heard of *Casablanca*, of course, because of the American victory there in the North African campaign and because it was the site, a little later, of the Roosevelt-Churchill conference with the Free French leaders. But in those days exotic places seemed to exist mainly as settings for heroic and historic happenings. Somehow one never imagined that they supported ordinary life as well, little human dramas like a lost love turning up suddenly and requiring gallant assistance. Amazing! The human side of the news.

Of course, even then I understood that the events of the film were romantically colored. Obviously nothing like them could take place on our suburban block. Even so, they were acted out by recognizably human beings. It required no great leap to imagine that, if one could project oneself into a suitably romantic clime, one might have the opportunity to behave with a similar worldliness and coolness under pressure. Better still, after a movie diet composed of roughly equal parts of suitable-for-children fare and of straight adventure stuff, in which all motives were simple and the characters seemed to exist only in and for the heroic moment, without a past or a discernible future, I was thrilled in a new way by *Casablanca*, thrilled by its ambiance (at the very least it was my first nightclub picture), thrilled by its gray moral world (where people did right for the wrong reasons and vice versa), thrilled by its cynicism and its touches of pessimism (so at odds with the peppy, cheerful air of my native ground). It was like being permitted to overhear an adult conversation—and discovering that you could follow its twists and turns, its unspoken meanings.

Is it too much to say that in seeing it I began the process of losing my innocence? Probably. No doubt a lot of less memorable events were taking place around the same time and contributing to that process. Nevertheless, it is some kind of convenient benchmark in

RICHARD SCHICKEL

my personal history, a point from which it's possible to date the beginning of a change in sensibility.

But that is too bland a phrase. I have, of course, become as pessimistic and as cynical as Bogart presents himself at his worst in *Casablanca*—how can one be otherwise, having come of age in the fifties and sixties? But in my secret heart I still think that, if put to the right test, in the right atmosphere, I would be capable of the kind of romantic renunciation he managed there. It is not my fault that no cause appears to be as valid as the one that finally moved him. The important thing is that one believes such a cause may yet appear in the course of human affairs, that one may still be given the chance to serve love, decency and a good abstract ideal in a single grand gesture.

No doubt *Casablanca* succeeded commercially because it was a paradigm for personal commitment that appeared at a moment when many were in the process of making, or trying to make, personal—as opposed to merely political—commitments to the fight against fascism. No doubt it worked because so many who worked on it were themselves essentially apolitical and their work, like the minds of the audience to which it appealed, was untainted by prior ideological commitments. But I treasure it, finally, for more subjective reasons—because it was my first delightful, appealing primer in a problem that is to me endlessly fascinating, never fully resolved —the one of balancing the demands of the heart and the dictates of belief. Bless its sincere and slightly kitschy heart for undertaking so sober a task with wit and style and grace under commercial pressure, for somehow transcending the conventions of its cinematic moment at the same time it seemed to summarize them. Yes, that dialogue *is* wonderful, but it is only one obvious example of the professional skills that were deployed throughout this film, skills that were always present in the old Hollywood, but rarely orchestrated as they were in this superb example of what the studios could do, might have done more often, when they really tried.

The world grows old. And we along with it. But *Casablanca* reminds us of how it was when all of us were young and eager both to believe and to suspend disbelief, the better to touch and be touched by good romance.

13. A Few Notes on Jerome Hill's Film Portrait

JONAS MEKAS

I DO NOT HAVE *one* favorite movie; I do not have *one* favorite filmmaker; but I do have one hundred favorite movies, and twenty or more favorite filmmakers. Here are some: Carl Dreyer, Stan Brakhage, Luis Buñuel, Kenneth Anger, Sergei Eisenstein, D. W. Griffith, Georges Méliès, Gregory Markopoulos, Lumière Brothers, Michael Snow, Andy Warhol, Jean Cocteau, Harry Smith, Dziga Vertov, Jack Smith, Bruce Baillie, Ken Jacobs, Robert Flaherty, Joseph Cornell—and I could continue with another ten names. You'll notice from my list that I do not make any distinction between narrative and non-narrative films in my idea of cinema. No doubt most of the other writers in this book will make this distinction. To me the cinema embraces a large variety of styles, forms, techniques and creative temperaments. I consider the attitude displayed by most of the contemporary film critics—according to which cinema is a popular, commercial genus of narrative—as naive, primitive and vulgar. And of course they are also completely unaware of the most exciting achievements of the cinema of the last fifteen years. They are uninformed, unenlightened, and they are the true enemies of the art of cinema.

I chose to write about Jerome Hill's *Film Portrait* because of several very simple reasons:

1. *Film Portrait* is a very good film. It is one of the most representative works in the comparatively new genre of autobiographical-diary film.

2. Since *Film Portrait* doesn't fall into the familiar commercial storytelling film category, this film, like many other good films, will be condemned to obscurity by "official" film critics. I feel it is my duty to bring it to the interested viewer's (and reader's) attention.

3. This beautiful film illustrates another case of a great artist working in cinema without any recognition, while all the newspapers and magazines (including all the magazines devoted to cinema—with the obvious exclusion of *Film Culture,* are grinding out daily, weekly and monthly praises to mediocrity. Jerome Hill died in November 1972 without seeing his work recognized for what it really is. This piece is my tribute to all the unrecognized artists of cinema who work in silence and darkness—and leave us works of angelic light.

Jerome Hill's *Film Portrait* is one of the key works in the comparatively new genre of the *diary* film, the *autobiographical* film. It's a genre in which the filmmaker works with the footage that comes from close around his own life. By means of this footage and the diary-autobiographical form, he takes us into the place, the period, the class from which he comes and into the world of his personality.

In this particular case, via the *Film Portrait,* among many other things, Jerome Hill leads us into a social background that is not only very uniquely American, but which is also about the least doumented in cinema—at least not as genuinely as Jerome Hill does it in his film: the life, the feeling and the style of the well-to-do American class at the beginning of the century. Specifically, the film deals with the family of James J. Hill, the family that helped build the railroads of America, and the development of Jerome Hill himself as a young man and an artist. Since the period dealt with in this film coincides with the development of cinema as a young art and with the development of the avant-garde film as a form of cinema, *Film Portrait* becomes also a film about the art of cinema, and a film about the avant-garde film.

To come back to the family. Of course *Film Portrait* doesn't go into the details of the family background. The film concentrates on Hill's own personal experience. That experience is unique and with no precedent. Or is it really unique? It is a slow and agonizing growth of an artist in a family and class climate which exerted all the pressures of tradition and opinion it could muster upon the sensibilities of the young artist, the sensibilities which seem to lead him from the very beginning toward the lines of the avant-garde. It is curious and also, I'd say, dramatic, to watch how, through the years, this sensibility is being kept in the background by force, and how it shoots out on occasion until, beginning about 1965, it suddenly explodes, without anybody being able to hold it or stop it as it comes out in glorious bursts of colors, forms and images that belong to the most beautiful in modern cinema. This is still more unique and, as I said, dramatic, when one discovers from the film against what odds Jerome Hill, the artist, had to fight for his personal and aesthetic liberation. He had to work with the knowledge that his creative work would always be measured by his contemporaries (and so it has by unscrupulous critics) against his grandfather's railroads. So besides being all other things—a film about the passage of time, a film about cinema (about time going backward and forward), a film about the passing of a whole era, a film about a style of life as reflected through one American family—Hill's film is also about personal liberation. It's about the liberation of an artist from the bonds of his family, his class and from the fashionable art styles of his contemporaries. And what is most unique about it all is that this liberation came about by way of cinema, by means of the motion picture camera.

But no matter how deeply Hill seems to be involved in the modern film sensibility, and no matter at what great cost it took him to arrive there—the cost of many wasted years—we find in this film as much love for the images of his childhood as for the modern film image. Yes, always the childhood, always the mother! The images of Hill's childhood, as given to us in *Film Portrait,* are among the most tender childhood images I've seen. There is one scene in the film, a scene where, through animation, Hill shows his mother putting him to bed, that is so full of tenderness, of such unique nostalgia, that it is truly one of the great moments of cinema.

And then—the color. Hill also paints, and I have always admired the color of his flowers in the paintings. But it seems that in this film, in the frames of *Film Portrait,* his brush came to a special kind of life. There is one sequence in *Film Portrait* which shows the early Paris. The scene is old and familiar: the roofs, the streets, the bridges of Paris. The footage itself is old footage. But Hill's brush went over every frame, and transformed them all. As Paris is seen now through the vibrancy of Hill's colors, it comes back alive, all the way from the twenties, with a double-edged force: one edge is that of nostalgia, through the distance of time and aged footage; the other edge is the excitement of remembering, of seeing it again "as if for the first time," as expressed through the vibrancy of Jerome Hill's paint pigments. It is through these pigments, through this vibrancy, that this scene gains its content—what it means, or meant. Into one's mind comes Gertrude Stein and Hemingway and Henry Miller and Fitzgerald and all the Americans of Paris.

In a sense, Hill's brush treatment of these frames (and of many others in this film) becomes a treatment of time, or a time treatment: rejuvenation of memory. Yes, Jerome Hill's brush becomes an elixir of memory that conjures up the vibrancy of the first, gone-by experiences. The artist as Time. Somewhere in the film, if I remember rightly, Hill says something to this effect in very similar words. Without the artist, the footage, even old footage, is just footage, just a documentary. It's with his paints and brushes and pens (you should note that I don't include scissors, which are so important in the classical cinema), that Jerome Hill becomes the magician of time. It's with his brush that he freezes the brief moments of presence on film into eternity. And it's by means of his brushes that he merges himself totally with his images. Here is an artist who locks himself in his "editing" room, and who works for years, since 1965, on this old footage, and he works with a fury close to blindness—Hill literally came close to losing his sight while working on these frames, and he was told to stop; he works furiously on these frames, twenty-four frames per second, and he burns himself into these frames now, thirty years later, forty years later. Here the reality of the old celluloid, the reality of the old image merge completely with Hill's sensibility and personality, and the film speaks and vibrates and sings —finally! Such is the power and glory of the artist.

A little bit more about Hill's color. As in Hill's paintings, so in his film, in the *Film Portrait* (as was also the case in *The Death in the Forenoon* and *Canaries*), the color stands out; you can almost feel it. In Brakhage's work, when Brakhage paints on film, the color becomes integrated into the total abstract design. But in Jerome Hill's painted, animated sequences in *Film Portrait,* what comes through most is the presence of the colors themselves: you see them, you feel them, you are struck by their extraordinary screen presence. You look at the screen, you see the images, you see the colors—and you still feel the paint and splashes and strokes; you see both the effect and the medium itself, you feel them both at the same time. I find· this may be the most unique aspect of Hill's painted, animated sequences—this very special quality of the screen presence of the pigments themselves. When one faces a unique work of art, one can go around and around and look at it from always-new angles and discover always-new lights and new insights and new ecstasies. To me, such a work is Jerome Hill's *Film Portrait.*

The filmography of Jerome Hill runs as follows:

Tom Jones (1927). Co-director: Bill Hinkle. 2½ hours. Based on the classic by Henry Fielding. After a limited Yale University run, it was deposited in the Yale University archives.

The Magic Umbrella (1927). An early avant-garde work. Shot and edited, not released. (Incorporated in full in *Film Portrait.*)

The Fortune Teller (1932). An early avant-garde work. Shot and edited, not released. (Incorporated in full in *Film Portrait.*)

Snow Flight (1938). A documentary study of the skiing techniques of Hannes Schneider, with Otto Lang. Released through Warner Brothers under the title *Ski Flight.*

Seeing Eye (1940). A promotion film about the training of dogs for the blind.

Grandma Moses (1950). A documentary on the octogenarian artist. Released through Radim Films.

Salzburg Seminar (1950). A documentary on the international music seminar.

Cassis, or *How to Be Happy though Healthy* (1950). An autobiographical, humorous sketch.

Albert Schweitzer (1950-57). 82 minutes.

The Sand Castle (1961). 64 minutes. A Jungian allegory.

Open the Door and See All the People (1964). 82 minutes. A Jungian
   comedy.
Schweitzer and Bach (1965). A sketch on Albert Schweitzer playing
   Bach on the organ at Gunsbach.
The Death in the Forenoon, or *Who's Afraid of Ernest Hemingway*
   (1965 [filmed in 1933]). 2 minutes.
The Artist's Friend (1966). A humourous sketch. Not released.
Merry Christmas (1969). (Incorporated in full in *Film Portrait.*)
Canaries (1968). An animated sketch.
Film Portrait (1965-71). 90 minutes.[1]

As we can see from the filmography, Jerome Hill's avant-garde
sensibility has been playing a hide-and-seek game throughout his
entire work. It comes out, in 1927, in the footage of *The Magic
Umbrella*—and hides again. In 1932 it breaks out again in *The
Fortune Teller*—again to hide for years. Only beginning in
approximately 1965, with *The Death in the Forenoon,* does it come
into the open, never to disappear again. As far as I know, one of the
main causes for this radical change in Jerome Hill's creative life
was his growing identification with the ideas of the American avant-
garde film. It acted upon him not so much as an influence as, rather, a
confirmation of his own original dreams and visions. So he made
this jump from a respectable and recognized popular artist (recognized with two Academy Awards) to the precarious and unrecognized life of an avant-garde artist. It may seem to some that there
is nothing to it. But I do not know of another case in cinema of a
similar conversion. In most cases we find just the opposite: that a
filmmaker who began as a promising avant-garde artist is slowly
consumed by the temptations of the industry.

It is of interest to see how the history of cinema, and particularly
that of the avant-garde film, unfolds through *Film Portrait.* The
early version of *The Magic Umbrella* shows the sheer excitement
with the mechanical possibilities of the camera—an element that
played such an important part in the early avant-garde films. *The
Fortune Teller* moves through the dream and the surrealism. *The
Death in the Forenoon* takes us into the color, into the pigments, into the celluloid itself, the medium of cinema itself.

[1] The films of Jerome Hill are available from Monument Film Corporation,
267 West 25th Street, New York, N. Y.

Grandma Moses. Jung (in an unfinished film). Schweitzer. Complete, rounded lives. And in *Film Portrait*, Hill himself, also a rounded circle. Hill is attracted by complete, rounded circles of life. He has a very special interest in the architectural monuments of Europe. I have watched Hill during some of his travels. I know of his encyclopedic knowledge of the art history of Europe. Everything that has a roundness of being interested Jerome Hill. Not the fact that it has come to an end, but the wisdom and the attitude inherent in it, the depths of perspective. Like the compost pile he made in Cassis, where he recycled all the waste materials that came from the house, placing it all, layer after layer, on the pile, making it round again, making it go the full circle, another circle. As did his own life. I had often been amazed by Hill's ability to circulate, to move from one set of his life to another with an amazing easiness; from New York to Cassis, to Paris, to St. Paul, to California; from cinema to music to architecture to stage designing to art history. There is a roundness and a circle there, too. And so with his own most important creative work; he couldn't begin his own real creative work—at least so it seems to me—until he could look at his own life from a full circle's perspective.

This roundness, this completeness, this circularity of his life and his work is the paradoxical meaning, or the paradoxical edge, of the avant-garde. The avant-garde line or point is that point where the future and the past meet. The other paradox is that there is an avant-garde which comes like lightning from the sky, blindly, and strikes everybody numb, and it takes years to adjust to it; and then there is the other edge of the avant-garde that cuts silently, and with an invisible light, straight across all the rumble and bustle of the world and right into the heart of the future. Such is the work of Jerome Hill. It is round, it is circular, it is marked by a deceptive quietness. His work doesn't have any of the shrill contemporary notes. His work (like that of James Broughton on the West Coast) moves within certain rhythms of thought and knowledge and form that are eternal, that transcend all fashions, that gains more vitality and relevance as time goes by, as all the other, more immediately successful works begin to fall a step behind, falling into the patterns of time.

14. Madame de: *A Musical Passage*

MOLLY HASKELL

Everyone agrees, and a good deal of criticism is based on the fact, that our response to film is intensely personal and mysteriously chemical. Despite their growing academic respectability, movies still have the power to start violent arguments, to turn mild-mannered vegetarians into carnivorous beasts, to become the soapbox for every passing ideologue, to blight budding relationships and dissolve secure ones. A reviewer's love of a film is subject to all the vagaries of love—or friendship—between two human beings, and while loyalty and a certain steadfastness are desirable, his favorite film will change from year to year according to shifts in his moods and preoccupations. This is as it should be. Cinema is still a popular, living art in which the word "masterpiece"—which is as much a term of critical consensus as a statement of intrinsic merit—has little authority.

All the same, such terms must be applied and such choices, however mutable, must be made. The idea of a "favorite film" is a controversial one—I would be the first to denounce the use of such categories to elevate one work of art at the expense of others, or one director on the shoulders of another (the refuge of film criticism which is ashamed of its subject)—but it is ultimately a defensible one. For the reviewer who tries both to keep up and catch up, the sheer quantity of film, of images hurtling together in the memory, is a factor to contend with. For me, then, making ten-best lists and declaring favorites is not just a way of giving recognition to a director, but also of bringing to a temporary halt the flow of images and sorting them into the patterns which have meaning for me and by which I define my aesthetic.

I admire and respond to Max Ophuls's *Madame de* for all the reasons which follow, but also because it speaks to me at this moment in time as a woman halfway between tradition and liberation, a woman who will honor every step in the direction of presenting and encouraging a more complex view of woman without abandoning the art of the past, especially—as in the case of *Madame de*—when a radical portrait is disguised in conservative clothing.

For the record, along with Ophuls on the top rung of my personal pantheon, I would list: Hitchcock, Renoir, Hawks and Keaton. And crowded on the second rung, occasionally spilling over to the first or the third, are: Lubitsch, Murnau, Lang, Mizoguchi, Sternberg, Cukor, McCarey, Preminger, Ford, Chabrol, Sturges, Godard, Bergman, Bresson, Dreyer, Griffith and Rossellini.

My other favorite films are: *Vertigo, Under Capricorn, Les Bonnes Femmes, Sunrise, Contempt, French Cancan, La Règle du Jeu, Sherlock, Jr., Rio Bravo, The General, Woman in the Window, Bringing Up Baby, The Searchers, Design for Living, Letter from an Unknown Woman, Morocco, The Magnificent Ambersons, Sansho the Bailiff, Holiday, Hail the Conquering Hero, Au Hasard, Balthazar, Strangers on a Train, The Man Who Shot Liberty Valance, La Femme Infidele, Gertrud, Ordet, Summer Interlude, Persona, Jules et Jim, Band of Outsiders, Showboat* (1936), *The Miracle* and *Oharu.*

But when it came down to choosing one film, I did not select any of these. Perhaps I had just written about one or the other. Or maybe I had just read an analysis that seemed to do temporary justice to one of them. Or perhaps it was just that I had seen none so recently and with such a powerful aftereffect as *Madame de.*

The image of women projected by most film directors has been

134   MOLLY HASKELL

shaped by one of three basic attitudes: puritanical discomfort, misogyny or (the obverse of misogyny) idealization. Max Ophuls is one of the five or six great directors—Mizoguchi, Renoir, Dreyer, Sternberg, Bergman—who place women at the center of their universe and honor them with a love that neither crushes nor sanctifies. The heroines of *Madame de, Lola Montes, Letter from an Unknown Woman, Caught, The Reckless Moment* are creations of a director for whom the passionate exaltation of the eternal feminine does not preclude the dispassionate exploration of specific women, just as delirium and determinism are the twin components of the director's style.

Like Stendhal, one of his favorite writers, Ophuls sees woman as a creature at a distinct disadvantage in a society laid out by men, but in whom the gesture toward liberation, usually in the form of a commitment to love, becomes far more daring and heroic than the deeds for which men are crowned. In *The Second Sex,* Simone de Beauvoir bestows on Stendhal's women the words of praise she accords the creations of no other male writers, and they might equally well apply to Ophuls's Madame de:

> The so-called serious man is really futile, because he accepts ready-made justifications for his life; whereas a passionate and profound woman revises established values from moment to moment. She knows the constant tension of unsupported freedom; it puts her in constant danger: she can win or lose all in an instant. It is the anxious assumption of this risk that gives her story the colors of a heroic adventure. And the stakes are the highest there are: the very meaning of existence.

In the period context in which Ophuls has cast her, Madame de represents the romantic incarnation of the liberated woman, a figure whose true nobility is often clouded by the general disrepute of "women's fiction," a genre Ophuls both cherishes and transfigures. While giving special attention to this aspect of *Madame de,* I have no intention of turning the film into a Women's Lib tract(*Ms de*)! For one thing, the characters of the two men, played by Charles Boyer and Vittorio de Sica, are too important, and Boyer even draws audience sympathy away from Danielle Darrieux's Madame de. If she is the most obsessed and audacious of the three, she is not morally superior to the men (or at least to Boyer), the way Bergman's women often are to his men. Madame de does not achieve her spiritual splendor through the tarnished souls around her, but through a solitary struggle in which she surrenders the lesser part of herself for the greater part—"The woman I was made me the woman I am."

Just as Madame de progresses from self-centered society lady to saint, the film moves from soap opera to sublime art, redeeming itself and its heroine in the process. But even the most unredeemable soap opera, we should remember, has served as compensation for women who, denied the outlet of challenging work, and strung out on the interminable trivia of household chores, can feel an inverted sense of superiority in submission and self-denial. The trouble is that in pushing the ecstasies of martyrdom, soap opera has recruited more victims and reinforced rather than relieved the inequity of male-female roles.

Perhaps a key difference between soap opera and serious art on the same subject, apart from the crucial factors of intelligence and style, is that soap opera is a sedative, a kind of artistic Catholicism, which encourages passive resignation to what is seen as a general and unalterable law. Real art, on the other hand, has the opposite effect, since it shows people who dare to rebel, who break the rules, people poised on a moral precipice in which any move may be a fall but in which it is not only possible but imperative to choose the direction.

The difference between the two is the difference in *Madame de* between a tragic ending which involves the three main characters (and the death of two) and a denouement in which Madame de leaves each man one earring, or, in other words, the difference between Ophuls's film and its source, a novel by Louise de Vilmorin. The latter, an ironic, sub-Maupassant tale written and set in the thirties, was very much a "woman's story" in the pejorative sense. The circular plot (transposed by Ophuls into an aristocratic, turn-of-the-century setting) concerns the fate of a frivolous society lady who, in pawning a pair of earrings given her by her husband as a wedding present, sets up a chain of circumstances which, when she falls seriously in love, closes in and destroys her. In its skeleton form, it is a tale for which the American title, *The Earrings of Madame de,*

MOLLY HASKELL

would have been appropriate had not Ophuls transformed it into a masterpiece of visual narration in which every image, expression, line of dialogue, camera movement and dissolve has both emotional weight and structural significance.

The screenplay by Ophuls, Marcel Achard and Annette Wademant is a gem of succinct exposition and expressive dialogue, phrases reiterated but with different meanings. For example, in the magnificent ballroom scene, in which Danielle Darrieux and Vittorio de Sica waltz in one continuous motion, across the weeks and into the depths of love, the phrase "les nouvelles sont excellentes" occurs three or four times. It is uttered by Madame de, first seriously then ironically, in reply to De Sica's inquiry after her absent husband's health, and indicates both the passage of time and the growth of intimacy. The next and last time it is used, it is Boyer who reassures his wife that De Sica is well after his fall from a horse. "Je sais," she replies, using the words De Sica had used in their last exchange.

Another example of Ophuls's deepening and transfiguring of the original: the story seems to hang heavily on coincidence and chance, not just in the peregrinations of the earrings, but in the attention given fortune-telling cards, the number 13 and other signs through which luck is raised to a guiding principle. But Ophuls, while retaining the references to chance—largely as character details—emphasizes, in a beautiful observation by Boyer, the supreme naturalness of coincidence. He makes it clear that the drama lies not in the whereabouts of the earrings (except as their movement imitates an inner journey) but in their symbolic importance: the value placed on them, the lies told for them, the consequences of the lies—all the interlocking moves in a game of character, not chance, a game in which the outcome has the inevitability of tragedy.

Oscar Straus's beautifully sentimental score adjusts itself, without breaking stride, from the rapturous lilt of the waltz to the wistful and finally desolate strains of loss. It accompanies every appearance of the jewels except one: when, in a ruse to deceive her husband, Madame de lets them drop from the gloves where she has concealed them. They fall onto the table with a frightening finality, with no music to attenuate their impact at this turning point of the film. Actually, turning point is the wrong word because, although the story is full of turning points, the film itself is always turning. The movement is not only circular but spiral, so that when it comes back to the same place—as in the ballroom scene, the jewelers, the church, etc.—it has reached a deeper (or higher) level. Circles occasionally give way to straight lines, as in the movements and visual motifs of Boyer, a general, and in the single stretch in which Madame de, traveling to escape from her love, takes a long walk up the beach, trying in vain to control an emotion that is as vast and overwhelming as the ocean.

The women of Stendhal and Ophuls are not ordinary women. They are among the few who escape, who awaken from the dream-sleep—society's lifelong anesthetic—and overcoming the taboos of both society and their own inhibitions, embark on what Simone de Beauvoir calls "the adventure of liberty."

That this is one of the greatest themes of fiction—and most beautiful in Ophuls's hands—is a notion which makes so-called serious critics uneasy. Agreeing that Ophuls is a consummate stylist, they nevertheless refuse to take him seriously, on the grounds, presumably, of his choice of subject matter and feminine orientation, and the suspicion that nothing tragic can be expressed in so nearly painless a style. To this, Jean-Luc Godard gave the answer in his remark on Hitchcock and Rossellini (cited by Andrew Sarris) when he said of Hitchcock that where there is so much form there must be content (the converse applying to Rossellini). One has but to watch and feel *Madame de* to realize that Ophuls's style is, in the words Boyer uses to describe his marriage to Darrieux, "only superficially superficial." The perpetual motion of Ophuls's camera is both circular and progressive, the representation in time and space of the human journey through eternity. Each staircase climbed and descended, each corridor traversed, takes the body one space further toward the grave, and each lilting, contrapuntal swing of the camera suggests the soul's freedom to fly. This is a more complex and ultimately more tragic vision than Louise de Vilmorin's, or even Arthur Schnitzler's, whose plays Ophuls adapted, to the horror of the literati and the glory of film history.

The dismissal, or downgrading, of Ophuls as a "woman's director," seems to rest on a cultural and (male) sexual prejudice that is as old as art itself: a belief that the life of the heart is somehow a

MOLLY HASKELL

less worthy subject of serious treatment than such "large subjects" as wars, politics, religion and social causes. Treated seriously, it is soap opera, and people are likely to overlook the fact that what in one man's hands is soap opera is, in the hands of another—say, Euripides, Racine, Stendhal, Samuel Richardson, Jane Austen, E. M. Forster, Virginia Woolf, Proust, Mozart and Ophuls—the stuff of art. And now, with the relations between the sexes at an all-time low, the concept of love is in danger of dying altogether or of being reduced, by medical authority, to a conditioned response—the saliva of sickness or need. It will be up to the French, who have always been more alert to the subject than the rest of us, to remind us that if love is an uncontrollable emotion, *to love* is a choice and therefore a moral act. Max Ophuls, German-born, a man of the world in exile, but a spiritual Frenchman, understood that the heart's engagement is lonelier and—in the eyes of the world—less glamorous than political engagement. Love takes greater risks because it gains less credit than the socially honored heroics of battle and public gesture.

This is an odd notion, and film, for young people today to appreciate, particularly if they are Americans. In a permissive society, or among a permissive generation, the idea of risk and retribution has no meaning, and the rigid, unspoken rules of a French class society are as remote to college students as kinship patterns among the Hopi tribes. This, unfortunately, indicates once again that sexual liberation actually works against true liberation: that constant, soul-defining struggle with parental authority, social restrictions and private inhibitions in which some principles are guarded, some modified and some abandoned.

So widespread is the current sense of alienation that there is no established, homogeneous majority which can represent "society." For Ophuls there was, or had to be, which is why he preferred and was most eloquent in prewar Europe as a setting. Ophuls's society, like Stendhal's, was not just an abstract idea but a system, both blessed and cursed, a collectivity of real faces ready to serve, support or censure according to the events and their role in them. And it was against such a solid ordering of human destiny that the individual flaunted his or her obsession and took the consequences.

Vittorio de Sica, Charles Boyer and Danielle Darrieux, in their incarnations as the baron, the count and Madame de are extraordinarily beautiful, radiant, rich, aristocratic—stars in every sense of the word, yet Ophuls places them firmly within a society in which every position is clearly defined and interconnected. It is the cosmic order in miniature, its regular movements reflecting the orbit of planets, its irregular passions the trajectory of meteors. In such a universe, it is the most natural thing imaginable for A to advance to B, and B to bump into C, and C to charm D, and D to dance with E, and E to end up sitting next to F, and F to fall into the arms of G, and so on. So on, that is, as long as they keep moving. For to stop is to cause a ripple, and in Madame de's world, a ripple is a tempest. The wealth and leisure of the aristocracy entitle them to certain freedoms denied the lower classes, but the rules are subtler and stricter, and the tiniest infraction reverberates from the orchestra to the galleries. In the marvelous and characteristically Ophulsian opera scene, the opera (Gluck this time, not Mozart) is interrupted —always a faux pas!—by Madame de's revelation that her earrings have been stolen, with the consequence that her husband is obliged to turn the opera house—and all Paris—upside down in search of them. In a stylish cacophony of hushed voices (whispers which ring out like bells), doors (inner and outer) opening and closing, rumors spreading, ushers leaping to their feet, we are given a comic vignette of a hierarchical society and the chain of command in which servants jump to their masters' bidding and masters in turn scrape before their mistresses. There is a beautifully edited sequence in which Boyer, having gone home to search for the earrings, calls the servants. In one shot, we see the entire household staff leaping at different speeds up the stairs. The next shot, with precisely the reverse motion and meaning, shows Madame de, surrounded by admiring beaux, descending the stairs of the opera with careless grace. Thus in one lyrically lighthearted episode, Ophuls gives us sociology and psychology, the world of Madame de and the disruptive influence she is to have on it.

At one point—in the jeweler's—we see Madame de gracefully swooning. At another—after De Sica's accident—she faints for four minutes instead of three, and Boyer is alarmed. This is a society which permits, even encourages, a woman to enjoy flirtations as long

MOLLY HASKELL

as she abides by the unwritten rules governing such affairs. If she falls in love—already bad form—there are even allowances for that, provided she doesn't impose her feelings on others, or compromise her husband's honor. Ophuls's complex pattern of camera movements—rapturous, lyrical pans and tracks and occasionally sudden swings, within a larger, strictly observed symmetrical system—reflects the paradox of Madame de's social situation and, on a larger scale, the mystery of free will and determinism.

Madame de, one of society's crowning jewels, rejects her "setting" (one thinks of the first time we see her, her face framed in a mirror), thus enacting the primal conflict of tragedy, the individual against society. But in one sense she, like other tragic figures, has been outside society all along. The spoiled and petted darling of the beginning of the film is no more in touch with reality than the mystically redeemed saint of the end. And when, in her passion for De Sica— loving him, then losing him—she turns her back on society, it is not just its luxuries and ornaments she rejects but its premises: her role as wife and mother. This is clear in the scene in which Boyer takes her to the country house, teeming with children of his poor relations, and forces her to make a gift of the earrings to a niece who has just given birth. Madame de tosses the earrings to her and, in a touchingly comic gesture, hastens to the crib where to hide her grief she makes a pretense of admiring the baby—a baby that arouses no more feeling in her than a harmless insect, the product of a cycle of nature in which she wants no part. If this isn't a radical gesture, I'd like to know what is!

In the beginning is the end, and in the first two and a half minutes of *Madame de,* in an extraordinary single-take sequence, we are given the particulars of her life which foreshadow her death. In one of the most graceful bits of exposition in all cinema, Ophuls introduces Madame de to us through her possessions, as she is pondering which to surrender. At first all we see is her hand as it searches with sensory pleasure among her jewels and furs and dresses, up and down, across, over and back, rejecting first one and then the other. In the course of this inventory, she drops a Bible, holds it for a second and replaces it; regrets aloud the absence of her mother who "would tell me what to do"; holds her cross fondly and at the idea of pawning it cries, "Oh, no! I adore that"; and finally settles on the earrings her husband gave her, on the grounds that "I can do with them as I please."

During this sequence, Ophuls has told us Madame de's preoccupations, her character, her attitude toward and relations with her husband, with her mother and with God; in what she lacks, he has prefigured what she will come to have, and in what she possesses, what she will no longer have. The reference to her mother reveals how she has been spoiled, that she misses her mother and that it is to her mother, or her mother's memory (at the expense of her husband), that she has always turned for help. In the array of her possessions and the affection she lavishes on them, we see that they are everything to her and are no doubt compensation for a loveless marriage. In her almost sensual familiarity with the Bible (which she keeps among her furs) and the cross, she reveals a direct, childish sense of closeness to God, of whom she can ask favors and expect the indulgence of a doting parent. The decision to sell the earrings given her by her husband—not just as an ordinary present but as a wedding present—constitutes an explicit rejection of him and a repudiation of their marriage. Her comment that she can do with the earrings as she pleases is another way of saying that, having no affective value, they have no power over her (even here, at her most materialistic, she avers that the claims of love are the only binding ones); and this is in sharp contrast to her later deranged behavior toward, and possession by, the earrings when they have been given to her by the baron. Invested with the "revised value" of love, they are now as binding and inescapable as religious vows; she is at their mercy, no longer free to "do with them as (she) pleases," and thus does passion become fate.

Almost every action in the first half of the film has its double, or mirror image, in the second half, only they express the opposite relation to each other: the first images are the mirrors, the echoes, of the deeper and truer essences which will emerge.

Madame de's first visit to the church (on the way to the jeweler's), where she perfunctorily crosses herself and asks God to "make him understand and I'll never forget you," has its double in the end where she, near death herself, prays in anguished sincerity for the life of De Sica, who is about to meet Boyer in a duel. Her prayer appeals to the spiritual nature of her love: "You know we loved in thought only." And this is followed, after the duel and Madame de's death, by the third and final shot in the church in which, after a long, stately track to the altar, the camera pans from the altar to a small shrine where Madame de's earrings have been placed in memoriam, thus joining, gently, comically and reverently before God, the material and spiritual sides of Madame de, sanctifying her love and redeeming her life.

The first time we see Madame de, it is her reflected image in the mirror on her dressing table, framed by the luxuries which are an extension of her being and without which she is nothing. As the film progresses and her love grows, she dresses more severely, becomes physically wasted, and even her surroundings take on an ascetic look. She is perhaps no longer beautiful by society's standards, but she is more beautiful by the higher and more demanding ones of the spirit. In her last agonizing and comical encounter with De Sica, she has rushed to warn him about the duel, knowing he no longer loves her, but still daring to hope.

"I am not even pretty," she says sadly.

"More than ever," he replies.

"Really?" her eyes light up, with a coquetry that shows how much she is still herself. Then just as quickly, "I'm incorrigible," she confesses, with an awareness that shows just how far she has come.

One of the glories of Ophuls's conception of Madame de is that even as she is ennobled by her love, she retains some of the myopia and weakness of her former self. Thus the brutal lesson of her suffering teaches her nothing of the pain she has caused her husband, and her eyes are never opened to the mute misery he endures in loving her.

As a general in charge of an artillery unit headquartered in Paris, Boyer has the rectitude, the faith in social conventions and a certain lack of imagination characteristic of the Ophulsian military figure. At the same time, he has a stern formality that we come to realize has been forced on him and is alien to his disposition. In a heartbreaking moment late in the film, as Madame de is languishing on a chaise longue, Boyer confesses he never had much taste for the image she had of him and for the role she made him play, but she is too far gone in her own unhappiness to hear. The brilliant subtlety of Boyer's performance, with its suggested reserves of feeling, becomes more apparent with successive viewings of the film. We begin to sense that every care lavished on Madame de—from her family, her personal servant Nanou and friends—has been love withheld from him, and that his gentleness, increasingly obvious to us, is forever hidden to her. She refuses to make the sympathetic leap, symbolized by the vast space between their beds, necessary to unleash the passion smoldering within him. Ophuls permits us to glimpse Boyer's passion, through the correlative images of fire, that is in some ways more magnificent than Madame de's for being undeclared. Unlike the simpler character of De Sica, whose love is destroyed when his honor is insulted, Boyer allows his honor to be defiled, but not his love. By not acknowledging his love or accepting his friendship, Madame de unconsciously wills his death; in order not to be turned into an object, Boyer must challenge De Sica to a duel.

The two men—one worldly, the other more innocent—react in ways perfectly justified by any normal criteria of human behavior, but they are criteria by which Madame de can no longer be judged. She has bypassed good and evil and conventional morality in the total—religious, romantic, neurotic and heroic—sublimation of her entire being into a passion which refuses to make room for anything else. The men, gentlemen and standard-bearers of the masculine code, are prevented by their straightforwardness from imagining the depths of her commitment, or from understanding the difference between her lies.

Knowing Ophuls's fondness for Stendhal and Mozart, critics have often wondered why he never used their work as the textual or musical basis for his films. He never adapted Stendhal, and he restricted his use of Mozart to the opera scenes within his films, but it is precisely by not trying to transfer classics from one medium to another that Ophuls created something comparable in his own. The whorl of *La Ronde* is closer to the sustained lyric and comic ecstasy of *Così fan tutte* than a film like *Sunday, Bloody Sunday*, which uses the score throughout. And *Madame de* is closer to the world of Stendhal, both in style and in its harsher view of risk and redemption, than Claude Autant-Lara's film of *The Red and the Black*. Ophuls uses objects and images the way Mozart uses music—to define character and feelings and the subtle alteration in each. Like Mozart and Stendhal, but in his own uniquely cinematic language,

Ophuls conveys shifts and transitions, the crossover from playfulness to passion, without ever deviating from the elegance and grace of the original style and the world it sustains. People who are attuned to more blatant histrionics may miss the clues, expecting Wagnerian sonorities when a magic flute or a flutter of paper signals the transition.Through a conceit of cinematic metamorphosis reminiscent of Keaton's *Sherlock, Jr.,* Ophuls shows us such a transition, as the pieces of a love letter Madame de has torn and thrown from the train window metamorphose into the snow flakes of a crystallized love. To accept the fate of Madame de, you must believe that the depths of love can be rendered by a flurry of snowflakes and that the distance between death-in-life and life-in-death, symbolized by the journey of a pair of earrings, can be crossed by a moving camera. The film never stops to underline its purpose but, like a Mozart opera, is in constant motion, incorporating every moment into the highest and purest lyrical expression. Sometimes you long to catch it and hold it, to stop it in its tracks and luxuriate in an image, even as you know that its beauty is movement and that its very essence lies in the poignancy of its passing.

15. My Favorite Movie—Madame de

PETER HARCOURT

WHAT IS MY FAVORITE MOVIE? Difficult though it may be to answer such a question, I find it easier than choosing the top ten films of all time. For I have long felt it should be possible to separate the objects of one's affection from those that one recognizes as having great value. Of course, *Battleship Potemkin* is a very great film, but is it anyone's favorite, at least nowadays? A favorite movie, to my mind, implies a film for which one feels a particular sympathy, whatever its eventual worth. To write about one's favorite movie is thus to write more personally than judiciously. It is to share one's excitement about the inner rhythms of a work of art more than it is to pass judgment on a film.

What, then, is *my* favorite movie? It is generally the one that I have most recently discovered—*Five Easy Pieces,* from two years ago; *Bonnie and Clyde,* from a few before that. Yet when I look back over the years at the films that have most engaged me, I know that repeatedly I have been excited by what many critics might describe as stylistic excess. While I greatly value the firm pessimism of the films of Louis Buñuel and admire the austere worlds created

146

by Robert Bresson and Erich Rohmer, I know that in some deeply personal way I reserve a particular delight for works of art that give a sense of life as play, that—through the energy of their own forms—convey an energy within the artists themselves, an energy which seems an affirmation of life.

Hence, Renoir's *La Règle du Jeu,* Bergman's *Smiles of a Summer Night,* Truffaut's *Jules et Jim,* Godard's *Pierrot le Fou,* and—supremely—Fellini's *8½* all successfully counterbalance the gloomy implications of their view of life by the vitality of their forms. In spite of their thematic concern with defeat or death, these films all leave us with the feeling of joy, of despair transcended. Furthermore, I must confess to a kind of private delight (perhaps somewhat snobbish) in detecting beneath the surface of a film, which many quotidian reviewers have dismissed as banal, the hint of a profundity lurking underneath. It is this suggestion of profundity that my senses respond to and that my critical mind seizes upon in the effort to convey my own delight to other viewers who may not have noticed it. Indeed, it is this sense of something deeper within the apparent superficialities of the film that has led me to choose as my favorite movie, arguably the supreme achievement of his whole career— Max Ophuls's *Madame de.*

> *L'amour, en traversant les âges, marque d'actualité les événements qu'il touche.*
>
> —LOUISE DE VILMORIN [1]
>
> *Je crois que le véritab!e but de l'artiste, c'est de nous donner, du monde, une vision nouvelle. Tous les sujets, au fond, arrivent à se ressembler. C'est la vision personnelle que nous avons d'un milieu ou d'un être, c'est la forme que nous leur commuiquons qui les différencient . . .*
>
> —MAX OPHULS [2]

In a world hungry for film *auteurs,* Max Ophuls has been curiously neglected. Except for Andrew Sarris's splendid tribute in *The*

---

[1] "Throughout the ages, the events that love has affected have seemed more immediate." The opening lines of *Madame de,* by Louise de Vilmorin (Paris: Gallimard, 1951).

[2] "I think that the true goal of an artist is to give us a new way of looking at the world. Ultimately, all stories tend to resemble one another. It's the personal point of view that we have of a society or of a character, it's the form that we give to them, that makes them distinct." "Cinéma d'aujourd'hui, No. 16," in Claude Beylie, *Max Ophuls* (Paris: Editions Seghers, 1963), p. 123.

American Cinema,[3] there has been very little appreciation of him in English. In his little monograph on Ophuls published over a decade ago, Richard Roud usefully documents the shameful insensitivity with which Ophuls's work was generally greeted in England, an insensitivity that Roud substantially shares.[4] In North America, of course, the limited availability of his European films has not made for an easy familiarity, and the outcry caused by the recutting of *Lola Montes* after Ophuls's death has tended to obscure the fact that, even in its original form, it is, while extraordinary, not really his most satisfying film. That title must fall either to *Letter from an Unknown Woman* (as Robin Wood would argue) or to *Madame de,* the film which I prefer. "Our marriage is like ourselves," Monsieur de explains to his wife at a crucial moment in the film. "It is only superficially that it is superficial." So I would want to argue about the whole of *Madame de.*

In France the short novel by Louise de Vilmorin from which the film is taken enjoys a firm, if academic, reputation. Written in 1950, it evokes the sensibility of a much older era, seeming to belong more to the moral ethos of Constant's *Adolphe* (1806) than to any novel written today. Yet it is not without distinction. One of its great qualities is its sense of restraint. In a way that suggests the manners of the time, nothing is directly alluded to, no one is named. Indeed, we cannot know for certain where the scenes take place or what time in history is precisely intended.

If we are familiar with the novel, the most striking characteristic of Max Ophuls's film is the richness of its detail. Everything in the film seems so accurately *seen.* Of course, it would have to be, in order to become a film (one might argue); but the accuracy of the detail of its fin-de-siècle period is worth commenting upon: it is part of the film's ability to persuade us that everything we are witnessing is unmistakably real. Furthermore, if through the richness of its decor and the restless movement of Ophuls's camerawork, the film seems opulent, it also has, like the novel, an element of restraint. The restraint is most centered in the formality of the characters and

[3] Andrew Sarris, *The American Cinema* (New York: E. P. Dutton [paperback], 1968), p. 69 ff.

[4] Richard Roud, *Max Ophuls* (London: British Film Institute, 1958).

PETER HARCOURT

in the oblique way they deal with the passions of their lives. Reduced to its plot synopsis, *Madame de* might seem to epitomize the banal. It certainly might seem to depend too greatly on the fortuitous reappearance of a pair of diamond earrings. But in the hands of Ophuls, these characteristics recede before the swirl and intensity of the film itself.

The film opens with a gloved hand pulling open the drawer of a case full of jewels, revealing the fateful earrings, as we hear a voice mutter: "The trouble is, they were his wedding present." Then the camera travels right, along a whole collection of feminine treasures —more jewels, elegant dresses, and finally a fur wrap. We know immediately that these gloved hands are looking for something to pawn. As the camera travels back again and we see the gloved hands reaching up for a hat to wear, a Bible falls from the shelf and we hear the voice say: "Never have I needed it more." While this line seems curious at this stage of the film, it makes sense later on.

Only when the camera returns from its restless search for something that can be dispensed with and we see the hands decide at last upon the earrings do we catch sight of Madame de's pert face in a mirror, as she puts on her hat. "It's better to dress simply," as she had said a moment ago. We get the sense immediately of a somewhat spoiled woman who is rather pleased with herself, whose life is frivolous and self-absorbed. At the same time there is an energy within her as she bustles about—the camera once again following her right as she hurries out the door, where we cut to the top of a magnificent staircase and then follow her down the stairs, along a landing, and finally through an interior window into the library. Here we see her gulping down a cup of tea while arranging her hair. Meanwhile, a full-length portrait of her husband looks down on her from the wall, making her uneasy. We follow her again as she hurries out the door.

This opening sequence establishes many things. Not only does her life seem trivial and self-indulgent, but the world around her supports these values. We see objects before we see her. Indeed, we see her gloved hands before we see her face—and even then it is a face reflected in an elegant mirror. Afterwards, we see her through bannisters and then through panes of glass. Material objects thus dominate not only the way she thinks about life but her actual environment as well. Even her attitude to the Church partakes of this.

As she runs out the front door, pausing for a moment to catch a glimpse of herself in yet another mirror, we dissolve to a cathedral where we see her scuttling down the center aisle. Her deportment is the antithesis of anything we might want to call devout—a comic discrepancy emphasized by the presence of a young man in the front pew who is distracted from his attempts at prayer by her handsome form flouncing past his eyes. She has come to church to pray that the jeweler will accept her earrings! It is one of the miracles of Ophuls's compassionate observation that we can still be somewhat charmed by this woman.

At the jeweler's, when Monsieur Remy suggests that he should think about the matter first, implying (we suppose) that he might like first to consult her husband, she feigns a swoon. The feint works and he agrees to take the earrings. So once again we see her hurrying down the little spiral staircase in the jeweler's shop and out into the street, while the jeweler, his son and his assistant watch her through the window, as if in amazement. We then dissolve to the back of her head in her box at the opera, with Gluck's *Orfeo ed Euridice* now on the soundtrack,[5] while we watch her stage one of her most successful scenes: she pretends she has lost her earrings on the way to the opera. In spite of assurances from her husband and friends that she had none on when she left the house, she sends her husband off to look for them.

While it is perhaps tedious to re-create a film in words in this way, the details are important. Both the scene at the jeweler's and this scene at the opera are rich in comic observation, creating the kind of comedy which depends throughout upon master-servant relationships and their obsequious hypocrisies. If Madame de's rank invites the jeweler to be somewhat servile towards her, the jeweler's son is equally servile toward his father—especially in the next scene where we see them together, the son running up and down the staircase, fetching this and that, as his father shouts orders from below. Similarly, the flunkeys at the opera house who snooze through all the performances and whose job it is simply to open the doors for

[5] The music is by Gluck, not by Meyerbeer as listed in the credits for *Madame de* in Claude Beylie's book, p. 197.

PETER HARCOURT

the nobs who inhabit the boxes are presented with great comic effect, as Monsieur de keeps moving in and out, from one box to the next, searching for the missing earrings. Similar too, later on in the film, will be the sentries outside the army barracks, who perfunctorily salute every officer that goes by but have a keen sense of when it is not worth their trouble—when "it's only a tradesman."

Thus, in the first scenes of *Madame de*, Ophuls has created not only a woman but an entire world. If at first glance Madame de seems vain and self-satisfied and given to petty deceptions, in this way she simply reflects the values of her society. In fact, depending on our response to Danielle Darrieux in the part of Madame de, we might even by this time have come to feel that, in comparison with this world, Madame de has an energy and a charm that sets her somewhat apart.

For it is a very male world that she inhabits. In spite of the opulence of all her surroundings and the sense of infinite leisure that pervades her life, the men call all the shots. Her husband, whose walk in life remains unspecified in the novel, in the film is a *militaire* —a professional soldier. He is, in fact, a general who is accustomed (as we shall see) to being obeyed. Though portrayed with great sympathy by Charles Boyer, he is the kind of man who ultimately will put his own sense of honor above the needs of his wife. In the best bourgeois tradition, the only liberties allowed a woman of her class are her vanities and little wiles (*mensonges* is the word that recurs throughout the book), along with her playful flirtations with other men. Thus in this indirect and often comic way, Ophuls encourages us to recognize that the values of Madame de, as we see them at the opening of the film, have been to an extent forced upon her. They are the values of the culture in which she has grown up.

If the world that Ophuls has created for us is the conventional, bourgeois world that we find in nearly all nineteenth-century novels, he also, through his style, implied a distinct way of looking at it which is both appreciative and critical. Ophuls is obviously attracted by all that elegance, an elegance which he reinforces through his own camera movements. At the same time, his habit of repeatedly shooting through glass and of traveling past pillars gives us the sense of this world as a cage, and his constant dwelling on elements of decor very quickly makes us feel that material objects dominate these people's lives.

When the general, Monsieur de, first goes in search of those elusive earrings, his sword falls off a hanger as he is searching through a cloak. A simple effect, this, yet superbly right as well. The sword seems to stand for something in the general, just as those earrings, as the film progresses, will come to stand for something that Madame de is discovering about herself.

Though I have already mentioned the astonishing sweep and gracefulness of Ophuls's camerawork, it is important to point out that this graceful style is not used throughout the film. The scenes both in the jeweler's shop and in the army barracks are shot in a more conventional way, with a far greater number of cuts and the standard narrative device of action/reaction shots. The graceful style is reserved for Ophuls's graceful people, both as the accompaniment and the celebration of their lavishly indolent lives. Furthermore, if Ophuls wishes to create a different kind of mood, he has other techniques he can draw upon.

For instance, later on in the film, after the general has retrieved the earrings from the jeweler, and with a pleasing sense of ironic appropriateness, given them to his mistress who is on her way to Turkey, we have a scene at home with Monsieur and Madame de where they are getting ready for bed. We dissolve in on two washbasins, sitting side by side on two stands. We pan right to pick up the general coming into the room and follow him left, over to his mirror, where we watch him comb his hair and moustache and pluck his eyebrows as he is talking to his wife about the earrings. We then pan left with him again as he crosses what looks like an enormous room—their shared dressing room—to the glass doors of her bedroom, where we see her sitting up in bed, as if miles away.

The general is obviously enjoying this game of married deceit that they are playing together, as they speculate, with shared hypocrisy, who might have stolen the jewels. The scene is too delicately nuanced both in style and in characterization to re-create in detail, but several points of interest might be mentioned. First of all, while Ophuls pans quite a bit in this scene, following the general as he paces back and forth between the glass doors to his wife's sleeping quarters through the glass doors of his own, Ophuls uses a large number of cuts as well to emphasize their separateness. Furthermore, the wide-angle shooting, which gives this scene as much of a Wellesian as an Ophulsian flavor, also serves to emphasize the space between them. At one point, we cut to a shot of her in bed, the canopy of her four-poster encompassing her like the decoration around a valentine (and like the decoration around the titles at the opening of the film). Once again we have the feeling, slightly, of a sense of confinement, yet at the same time of great luxury and of perfumed femininity. Finally, however, I would suggest, that in placing this shot at this moment in the film, Ophuls confirms our sense of the falsely idealized role that, as a wife, she is expected to assume. She is thought of, by this society, as a china-doll creature, whose little "indiscretions" are to be expected (*étourderies* is the word in French), but who can be allowed no real passion, no vital life of her own.

This scene is filled with the characteristic Ophulsian wit and charm as it explores the characters' relation to one another and to the world in which they live. Yet at the same time, there is a most compassionate observation of both of them, an observation full of little ironies. The scene ends with both of them in their separate sleeping quarters at opposite ends of their shared apartment, blowing kisses to one another through their open doors, while Madame de reaches up with her extinguisher and snuffs out the candles around her bed. We then have the first fade-out in the film.

This piece of punctuation is worth mentioning, for it not only marks the end of the first act. of our play and thus makes way for a little bit of plot business in Turkey, allowing the earrings to come into the hands of an Italian ambassador who is on his way to Paris; but also because the sense of warmth, distant though it may be, of this going-to-bed scene followed by the extinguishing of candles and then a fade to black anticipates another similar, yet far more passionate, scene, later on in the film.

If the fortuitous reappearance of the earrings adds a note of chance to this story, the appearance of the ambassador, Fabricio Donati, in the life of Madame de also occurs by chance. By chance, they first see one another at a railway station in Basle, where Donati (suavely played by Vittorio de Sica) is clearing the earrings through customs; by chance again, they meet in Paris, when the wheels of their respective carriages interlock while passing one another in the street. Finally, it is by chance yet again that they meet at a ball, and by chance too that they find themselves seated next to one another at the dinner table.

The sequence that follows provides one of the highlights in Ophuls's career. If it is true, as Andrew Sarris has nicely said, that Ophuls "gave camera movement its finest hours in the history of the cinema,"[6] this sequence represents these hours at their most distinguished.

On the level of characterization, it is the first time in the film that we see three main characters together—the general, Madame de, and Fabricio Donati. There is a huge banquet table elevated above the dance floor, at the back of which is an equally huge mirror. Thus, during the dialogue scenes that take place at the table, we can see the reflection of the crowds of people dancing below. When the general first enters the scene and finds Donati talking to his wife, he seems genuinely pleased. "You'll get on well together," he declares. Then when Madame de is called away by an American admirer with whom we see her quite deliberately flirting, we cut back to the table where the general is talking with Donati. From the preceding moment, it is easy to believe him when he warns Donati that his wife "is a flirt. She is adept at making you die of hope." As these words are spoken, we can still see Madame de in the mirror, teasing her American on the dance floor below.

Then Donati asks her to dance and the film's waltz begins, with a tune which plays a crucial part in the film. Whether by Oscar Straus or Georges van Parys (the credits do not make this clear), its slowly ascending melody neatly embodies all the longing and aspiration of their relationship. Meanwhile, the camera follows them as they dance round and round one way, and then we cut to pick them up as they dance back another. Then a dissolve (and a modulation to a higher key) as we see them dancing again—but obviously at another ball. "Four days without seeing you," Donati exclaims; and the camera follows them right as they dance past a whole series of pillars and couples passing left in front of them.

The sequence continues in this way, dissolving from ball to ball,

6 Sarris, *op. cit.*, p. 70.

PETER HARCOURT

but always the waltz is the same. "Two days without seeing you," he says the next time; and then, "Twenty-four hours without seeing you," as we dissolve into the last dance. What is so extraordinary about this sequence is not just the elegant choreography of couples and camera movement (though this would be enough) but the sense of vertigo that the sequence creates. As we see that the couple are growing genuinely attracted to one another, we see as well that they are literally spinning out of control.

More complicated still is the dialectic tug of other elements in this staging. The sequence begins with a room full of people, with a kind of public gaiety reflected in the mirror on the wall, and with the sound of a full orchestra confident on the sound track. However, the final section of this sequence begins with a dissolve onto a chamber orchestra, also with a mirror behind them, but this time with no couples at all reflected from the floor. Of course, it is late and the musicians are preparing to leave. "Count or no count, I'm going," one of them exclaims as he packs up his violin and blows out his candle. We follow him left as he gets a light for his cigar from a valet, and we continue left with him towards the door. As the camera pans, it picks up the dancing couple, now very close, yet with their overcoats on, a single piano now playing their waltz on the sound track. Donati and Madame de move in left, from long shot to mid-shot, in front of a mirror now with no one reflected in it, not even themselves.

Thus, while the sequence has created a vertigo of joyful ecstasy, in the space of some seven minutes it ends on a chill note, with an increasing sense of cold and isolation and of disappearing light. "Your husband comes home tomorrow," Donati simply states, as we pick up another footman with an extinguisher in hand, snuffing out the candles in the candelabra at the center of the room. Then, in sharp contrast to all the energetic swirls at the first part of the sequence, the camera slowly follows this footman in what is at least a 180-degree pan, as he goes about the dance floor putting out the candles. As he passes by the orchestra platform, we see another musician filling the screen with a dark cloak that he is putting over his harp, as we fade out to black.

This is surely one of the most extraordinary sequences in the history of the cinema, a far cry from mere "visual frou-frou," which was how Lindsay Anderson responded to this element in the film.[7] It is a sequence that creates within its own style the emotions of the characters—first their sense of hope and their excitement at being together, but finally the chilling recognition that their waltzing dream has ended. A society that lives by such superficial rituals will not allow so "serious" a flirtation to occur.

There are many other elements in the film and many fine sequences. Particularly telling is the general's attempt to talk to his wife about what is happening to them, about the degree of her involvement with Donati, which he has come to sense. It ends with his decision not to go out but to stay at home with his wife. Yet, as he goes to close the windows for the night, we cut to outside the house as the camera travels along a number of windows that we see being closed—until the last one, when the camera stops, and we see the light go out as well. Thus, while we recognize the general's attempts at compassion and concern, we get from the sequence the sense that his wife is trapped.

Equally fine is Donati's visit to Madame de on the eve of her departure for the Italian lakes, in an effort to forget him. As he waits in the library for her to appear, he seems dominated by portraits of her husband—the full-length portrait that we saw in the opening sequence of the film as she was gulping down her tea, but also another little one on the other side of the room. He has brought her back her earrings, which suddenly take on meaning for her. Her look of ecstasy as she tries them on in her bedroom in front of a little ornamented mirror (again, this time ironically, making her look somewhat like a valentine) is in sharp contrast with the pert, self-confident look that we saw reflected from another mirror at the opening of the film. Now her emotions have become seriously engaged, and while the trappings of her life remain the same, we no longer feel that her life is frivolous. She wants to wear the earrings when she goes down to greet Donati in the library but cannot because her husband has come in. As she escorts Donati to the door, she seems deeply distressed. She places her cheek against the door and closes her eyes as he is leaving. *"Je ne vous aime pas, je ne vous aime pas, je ne vous aime pas,"* she whispers as he

[7] Quoted in Roud, *op, cit.,* p. 37.

PETER HARCOURT

goes out, as if trying to make the words come true: "I do not love you."

Madame de records the transformation of a vain and spoiled woman into a tragic heroine, As in Tolstoy's *Anna Karenina,* however, the world she inhabits defeats her passion and brings about the death of both her lover and herself. Yet, interestingly, in *Madame de* it is less the passion in itself that defeats her than her inability to free herself completely from her pattern of little lies. It is when she lies to Donati—again about the earrings, trying to keep him from knowing that they had been given to her by her husband—that he loses faith in her. She learns her lesson—only too late. The earrings that meant so little to her at the opening of the film have become inseparable from her faith in life itself, in the validity of her own feelings. Yet she has told so many lies about them, both to her husband and to Donati, that her attempt to hang onto them literally causes her to languish and die. Furthermore, the fuss that she makes about them so humiliates the general that he is finally driven to challenge Donati to a duel, bringing about (we must suppose, as it happens off screen) Donati's death as well.

As we watch the film, increasingly we have to ask ourselves what these earrings are, finally. Are they just a plot contrivance, or are they something more? Initially, they might seem to have symbolized the luxurious vanity of Madame de's life and of the society she lives in—costly, but not yet precious, ornaments which she is prepared to give away. In the course of the film, however, their associations change. What was once simply ornamental and therefore intrinsically valueless becomes something of extraordinary value—a reminder of the only deep human relationship she has ever known.

Yet in the film neither Madame de, nor the general's mistress, nor later on the general's niece, are able to hang onto them. It is as if their value, once appreciated, seems too great for human beings to handle. Finally, in deliberate contrast once again with the opening of the film, Madame de takes them to the cathedral in a much more devout kind of visit. She leaves them on the altar, hoping that her God will forgive her and spare Donati's life. But as so often in Ophuls, her request is too late. The offering is in vain.

Primitive man may have had a symbolic relationship to the whole world around him. Objects took on meaning for him according to the degree that they affected his life. Civilized man, however, has lost this directness. Objects still have meaning for him, but chiefly as the outward signs of his station in life, of his wealth or his class. It is only in moments of great stress that the same objects may come to stand for something inward. In Buñuel the isolation of the characters often imbues everyday objects with fetishistic force. In Ophuls, on the other hand, objects that seem at the outset just part of the decor, gradually take on a special significance.

In *Madame de,* not only are there the earrings, but there are also the staircases and carriages which form so much a part of his characters' lives. With their sense of grandeur, the staircases might well remind us again of Welles and *The Magnificent Ambersons,* but also of Ophuls's own *La Signora di Tutti* or *Letter from an Unknown Woman.* On a practical level, of course, they provide a convenient space on which to move people up and down in a choreography of movement; but more than this, especially when contrasted with the little spiral staircase in the jeweler's shop, they seem to stand for the sense of self-importance that dominates these people's lives, a self-importance that finally proves so vain.

Equally meaningful are the carriages in *Madame de* and the way they are used. At one point in the film, after the hunt scene, the general is mildly chastising his wife for having swooned for too long after Donati had fallen off his horse. They sit side by side, and everything is formal between them. In contrast to this scene is the one where Madame de and Donati are in a carriage together. It is the moment of their longed-for rendezvous, the consummation of their love. She sits across his lap as they hold one another. "I do not love you," she keeps whispering, urgently as she had done before, but this time with a smile on her face.

Finally, during the last sequence in the film, Donati and the general both arrive at the dueling grounds, not only in separate carriages but by separate roads; and later on, after Madame de has been to church, she is seen traveling in yet another carriage on yet another road, trying desperately to arrive in time to stop the duel. In such a way, by making use of the everyday trappings of the characters' natural surroundings, Ophuls lends emphasis to the breaking apart of their lives caused both by the passion and by the intrigue that has accompanied it.

PETER HARCOURT

Like Renoir's *La Règle du Jeu,* Ophuls sees his world as both positive and negative. It is a world formalized to the point of coldness, and polite to the point of hypocrisy. *"Cher ami,"* is what the general calls everyone, no matter what his feelings. Yet, while he might kiss only his wife's hand as she is going off in the train, he refrains from saluting her as he had, in fact, his mistress, even though he had previously kissed her on the cheek.

Respect and dignity are bound up with formality, a formality which apparently does not allow the passions to grow. At the same time these qualities hold the world together, masters and servants, husbands and wives, however one may feel. "His elegant characters lack nothing and lose everything," as Andrew Sarris has said.[8] As in *La Règle du Jeu* and in *Anna Karenina,* to attempt to act out your passion is to break the rules that hold this fragile world together, and there is apparently no other that the characters can reach.

Claude Beylie has taken pains to emphasize the Christian side of Ophuls's work,[9] and even the secular Andrew Sarris refers to the "mystic" reprise at the end of *Liebelei.*[10] Certainly, there is the sense in *Madame de* that our most precious feelings can scarcely find expression in this imperfect world. So the earrings, that have come to stand for this search after something more precious and more inward than the formalities of life, end up in church. After we have heard the pistol shot from the dueling ground and have seen Madame de collapse beside a tree, we dissolve to yet another one of Ophuls's exploratory camera tracks—this time down from inside of the cathedral tower, left past a now-empty nave, up and around a pillar to the icon of the Virgin Mary and then down towards the altar. As we hear the cathedral bells ringing, with harsh brass chords punctuating the theme song of the film—a theme which, in its down-falling cadence, forms the musical antithesis of the waltz theme that we had heard earlier—the camera cranes down upon the earrings on the altar, beside which is a placard reading, "Given by Madame de." Perhaps only here, this final scene might imply, will these earrings and all that they have come to represent find their final resting place. They have proven too much for this world.

8 Sarris, *op. cit.,* p. 72.
9 Beylie, *op. cit.,* pp. 9-116.
10 Sarris, *op. cit.,* p. 71.

16. The Seaweed-Gatherer

ROBIN WOOD

GREAT ART IS THE PRODUCT of a sensitive intelligence deeply involved with life. Such a formula may appear at once vague and obvious but, confronted with that elusive Protean ogre, Film Theory, I consider its vagueness, at least, an asset. One should, according to Theory, admire a film because (a) the cinema is the art of editing, (b) the cinema is the art of camera movement, (c) the cinema is the art of the "real," and (d) the cinema is the art of illusion. Of course, it's all nonsense. One admires a film as one admires a poem, a painting, a novel, a piece of music: when one makes contact through the work with the searching and guiding intelligence (by which I mean much more than intellect) of the artist, and experiences that shock of simultaneous empathy and enlightenment, the sense at once of novelty and recognition, as if one has just been brought to awareness of something one has always known. Any theory of film aesthetics that is not strictly subordinate to this—in particular, any that would impose limitations of any kind whatever on the use the artist may make of the complex technical means at his disposal—is instantly disqualified. The critic's

160

job is to discuss the quality of the result, not to lay down rules.

The concept that certain possibilities inherent in the medium are more "cinematic" than others has been repeatedly proven a chimera. The pursuit of elements that distinguish film from the other arts is neither pointless nor unrevealing; but it is equally valid to find the richness of film precisely in its manifold resemblances to the other arts. Film is like drama in that it uses real people enacting roles within a decor; it is like the novel in that its narrative possibilities are not restricted by considerations of time and place; it is like painting in the possibilities it offers for visual composition within a frame; it is like music in its aspect of complex movement—within the frame, of the camera, from image to image—and temporal continuity; it is like poetry in the opportunities it offers for the organization of recurrent or connected imagery. Nor are these affinities in any way mutually exclusive. All are inherent in all filmmaking. Different filmmakers may veer toward any or all of them, synthesizing them in rich combinations: *Sunrise*—painting, music, poetry; *La Règle du Jeu*—music and theater; *L'Avventura*—painting and the novel.

The fatuity of seeking some specifically "cinematic" essence can be illustrated by juxtaposing and contrasting two classic dialogue scenes: the sequence in Nicholas Ray's *Bitter Victory,* where Richard Burton and Ruth Roman, former lovers, meet unexpectedly after an interval of some years under the suspicious eyes of the man she has married (Curt Jurgens); and the celebrated kitchen scene in Welles's *The Magnificent Ambersons,* wherein Fanny (Agnes Moorehead) tries to get information out of George (Tim Holt) without betraying her emotional involvement, while the latter stuffs himself with food. The most simplistic notion of the "cinematic" is that which insists on a sharp distinction between subject matter appropriate to the cinema and to the theater, so let it be said at once that in terms of content—of action and dialogue—there is nothing in either scene that couldn't have been done on a stage: a single set, with three people sitting or standing around a table. The intensity of the Ray—it must be among the most electrifying dialogue scenes ever filmed—arises partly from the cutting. The situation is quite commonplace, the dialogue unremarkable, the actors scarcely my favorites; though they offer notable demonstrations of the general truth that Ray can get fine performances from the most unexpected people, the fascination of the sequence does not lie merely in the acting. Ray has conceived the whole scene in terms of exchanged or intercepted looks; the significance, instead of being extracted from the text, is conferred upon it by the way the characters look at each other. The cutting stresses (but not crudely) the significance of the glances, Ray using editing rather as a poet uses accent to obtain the most precise inflections.

The *Ambersons* scene, in contrast, uses editing only negatively, through its absence: the whole scene is done in a single take, and we keep waiting (if sub-consciously) for a cut that never comes. The effect is, in an obvious way, much closer to theater—the camera is almost entirely static (there are two small pans) and we are compelled to watch a continuous action from a fixed position. The literary content of the scene—by which I mean the text abstracted from the visuals—is much stronger than the *Bitter Victory* sequence; one can imagine getting a certain pleasure from the script without having seen the film. The quality of the acting assumes a more autonomous importance—one could admire Agnes Moorehead's performance without necessarily admiring the film, whereas it is difficult to think of the acting in the Ray scene distinct from the editing. I take these points as simply descriptive, not as implying any comparative valuation. The effect of the Welles scene is quite different, but no less intense. Ray's cutting takes us right into the situation, putting us in the characters' places. We are led to empathize very strongly without becoming exclusively identified with any one participant, so that we experience the psychological tensions of the scene, the complex pattern of recognition, distrust and recoil in an almost physical way. Welles insists that we remain spectators rather than participants, examining characters' behavior critically (though not necessarily without sympathy); as Joseph McBride says in his book on Welles, the hesitations become as important as the gestures. The valid question is not "Is this theatrical?" but "Does it work?" and a cogent answer would involve some analysis of the whole film, and the relationship within it of style and meaning.

I shall anger the theoreticians—not for the first time—but I believe that *ultimately* the quality that makes a movie (or work of art) great is probably beyond quasi-scientific demonstration of a kind that would enforce universal agreement. This does not mean that I consider critical discourse meaningless or futile. If the critic cannot ultimately prove, he can *point toward*, and there are different methods of pointing, some more compelling than others, though in the last resort it will be our confidence in and sense of contact with the person who points that will convince us (together with our sense of *his* contact with the work in question). The quality indispensable to greatness in art is next to impossible to name with any accuracy or precision of meaning, being itself elusive, intangible, capable of embodying itself in innumerable forms. The nearest single-word definition I can offer is *aliveness*, a term which could mean anything to anyone or nothing to nobody. I can add to it a few other phrases and ideas that may make what I am trying to communicate clearer to the sympathetically inclined. In Chinese aesthetics there exists a complex term which can be rendered in English as "spirit resonance": it implies the artist's sensitivity to (or empathy with) the life principle in the universe, and his ability to become so attuned to it that he himself becomes one with it. To offset charges of mysticism (or mystification), and to remove from the concept any limiting implication that some form of rapt "Oriental" contemplation is essential to the production of art, let me set beside this the cumbersome but eloquent phrase of D. H. Lawrence's, "spontaneous-creative fulness of being." I am by no means deterred by the fact that Lawrence does not use this phrase in a specifically aesthetic sense, but as a life ideal. There are, obviously, certain characteristics that distinguish artistic creation from other activities, but they are not necessarily the most important ones (any more than are those that distinguish cinema from the other arts). Anyone who has experienced those rare moments (for me at least—more fortunate people may experience them frequently) of feeling fully alive and untrammeled, of being *caught up*—moments of untrammeled spontaneity of action or heightened perception, or both—will know what Lawrence's phrase means. "Creativity" is a concept of extension far beyond aesthetics, and such moments embody it in its intensest form—and are the most recognizable manifestations of a state of being by no means restricted to them. Quite disparate experiences—like being reciprocally in love, or performing with a sense of mastery a job (*any* job), or romping spontaneously with one's children, or simply feeling a sense of living contact, however momentary, with another human being—while they are not identical with artistic creativity, have a great deal fundamentally in common with it.

The kinds of feelings I have in mind are not incompatible with even the most extreme pessimism; indeed, their fusion with a pessimistic outlook is the essence of what we call the "tragic sense." But they *are* incompatible with negative, antilife impulses—cruelty, cynicism, disgust. To define by opposition the qualities that determine what are my favorite movies, it might help to allude briefly to one of my *un*favorites. Kubrick's *A Clockwork Orange* seems to me convincing proof that a film made exclusively out of hatred and contempt can only be hateful and contemptible. It has been acclaimed for technical brilliance by critics who only notice technique when they are hit over the head with it. For me, the technique of *A Clockwork Orange* is unremittingly crude and complacent, contrived to emphasize at every point the ugliness of the humanity depicted and the director's sense of his own superiority to it. If we feel that humanity stinks, perhaps our only salvation lies in the acknowledgment that we, as humans, stink with it.

I am not preaching the Romantic doctrine of inspiration—of the artist as Aeolian harp breathed on by the winds of heaven. Rather, what I have in mind is a spontaneous-intuitive sense of the unity of inner and outer worlds; a sense, in fact, of the interrelatedness of things—of interrelationships so complex and organic that reason alone could never trace them, though reason, interacting with intuition, can pin them down and clarify them. It is this sense of interrelatedness that the greatest works of art, working on the sympathetic, responsive consciousness, can communicate, and it is through this that analysis and some degree of rationalized demonstration become practicable. "Interrelatedness" is a concept emphasized by D. H. Lawrence in an essay on the novel; it is also central to the most valuable of recent "pointers" toward means of cogent demonstration, V. F. Perkins's Pelican book, *Film as Film*, to which I must express an already considerable debt accumulated during the month since I have read it.

It will be clear by this point that I can make no clear-cut distinction between "favorite" movies and "great" movies. My favorite movies are those that I feel have the richest experiences to offer, and

164   ROBIN WOOD

what other way is there of defining "great"? All the movies I would call great develop toward points analogous to those moments of heightened aliveness that I have attempted to describe, or are structured on a series of them. The function of such points is to draw together in a knot the interweaving threads of the film; they depend very largely on context. To lay such stress on a single moment in a film is merely to make a convenient signal that points toward a detailed analysis of the whole; it is not a suggestion that the greatness of a film can be gauged from an occasional isolated shot. It can be gauged only from our apprehension of the density of its interrelationships, an apprehension which the culminating points crystallize. Examples could be multiplied more or less indefinitely. Sometimes such a moment can be pinpointed in a line of dialogue: Anna Lee's "I can't see him any more—all I can see is the flags," in Ford's *Fort Apache,* which epitomizes the film's ambivalent tragic-heroic feelings about the cavalry, the individual submerged in the very tradition that ennobles and immortalizes him; Charulata (in Satyajit Ray's movie named after her) summoning her servant to bring the lamp that will illuminate her tentative, suspended reconciliation with her husband on the threshold; Ingrid Bergman, in Rossellini's *Viaggio in Italia (Strangers in America)*, discovering, after her experience of the Pompeii relics, that "life is so short." No one familiar with the films in question will imagine me to be talking here just about their scripts. The lines in question are devoid of autonomous "literary" distinction; in each case they knot together the whole complex of ideas, motifs, narrative threads of which the fabric of the film is composed. I shall, however, balance these examples with three purely visual moments from other favorite movies:

1. The more one contemplates Murnau's *Sunrise* the more of a mess it seems. Its intentions are bewilderingly confused, it loses its sense of direction in the middle to a degree that almost loses it the viewer's attention, its traits of false naiveté (ominously anticipated in the subtitle, *A Song of Two Humans*) frequently make one wince (that field of daffodils!—those circling cherubs!), its celebrated outbursts of expressionistic technical bravura appear less expressive on each viewing. Yet its underlying creative intensity, deriving ultimately from Murnau's personal predicament, that of a homosexual with an impossible, unrealizable yearning for an idealized norm of

marriage-and-family) transcends all its failings. The intensity—paradoxically perhaps—is most convincingly expressed in the film's quietest, simplest, most reticent moments. The whole opening movement of the film (on which one would primarily base one's claims for it) culminates in what is for me one of the cinema's most moving moments: the couple's exit from the church after their (metaphorical) remarriage, with the spectators who are awaiting the emergence of the actual bride and groom automatically falling into place for them as if in inadvertent acknowledgement of the reality of their union. In sharp contradistinction to the elaborate technical display for which the film is usually singled out, Murnau shoots this brief scene in one take, in long shot, from a fixed position, leaving the action to speak quietly (but most eloquently) for itself; the scene's great force of affirmation and its power to move are enhanced rather than negated by the fact that it is also funny.

2. In Kazan's *Wild River* Carol (Lee Remick) takes Montgomery Clift back to the house she lived in with her late husband. It is the first time she has revisited it since his death. She and Clift are trying to find ways of persuading her grandmother to move off an island that will soon be flooded in the interest of "progress." The scene—among the finest things in the American, or any other, cinema—has a delicacy and sensitivity not easy to parallel in Kazan's other films. Of its many moments, gestures and exchanged looks that are rich in implications, I single out one: Carol, wondering if her grandmother could be persuaded to move into *this* house with her, sits down in a rocking chair in front of the window. It is Ella, the grandmother, whom we have come to associate with rocking chairs. Carol's action reminds one of that "sympathetic magic" practiced by primitive peoples: you make what you want happen by enacting it. But beyond its unobtrusive psychological rightness, the action, comparing Carol with Ella, beautifully draws together the film's thematic and narrative threads: we are led by the setting to think of Carol's loss of her husband Jim, and to compare it to Ella's loss of *her* husband; we connect Ella's refusal to leave the island where her husband is buried with Carol's difficulty in finding life meaningful since Jim's death; we feel that the old woman's need to remain faithful to her past is as great as the young woman's need to break with hers. The film's complex attitude toward progress and the

166   ROBIN WOOD

past is thus rendered for us in precise human terms. Clift's presence is of course essential; he is not only the believer in "progress" who is trying to remove Ella, he also represents a possible future for Carol. But equally essential to the effect is the "presence" of Carol's husband and their past together, marvelously created for us in the wealth of suggestions in the decor, and the girl's response.

3. Finally, a single camera movement. Towards the end of Hitchcock's *Vertigo*, Scotty (James Stewart), having finally remade Judy (Kim Novak) in the image of the supposedly dead Madeleine, watches her put on a pendant, recognizes it from a portrait of Madeleine's grandmother, and realizes that Judy is in fact the woman he knew as Madeleine and that he has been the victim of a complicated deception. To render for us as vividly as possible Scotty's moment of perception and recognition, Hitchcock cuts in a shot of the portrait, as Scotty saw it in an art gallery, that looks at first glance like a simple flashback or memory shot. Yet there is a crucial difference: the earlier parts of the film, including the art gallery scene, were characterized by subjective forward-tracking shots as Scotty (and through identification, the spectator with him) was led deeper and deeper into the mysterious and haunting world of Madeleine and the past; here, the camera moves *back* from the portrait. The sudden movement of recoil (again done subjectively so as to be shared by the spectator), in the context of all that has preceded it, marks a point of culmination in the progress and structure of the entire film.

I shall end by examining the closing scenes of two films that, as well as any, for me represent the finest achievements of which the cinema (as we know it so far in its short history) is capable, and which already justify any claims for its position beside the senior arts: *Letter from an Unknown Woman* (Ophuls) and *Sansho Dayu* —"Sansho the Bailiff" (Mizoguchi). Both are works that would respond to the most detailed and meticulous analysis; works, that is, in which every detail exists both for its own inherent expressiveness and for its reverberations throughout the total structure.

Letter from an Unknown Woman is one of the cinema's most perfect film-poems, constructed as much on an intricate system of internal balances, correspondences, echoes, as on a forward-moving narrative. Its forward movement is in fact dual: Ophuls counterpoints the few hours during which Stefan reads Lisa's letter with the many years its narrative covers; both converge upon a single point, Stefan's moment of realization—of Lisa, of himself, of their meetings, of the past now irretrievably lost—and his resulting decision not to evade the duel with Lisa's husband that he knows can only end in his own death. Time, and the sense of people's entrapment in its inevitable progress, has always been one of Ophuls's central preoccupations. The flashback structures of this film and *Lola Montes* perfectly express this (never has the flashback seemed a less arbitrary narrative device); so does Ophuls's celebrated style, characterized by long, graceful, predetermined tracking shots in whose movement the characters are caught. The other central concern in Ophuls is with the yearning for a romantic Ideal, which may be unattainable and may be illusory, but the striving for which confers on his characters their beauty, even as it renders them incapable of adapting to reality. *Letter from an Unknown Woman* is at once an elegy to the tragic waste brought about by this immersion in an impossible dream, and a celebration of the triumph of the dream over time; in the paradox lies the film's poignance.

Although the main body of the film is a visualization of Lisa's narrative, Ophuls never traps us wholly in her vision, permitting himself the license of showing us details of which Lisa couldn't have been aware (the sausage-eating, beer-drinking ladies of the orchestra) or showing us events from a point of view (physical and attitudinal) that Lisa couldn't have shared (the ironic overhead shot of her return home with Stefan the night they become lovers). The film is centered on Lisa's romantic vision, but we are given the freedom to adopt other viewpoints if we wish, to respond to her vision in ways more complex than simple identification. When she visits Stefan for the last time, we know (as Lisa doesn't) that her son is going to die of typhoid; we are aware that she has wilfully destroyed her marriage and unwittingly caused the death of her child. The sequence is crowded with intimations of waste and loss, of time running out—from the moment when Lisa, in memory of her first night with Stefan, buys the last few white roses from the very old man who has taken the place of the friendly woman of the earlier scene. Stefan's line, "For us, all the clocks in the world have stopped,"—a part of his practiced technique of seduction—is among the most poignantly ironic ever uttered on the screen. When

ROBIN WOOD

her lover, father of her child, has failed to recognize her, treating this again as one of an interminable series of casual encounters even as he expresses his own frustrated yearning for the perfection she has always wanted to offer him, Lisa leaves, and Ophuls ends the scene on a "still life" of the roses and a guttering candle.

Stefan finishes the letter, reading of Lisa's death, and his eyes filling with tears, recalls moments in their meetings, going back through the years, recognizing what he has lost. The carriages arrive, and he leaves for the duel. At the gate he pauses, turns, "sees" Lisa at last as she was as a young girl, the very first time he saw her, from this exact position. The image fades, leaving an empty doorway; the sense of the lost years is overwhelmingly strong, with that Ophulsian sense of "too late." Yet the effect is counter-balanced by the triumph of memory. Stefan leaves for the duel, a slight smile on his face. In accepting death at the hands of Lisa's husband, he affirms his acceptance and appreciation of Lisa's love, his sense of the potential supreme value of all that might have been.

The end of *Sansho Dayu* achieves, by very different means, a similar fusion of loss and affirmation. The central theme here is the attempt to reunite a dispersed family. Towards the close of the film, Zushio, having learned that his father and sister are both dead, renounces temporal power to go off in search of his mother, who was sold to a brothel on the island of Sado. They tell him in the village that she is dead, one of the many victims of a recent tidal wave; but Zushio continues around the cape and finds his mother, pitiably wasted and blind but still alive. The extraordinary emotional depth of this sequence depends on the accumulation of ideas, images and associations throughout the entire film. I shall list here some of the crucial factors:

1. Earlier, as slaves in Sansho's terrible domain, Zushio and his sister Anju discovered that their mother might still be alive when Anju overheard a young girl from Sado singing a yearning song, "Zushio, Anju, I long for you . . .," which could only have originated with their mother. As he crosses (it is low tide) the little inlet recently devastated by the tidal wave, Zushio questions an old man gathering seaweed. As the man tells him of the many deaths, the mother's voice, enfeebled to the very verge of audibility, is heard in what is just recognizable as the melody of the song; it is the per-

sistence, lingering on long after conscious rational hope has left her, of the desire for her children, that calls Zushio to her.

2. The little cape Zushio rounds is the place where earlier, degraded and lamed, the mother climbed to call her children's names in hopeless longing across the sea; the bay was the scene of one of her desperate attempts at escape, which resulted in her laming. She called their names similarly when, as young children on their way to rejoin their father in exile, they were cutting sticks to build a shelter; in adulthood, as slaves, they heard, or seemed to hear, the voice calling their names at a moment when circumstances evoked memories of the incident. The plaintive cry of "Zushio . . . Anju . . . " echoes through the film, becoming an emblem for the triumph of the spirit over time and space.

3. The visual presence of the sea throughout the final sequence relates to the use of fire and water imagery throughout the film, too complex to be more than touched on here. Suffice it to say that fire is generally associated with violence, destruction and cruelty; water with patience—especially of the women of the film. In order that her brother might escape, Anju, who is given the name Shinobu, which means "patience," committed suicide by walking into a lake. Water is associated with fidelity and remembrance (the father's grave is on a hill overlooking a lake), but also with separation; it accumulates complex emotional overtones during the course of the film which greatly affect our response to the last scene.

4. In defying the authorities in order to perform a noble action, and subsequently renouncing power, Zushio has repeated the action of his father, for which he was exiled and which constituted the starting point of the action; Anju's suicide has made possible Zushio's subsequent actions (including the finding of their mother). Behind the reunion of mother and son, and giving it its full significance, is the *living* presence of the dead: we are aware at once of the sense of tragic loss, and of the unity of the family reaffirmed triumphantly in the face of that loss.

5. In the film's closing shot the camera cranes up from the embracing mother and son, passes over the sea, comes to rest on the seaweed-gatherer (in distant long shot) still at his work—an image of continuity, an acknowledgment of a wider world where other lives continue, but more than that. The seaweed, we realize, has

ROBIN WOOD

been deposited by the tidal wave, which has wrought havoc and destruction, causing many deaths; but seaweed is used as a fertilizer, and it is for this purpose the old man is collecting it. The symbolism is quite unforced, incorporated naturally in the action, yet it epitomizes the tragic-affirmative movement of the whole film, the hope and possibility of new growth wrested out of the most terrible devastation.

In *Sansho Dayu* Mizoguchi's style, with its perfect balancing and harmonizing of sympathetic involvement and contemplation, reaches its fullest maturity. Few artists in any medium have achieved such mastery of technique, mastery of experience, mastery of self (three aspects of the same process). It is the greatest movie I have ever seen.

17. My Adventure

CHARLES THOMAS SAMUELS

My FAVORITE FILM IS *L'Avventura*. Ordinarily, I would explain such a statement by immediately discussing the film, but the editor has invited his contributors to be autobiographical and theoretical, so I should first explain why I usually avoid expression of self.

For me, the critic is a servant. He helps his readers decide what films to see and, more important, to understand what films they have seen. By so doing, he also serves the artist, who wants a discerning audience. An evidential piece of criticism is useful even when we disagree; by forcing us to find contrary evidence, it sharpens our understanding. However, when the critic says that his judgment reflects his personality, he makes it difficult to argue with him and even invites us to pay less attention to the film than to his personal style.

Nevertheless, people usually deny that critics can be impersonal. They say that criticism is opinion and that there is no disputing about taste. But all judgments are opinions, requiring only evidence to make them disputable; if taste itself cannot be disputed, a given expression of taste can, so long as it is rendered as argument. If only the critic will cite the facts on which he bases an interpretation, we can judge his accuracy and logic. Evaluation is obviously more difficult to judge, but this too can be checked, if only aesthetic grounds are declared.

Behind the notion that critics express opinions having no special claim to truth lurks timidity. Since art is enjoyed as well as understood, when we claim that a critic speaks only for himself we are actually asserting the right of enjoyment without fear of censure. If, on the other hand, a critic might be truly a judge, when we disagree with his opinion we may also expose our deficiency. Those who march under the banner *"de gustibus non est disputandum"* are really saying, "hands off!"

Since the critic who writes as if he were seeing the truth thereby implies that we are not, we accuse him of being high and mighty. Yet there are many other critics trying to unhorse him, to say nothing of the film itself, which, should it prove a windmill rather than a damsel in distress, will effectively mock his pretension. So, far from being arrogant, this sort of critic invites exposure. He understands that he is part of a collective effort to get at the truth, and that if he is wrong he must be corrected.

Therefore, when I get down to explaining why *L'Avventura* is a great film, I want to tell you something about it, not about myself. I would rather be guilty of colorless, impersonal writing than of not giving evidence. I mean to provide an argument that tries to seem anonymous, an evaluation based on an interpretation, that you can use without feeling like a thief and deplore without feeling like a scoundrel. I heed the editor's call to autobiography only in the degree that "favorite" implies a personal element. I really mean to say that *L'Avventura ought* to be favored, though obviously the extent will vary according to the viewer's other experiences and his conception of what constitutes film art.

My experience is that Antonioni's film made me a critic. I had dabbled in writing about movies during my student days, but since movies were almost all I could see (few serious films reached the provinces), I gradually came to sense the anomaly of contemplating works that were meant only to be used and discarded. For me, as for most viewers, films remained a diversion. When I wanted to see life formed, and thus comprehended, I read books and—with decreasing frequency—went to the theater. But on one occasion when I attended a movie for fun, I stumbled on something different from but just as pertinent as the books and plays I liked. Thereafter, I began to need films in the way I had always needed literature; since I am fundamentally a teacher, I began to want to show other people why they should need them too.

In the years since the delightful shock of *L'Avventura*, I have seen hundreds of films, some of which strike me, for varying reasons, as serious works of art. Only with these, as both critic and teacher, am I concerned.

Like words such as "art" or "intellectual," the word "serious" is thought to be honorific, whereas it is only descriptive. There are bad and good serious films, yet all of them engage our powers of comprehension and empathy not only during the performance but afterwards. Each tells us something that is worth knowing in itself, and each invites us to reconsider both its meaning and its means. (Sometimes a film may be serious only in its art when that art has outstanding formal excellence; I think, for example, of films by Alfred Hitchcock or René Clair.) Only serious films need to be criticized because only they make thought necessary to appreciation, and only they reward a second look. Other films ask to be labeled, as when we indicate the malaise relieved by a given medicine, or they invite sociology (what society produces such things?), or stargazing, or technical attention to some device. Writing about film in response to such invitations has its value, but it is barely criticism.

L'Avventura insisted that I be a critic; this much it demands from all viewers. It precludes the passivity with which one customarily regards movies. It says something worth hearing in a way that no other art does. *L'Avventura* is my favorite film not only because it is so good but because, up to now, it so fully accords with my understanding of what film can do.

As a narrative art (and virtually all feature films tell stories), film can do most of what is possible in drama or fiction: it can show people talking and acting, as in plays; or it can describe, by means of the camera, what the novelist describes with his prose. It can use other arts: music, for example, with its powers of evocation, or a species of painting, with its visual signals. Film speaks in several

174

voices, but too often it depends on words. As Alfred Hitchcock says, most films are simply "photographs of people talking."

The simplicity Hitchcock is right to deplore is not simplicity of theme; in narrative, not meaning itself but its embodiment, causes a work to be simple or complex. Most films are simple because you can shut out their images or ignore scenes and events, and still get the point. Films that repeat their meanings or state them explicitly appeal to us only insofar as we go to the movies to be diverted not only from our cares but also from the bother of having to pay attention.[1] As a result, there is no need to think about them, and the enjoyment they provide is transitory and shallow.

Art, on the other hand, seeks to deepen our capacities to think and feel. Great novels, for example, expand the confines of personal experience or challenge us to see the familiar in a new way. For this reason, art wants to involve us, to make its challenge irresistible. Filmgoers who do not like being challenged dislike art; those who value art's invitation to growth understand that their participation is crucial.

L'Avventura makes participation more crucial than any film I've seen. It does so, first, by dispensing with a plot that sets up expectations which we merely sit back and see fulfilled. Or rather, *L'Avventura* rejects its own plot in order to assert that real human drama occurs without artificialities of climax and denouement. Seducing us with mystery that would conventionally be resolved through detection, it focuses on the more profound mystery of human behavior.

A girl disappears while she and her lover, Sandro, are vacationing with some friends. One of the latter, Claudia, joins Sandro in searching for Anna, but gradually they forget their purpose and fall in love. We are never told what happened to Anna because she disappeared from a world where nobody counts enough to be remembered. The plot of the film is the absence of a plot, the failure of the protagonists to complete their action and thereby experience fulfillment. Fulfillment comes only to the audience—when it understands why these people cannot succeed. Whereas the ordinary film

---

[1] There are serious and even good films that depend on words almost to the extent of being essentially theatrical, but they also make use of film's other languages. Moreover, works like the films of Bergman, *Children of Paradise* or *Grand Illusion*, to name some examples, are neither obvious nor repetitive, however verbal.

is a self-contained process that we watch, *L'Avventura* is an experience we undergo; what happens on the screen is only data for our developing comprehension.

Though rare, films were made about the spiritual or emotional rather than the active lives of characters before *L'Avventura*. However, unlike his predecessors, Antonioni doesn't permit his characters to explain themselves; he doesn't provide them with revelatory backgrounds or dramatic quirks;[2] we know them only because of what they do. Claudia, for example, undergoes the most profound personal revolution in the film, but neither her original innocence nor her final shame is stated. The former is displayed through many small moments, as when she reacts with simple pleasure to Sandro's speeding at the beginning of the film, though we and Anna see it as a childish reassertion of the virility Anna had previously mocked, or when the bored yachting party goes down the gangplank to the island and only Claudia stops to run her fingers through the water. Her final realization that she has become truly absorbed by Sandro's world of self-indulgence and disloyalty is expressed only by the look on her face and the slow relaxation of her hand as it moves forward to rest on Sandro's head.

The larger significance of the film is also revealed by what we see rather than by commentary. Sandro's shallowness of feeling is more than a personal flaw; it represents a culture lacking in vital commitments. This Antonioni demonstrates not only through the human drama but through the physical universe surrounding it.

Eloquence of background, Antonioni's greatest innovation, is perfected in *L'Avventura*. From the beginning, setting shapes our response. The first words spoken in the film concern physical surroundings. While Anna walks into the rubble of a construction site near her home, she hears her father complaining: "It won't be long now before this poor villa will be completely crowded out. And to think this was once all woods." By such a casual utterance are we alerted to a main point of the film: the actual deterioration behind the façade of progress.

Always Antonioni counterpoints the new and the old to the lat-

---

[2] One exception proves the rule because it is crucial to our understanding of Sandro. He wanted to be an architect but gave that up for the more lucrative job of appraising.

ter's advantage, as when Claudia and Anna's drive past a magnificent Roman arch is followed by Claudia's walk through an art gallery, whose modern paintings provoke a response that is suitably both derisive and pretentious. When Sandro visits the carabinieri in Messina, we see that their office has been formed by setting up ugly wooden partitions in a magnificent baroque palace. And as Sandro and Claudia cross the Sicilian mainland they move against a background of decreasing humanity, including a sleekly modern village, empty of people and dominated by a cathedral without a bell. When they recognize their mutual corruption in the film's last scene, Claudia and Sandro stand before a ruined church.

Such facts take on their full significance in the moment when Sandro vindictively destroys a sketch some young student has drawn of the splendid cathedral at Noto. In this act, the most violent we see, he expresses jealousy of all the life-enhancing commitments that his contemporaries cannot feel: work, tradition, spiritual reverence memorialized in things of beauty. When the yachting party finds a vase on the island during the first stages of searching for Anna, they express only curiosity about the object's use. Not being able to imagine anything suitable, they carelessly let it fall.

Among such people, the individual human being counts for little more. Since pleasure is the only use they can imagine and since pleasure can be provided by anyone, anyone, as Claudia must learn, can be replaced. Lust is depersonalizing in Sandro; in his friends it doesn't even inspire human adhesion. Giulia, for example, feels lust only as a way of avenging herself on Corrado. Some of the characters do not feel lust at all; when Raimondo attempts to fondle Patrizia, she expresses an indifference he lacks the passion to overcome.

Among the poor people in the film, things appear to be different; lust drives them implacably. When Sandro and Claudia stop at a small-town pharmacy to inquire after Anna, the pharmacist remembers the girl, or so he thinks, only because she had good legs, and while giving this information, ogles Claudia, though his wife of three months is plainly furious. On the train taking them to a friend's villa, Claudia and Sandro see a provincial rodent trying to seduce a maid by means of his transistor radio. When the couple stops in a small town, Claudia is encircled by a mass of men, their eyes heavy with desire. But if the poor feel lust more fully than the rich characters in the film, neither feels it as anything but an animal impulse.

As we watch *L'Avventura,* expecting to learn the simple fact of Anna's whereabouts, we fathom instead the depths of a culture's degradation. Yet to many viewers nothing happens in the film because they are not used to inferring from action rather than listening to explanations. Thus when *L'Avventura* was first shown at Cannes, the audience hooted at the screen. In the last sequence, when Claudia runs down the long corridors of her hotel, shouts of "Cut! Cut!" were heard. This sequence, however, is the best example of Antonioni's method for producing audience involvement; in the limited space alloted to me, I can think of no better way to suggest why this film is great.

Immediately before the sequence begins, Claudia and Sandro are bantering about their love:

SANDRO: Good night, love.
CLAUDIA: Good night. Tell me you love me.
SANDRO: I love you.
CLAUDIA: Tell me again.
SANDRO: I don't love you.
CLAUDIA: I deserve that.

Sandro then goes to the door, but turns back to say he was joking. Despite its mock-seriousness, this brief exchange precisely suggests the duration of love in this society. Claudia permits herself to be lulled by Sandro's recantation, though we see on his face how little he can live up to it.

Now Antonioni shows why love can't last. Sandro goes to the hotel's public rooms, which are filled with rich vacationers. He sees the prostitute he had first met in Messina, but he turns away from her, and also from a woman gazing at a mildly erotic painting and then at him. He meets Patrizia's husband, who reminds Sandro that he must prepare appraisal figures for the next day. Exiting, he sees the whore again. This time he is a bit more attracted, but again he turns away. He tries smoking, wandering, even television, but restlessness clearly overcomes him. All this is shown rapidly, in a tempo approximating Sandro's nervous avidity. Then Antonioni

CHARLES THOMAS SAMUELS

cuts to Claudia, sleeplessly waiting in her room, and time is distended so that we may feel the weight of her vigil. She paces, rummages through Sandro's valise, makes faces at herself in the mirror, aimlessly scribbles in a magazine while counting. The dawn comes up; Claudia is still alone and even more distraught now. She runs through the corridors of her hotel, an action that is represented almost at the pace of real life not because Antonioni can't foreshorten, but because he wants us to feel Claudia's anxiety and because the sight of her searching for Sandro in these empty halls declares her spiritual condition more vividly than words.

Foolishly, she enters Patrizia's room, saying she thought that Sandro might be with her husband. Though bemused and unbelieving, Patrizia, who sleeps in a room adjacent to that of her spouse (*comme il faut*), goes to him and inquires after Sandro. Ettore remarks sensibly that if Patrizia wants him she should ask Claudia, a comment whose very casual acceptance of the new affair provokes from Claudia her first critical utterance: "A few days ago, when I felt Anna might be dead, the very thought made me feel dead too. Now I don't even cry. Now I'm afraid she may be alive. . . . Everything is becoming so simple—I'm even depriving myself of pain." To which the perfectly adjusted Patrizia responds: "There's no need to be melodramatic."

Then with miraculous tact, Antonioni provides unmelodramatic proof of the total transcendence not only of good and evil—which melodrama consecrates, even if basely—but of all feeling in this world where there can only be numbness in self-recognition. While running through the hotel, Claudia is startled by a slight movement. Moving closer, she finds herself confronted by the prostitute, glaring in indignation at having been interrupted, and by Sandro, who tries to hide. Claudia runs off like a stricken animal, while Sandro attempts to disentangle himself from the whore's embrace. Then in a thin wheedling voice, the whore asks, not directly for money but for "a little remembrance." The thinness of her voice, our attention to the louder drama of Sandro's moral exposure, may contrive to make us pay less than full attention to these simple words, yet they ironically complete the adventure. A girl disappears; her lover demonstrates his feeling by looking for her, but soon that feeling devolves upon a new object; the new woman is also forgotten in her turn; finally, the lover is seen in the arms of a whore, and memory has withered into some crumpled lira notes. Antonioni's pitiless camera now trains on the whore's shoeless feet stroking the "remembrance." Poetry leaves images and phrases in our mind. A film like *L'Avventura*, in its own language of things seen, can leave images as memorable and no less eloquent. Here is one.

Another is the last meeting of Claudia and Sandro. Sandro leaves the hotel and goes to the parapet on which Claudia is crying. He walks past her and sits disconsolately on a nearby bench. For a long moment each is as isolated in his grief and shame as, we now realize, both had always been in their "intimacy." After awhile, Claudia moves toward Sandro. He tries to turn around and look at her, but he cannot. She hesitates, then places her hand on his head. Antonioni now cuts back to a long shot showing the two, joined in the knowledge of what they are; in the distance we see a blank wall and a not-quite-extinct volcano that eons ago formed this island on which so many people have since been lost. We began searching with them to find Anna; what we found was a colony of the abandoned.

L'Avventura is a bleak film, but like all great art it isn't depressing. It makes the unseen visible, the spiritual bodily; it takes nothingness, alienation, spiritual degradation as its subjects, but renders their reality in events and images which themselves bear witness to man's best powers. It opens film, for the first time, to the radical pessimism of modernist thought, yet it has room for affirmations of gaiety (Claudia dancing in joyful love) and even of wit (in the character of Patrizia, or the journalist who comments on the whore's triumphal entrance in Messina, or that scene itself). Most importantly, by making us infer, respond, examine, it reminds us of our own capabilities and thus of our own responsibilities at the very moment that it is exposing a denial of responsibility in its characters. Forcing us to comprehend enervation, *L'Avventura* makes us feel sentient and alive.

AUTHOR'S NOTE: The editor asked for a list of favorites that might convey the range of my taste. Had I compiled a list without regard to space limitations so as to include all the films I thought good, it would be much much longer. Had I limited myself to this length but indicated those films I thought great, it would include

CHARLES THOMAS SAMUELS

multiple titles for fewer directors. I decided to select one film by each filmmaker (or, as in the case of Zavattini and De Sica, a combination of filmmakers) so as to suggest how many types of excellence I have found in my moviegoing. The list is in alphabetical order: *A Man Escaped, Children of Paradise, Citizen Kane, Dr. Strangelove, Forbidden Games, Greed, Il Posto, Jules et Jim, L'Atalante, Le Million, Pather Panchali, Persona, Strangers on a Train, The Battle of Algiers, The Cabinet of Dr. Caligari, The Emigrants, The General, The Gold Rush, The Gospel According to Matthew, The Lady with a Dog, The Rules of the Game, The Third Man, The White Sheik, Umberto D.*

18. Antonioni: More from Less

RICHARD GILMAN

WE HAVE ALL HAD THE EXPERIENCE of watching a film which seems to be changing our perception as it unfolds, affecting the way we see and not simply offering us exotic or heightened images of what we have already perceived without the camera's intervention. And when we leave the theater we discover that the world, which we thought we knew, has changed to meet the new ways in which it's being regarded. This reciprocity—a new reality being summoned by a new perceptiveness and in turn compelling that perceptiveness into being—seems to me to be at the heart of the filmmaker's art and of the filmgoer's experience on the level of creative spectatorship. On any other level a film, like every object of popular culture, is there to console, divert, flatter, bludgeon or confirm—in any case to see to it that we remain unchanged.

In the preface to a volume of screenplays for four of his films, Michelangelo Antonioni has written that "the problem for a director is to catch reality an instant before it manifests itself and to propound that movement, that appearance, that action as a new perception." In its rescuing of the director from the status of a

182

recording agent who decides which aspects of established reality are to be photographed, this seems to me to be as useful a description of the art of filmmaking as we are likely to find. Or at least of one aspect of filmmaking; there is another, which is the *inventing* of reality I spoke of before, the making of something that hasn't existed before.

I'd like to think that Antonioni would agree that the two functions are ultimately the same, that the act of discovery of what reality is going to be next, the apprehension of its impending face, is a mysterious cause of the new, a procedure that brings it into being. If this weren't true, then the director would merely be prescient and his art only one of prediction. The artist is indeed a kind of prophet, but prophecy isn't simply prediction, but a force, a pressure on things to be other than they would be if left to themselves. And this power, while it may partake of or draw upon fantasy, isn't in its most serious uses a faculty of fantasy at all; there is nothing "unreal" or escapist in what it brings to birth.

Antonin Artaud spoke of the theater as a place where "what does not yet exist" can be made to exist. How much more true this is of movies, with their greater freedom from physical contingency, their greater spaciousness of arrangement and choice. So it was understandable that Artaud, whose love for the theater was that of a prophet for his beleaguered homeland, should have feared the film as a powerful rival and warned that it was displacing the theater as the "distributor" of the "myths of modern man." By myths Artaud meant crystallizations of centrally contemporary significances and dreams and more—picturings of our truest, previously unsuspected selves.

In the late 1950s Antonioni began to make a series of films that exemplified far more profoundly than any other works of the time the capacity of the screen to be a source of myth in Artaud's sense. These movies, linked to one another much less by subject than by sensibility and attitude, were creations that told us what we were going to be like next, how we were about to act and the kind of regard we would have for our actions. At the same time—and as a principle of these forecasts—they delineated the world with a scrupulously accurate sobriety, a refusal to enhance or "dramatize" what lay open to the ordinary eye.

Antonioni: *More from Less*   183

In response to the question asked by the editor of this volume I could easily write about any one of these films of Antonioni's, or at least any of the last four, from *L'Avventura* to *Red Desert*. This isn't because I think them all equally successful or admire them all with the same intensity, but because I can't help thinking of them as a group, dependent upon one another for a totality of vision—Antonioni's at this time—which is itself my "favorite" or preferred cinematic one. I ought to say this right out: I respond most to austerity and restraint and economy in films. Along with Antonioni the contemporary filmmakers I most admire are Bresson; Bergman in his wintry or unlavish moods; Erich Rohmer; Godard of *La Chinoise, A Married Woman* and the first part of *Weekend;* Ozu; early Resnais.

When I say austerity and restraint I certainly don't mean narrowness of imagination or skimpiness of theme. I mean a rigorousness of perception and a procedure by indirection, a cinema with silences and absences that can reveal more than the thick, dense presences, the hurly-burly activity it is all too easy for a filmmaker to clot our eyes with. After all, the world is indubitably there in its plethora of detail, and if that isn't enough there's always the studio in which to construct spaceships and saloons with swinging doors. There's always the Yugoslavian army or the Spanish.

But the austerity I'm thinking about isn't always a matter of a repudiation of physical sumptuousness, and in any case a cinema thick with objects and actions isn't necessarily the same as one with visual richness. A film like Rossellini's *The Rise of Louis the Fourteenth* triumphs by playing a visual opulence against an austerity of action, and so making the opulence, in its mysterious passivity, its resistance to having anything "dramatic" made out of it, become a sort of artistic action in itself, whereas a work like Fellini's boring *Satiricon* thrusts forward its gorgeousness, its Arabian-nights exoticism as a straightforward animated genre painting. Movies aren't paintings, but interactions of the externally visual and the interiorly personal, and the austerity I've been talking about concerns more than anything else the intelligence to resist handing over everything to the purely visual, to action and object for their own sakes.

Erich Rohmer's films illustrate what I mean. Physically hand-

RICHARD GILMAN

some and often splendid, they are controlled by a hard intelligence that works almost metaphysically to limit the things that "happen" and so to make the landscapes and interiors dispose themselves as mute backgrounds for meanings and not, as in "action" films, the meanings themselves. Against the beautiful lawns and lakefront of *Claire's Knee*, the film's characters do very little but talk, and this encounter of human speech, which is of course human thought made audible, and physical setting is the deepest event of the work. For this reason, when the protagonist does finally brush his hand against the knee of the girl, an action pregnant with significances that have been steadily and quietly gathering, the effect is more shattering than that of all the cavalry charges in the world.

After this digression, which I have to believe is no digression at all but a necessary frame in which to place my reply to the book editor's question and is probably half the reply itself (without it, it struck me that I'd be talking about my "pet" film, and who wants to hear about other people's dogs or cats?) I can go back to Antonioni's films of the late 1950s and early '60s, of which, after struggling to be obedient to the editor's request, I find myself unable to keep from writing about both *L'Avventura* and *La Notte*. The reason, as I mentioned before, is that I regard the series of films as an organic whole, any part of which would serve the purpose of communication about what *kind* of experience some presumably knowledgeable filmgoers have found important and satisfying, and not what particular one (my greatest summer vacation, my favorite Italian restaurant) they'd like to plump for.

In *L'Avventura* Antonioni introduced to the screen an almost unprecedented quality of randomness or indeterminate narration The long fruitless search for the girl lost on the island and her subsequently being entirely dropped from the plot were particularly striking instances of an imagination no longer concerned to use the screen for purposes of shapely, narratively consistent and logically unfolding dramas. And it was these gaps and holes, these seemingly aimless movements of the film's action, that were a chief source of the tedium felt by many of the film's first viewers, just as, on the contrary, they were the very basis of its supremely original beauty in the eyes of a minority who could look at it without preconceptions.

La Notte is composed according to the same principle of narrative indeterminacy as its predecessor—the same refusal to tell an easily repeatable anecdotal "story," and of course it proceeds from the same kind of insight into contemporary moral and psychic situations. The relationship between these two things is crucial, and I will return to it, but at this point I want to take up the general notion of Antonioni's "meanings." In regard to this, criticism has been all too thorough and self-confident; nearly every commentator seems to have been certain about what Antonioni was up to. Both films, their readings go, are documents of upper-class exhaustion, fables of sophisticated despair. Both testify to present anomie among the privileged, to the failure of sexuality to overcome existential ennui and to the spiritual aridity that accompanies all dedicated pursuits of pleasure.

To say these things is to say nothing of real interest, nothing that indicates why Antonioni's films might not be better as novels or why the works of this period are so much greater than, say, Fellini's *La Dolce Vita*, another picture on the theme of decadence and the moral crisis of the *haute bourgeoisie*. The critical failure has been in not seeing that Antonioni's films transcend their ostensible subject and milieu, as *La Dolce Vita* does not, that *L'Avventura* and *La Notte* are creations of universal validity and not simply portraits of a particular class or of a particular species of decadence. They are not really about decadence at all. Like Henry James's novels, these films employ privileged characters, men and women with the physical and economic freedom to choose their lives, precisely in order to exhibit the difficulties of such choice, the anguish of such freedom.

Thematically, Antonioni was treating of human connections no longer sustained by traditional values, or by any convictions at all, and so forced to abide with the most fragile and precarious of justifications. One might say that his films were the first truly existential ones. When I first saw them I was filled with a sense of discovery of a world—a visual one this time, and not a theoretical or abstract one as in Kierkegaard or Sartre—which no longer replied to the questions I had about it and gave no feeling of nurture or acceptance. And that is the way Antonioni's characters move through their environments, in a new and strange alienation, a condition very different from, and far more subtle, than what is suggested by the clichés of modern sophisticated awareness, all our talk about failure of communication, technological dehumanization, the fragmentations of society, and the like.

This new alienation is what we might call Antonioni's subject or theme, but that isn't the same thing as his art and it is a great mistake to think it is. The basis for my argument that Antonioni's films are not "about" a decadent class or the death throes of capitalism is that the visual world he composes, the one he discovers beneath appearances and calls into being, is the one we all inhabit, whether or not we have been summoned into any of its particular scenes. This is one reason why *L'Avventura* and *La Notte* are related in an indestructible unity; in the former we move through physical landscapes, nature, whitewashed ancient towns that seem part of nature, the sea, bare islands; in the latter through the city, the geometry of streets, a world of artifacts, the coldest products of modern materialistic "wit" and inventiveness, the new nature. Between them these hemispheres make up the world for us all. Antonioni's "characters" have been given the task of being its explorers—and its exhibited sacrifices.

Coherence, unity, connection between self and exterior reality are no longer sustained by a world of commerce and utility, so its inhabitants have to establish for themselves the very ground of their behavior. What is mistaken for boredom in Antonioni's characters is actually a condition of radical disjunction between personality and circumstance; a vital connection has been broken, the physical world has been dispossessed of the inherited meanings and principles according to which we had previously motivated our lives and structured its psychic and moral events.

In such a world the idea of a "story," in the sense of a progressive tale leading from a fixed starting point to a denouement which "settles" something or solves some problem, no longer has any use and is in fact inimical to the way this world is actually experienced. This is the reason for the broken narratives, the conversations in a void, the events leading nowhere—the search for the lost girl in *L'Avventura*, Jeanne Moreau's wandering without destination through the city in *La Notte*. For a story implies a degree of confidence in the world, or at least a trustfulness that the environment, no matter how painful or brutal it might be, is knowable, makes sense, hangs together. But of course there is a "story" in Antonioni's films, though not of the traditional kind. Will I be understood if I say that this story is in one sense the tale of the end of the stories which the screen, along with the novel (which art form films most nearly resembles) has heretofore beguiled us? I mean that our former modes of fiction—the love story, the romance, the adventure epic—have lost their power of conviction because the world we experience has lost its own. The essence of Antonioni's art in these films is to forge, in face of our lost convictions and acceptances of the world—convictions and acceptances we had based our narrative arts upon—a new, mercilessly stripped "telling" of our condition of bereftness and chill that refuses to find "endings" or resolutions or definitive images that reassure us. The quest for reality, and not reality as it appears to be, is Antonioni's subject; his discovery is that the real world is lying, is insubstantial, treacherous, an accomplice of our lovelessness.

Lovelessness, and the tiny, sorrowing, infinitely vulnerable gestures we try to make to restore the possibility of love—these, too, are Antonioni's subjects; they, too, make up the new reality he has discovered. Both *L'Avventura* and *La Notte* end in scenes of almost unbearably painful acceptance: of our having to be what we are, of there being no fiction that will exonerate or console us, no *ending*. Monica Vitti places her hand on Ferzetti's head in the most delicate, dry-eyed, yet anguished acceptance of what they are: frail, faithless, destined to defeat; the victory is in the recognition of this. And the couple of *La Notte*, writhing carnally in the dust on the rich man's lawn, struggle ferociously toward truth, or rather toward truthfulness. They do not love, they may love again, they have begun by acknowledging their suffering and despair.

I have spoken about the film's resemblance to the novel. It ought not be necessary to say that this resemblance is of an intellectual and aesthetic kind and not a physical one. Movies are obviously not filmed literary statements, but creations obeying their own principles and accomplishing their special, visual effectiveness. With this in

RICHARD GILMAN

mind, Antonioni's movies, like other great works of film art, can be seen as sharing in the flexibility and potential subtlety of imaginative prose that stems from the very abstractness of words, their not being "real" objects, just as film, being made of reflections cast on a screen, is not "real" either.

Every remark I've made about Antonioni's world of alienation and disjunction is exemplified not merely by what his characters do and say, but by the images they compose and that are composed as the context for their cinematic existence. I think now of Jeanne Moreau's head and shoulders traveling microscopically along the angle of a building; a figure gazing from the corner of an immense window in *L'Avventura;* the revelers eddying like dry leaves across the tycoon's lawn; the rain on the car window making a screen between the woman and her potential lover; the camera tracking slowly round the woman's room in *Red Desert,* painstakingly exhibiting every domestic object in its absolute separateness and indifference to her feelings. All these images are of a world newly forced to yield up its true face, to *look like* what we have secretly felt it to be.

"The fundamental problem of the cinema is how to express thought," the great critic and fountainhead of the New Wave, Alexander Astruc, wrote nearly twenty-five years ago. *L'Avventura* and *La Notte* are movies in which thought—indissolubly fused with image—lying behind it, selecting it and justifying it, produces an art worthy of ranking with any other.

19. "War!" said Scarlett. "Don't you men think about anything important?"

ELLEN WILLIS

As THE DEFINITIVE AMERICAN MOVIE HEROINE—
brilliantly played by an English actress, an irony that has too many
parallels in our popular culture to be coincidental—Scarlett O'Hara
has occupied a special place in my fantasy life, which is why,
if I have any one favorite movie, *Gone With the Wind,* the definitive
Hollywood romance, is probably it. Fascination with movie heroines was part of female culture when I was growing up. I learned
about being a teenager from rock and roll, but I learned about
being a woman from the movies. (The analogy isn't exact, of course:
rock and roll was mostly on my side, while the movies were mostly
against me—which didn't necessarily make their information less
valuable.) Movies about women shaped my aesthetic prejudices.
Emotions and personalities interested me more than action; the
images that were most vivid to me were faces. Many of my favorite
movies were adaptations of novels and plays. I was addicted to
movies about love, sex and female suffering—*A Streetcar Named
Desire, La Strada*, early Ingmar Bergman.

Conversely, war movies, westerns and most historical epics bored

190

me, not because I was intrinsically uninterested in war, the West or history, but because I didn't respond emotionally to the masculine myths about violence, competition, courage and honor on which such movies were based. Movies have done their part to perpetuate one of the basic sexual clichés: women are private, men are public. Thus movies about public events ordinarily take place in councils of state, on battlefields, on cattle ranges, wherever men with conflicting interests struggle for power. Occasionally a woman is depicted as a behind-the-scenes manipulator, almost always on behalf of a man or a child or some private goal irrelevant to the main issue as the movie conceives it. (Though she may contest one or another of the male myths, her challenge is rarely taken seriously except as an unholy temptation: "Women don't understand that men have to do certain things.") But mostly a woman's function in a "public" movie—when she is more than part of the scenery—is to provide "human," that is, sexual and emotional, interest to bring out the private man behind the public role.

This limitation does not simply reflect reality, for while men do dominate public life and set the terms of power struggles, women also participate in history. In fact it is precisely in times of social and political upheaval—the times that provide dramatic material for movies—that women have the most opportunity to break out of conventional patterns, challenge male prerogatives, move into power vacuums, exercise faculties that have been restricted. There is no reason (aside from the obvious one: that male moviemakers have not been interested) why we should not have developed a tradition of historical movies about women—movies that would explore the impact of public events on female fantasies and myths about revolt and submission, selfishness and altruism, sexuality and romantic love; that would transcend the artificial, male distinction between public and private; that in place of heroes insisting on their manhood would have heroines insisting on their personhood. As it is, *Gone With the Wind* is almost a one-movie genre, whose formula goes something like this: the destruction of the heroine's restrictive but secure world forces her to become her own woman; in the process she defies men's rules and finds out she can get away with it.

Morally and socially, Scarlett is a thorough pragmatist. Even before the war she has no use for Southern upper-class proprieties.

She plays the Southern-Belle game only to prove that she can manipulate men better than anyone else; when she wants a man she can't manipulate she is not afraid to approach him directly. (The ritual affectations required of Southern ladies are a perfect metaphor for female role-playing; long after they have become irrelevant to her life, Scarlett reverts to them whenever she is being dishonest with a man. Vivien Leigh exaggerates them with the comic relish of the Beatles doing Elvis. None of the men in the cast even have Southern accents.) She is no patriot; from beginning to end she sees the war as a useless, bloody mess brought on her head by men, their noble causes and their foolish "honor." She refuses to nurse the wounded and is barely dissuaded from leaving town and abandoning pregnant Melanie Wilkes during the siege of Atlanta. Later she unsentimentally lies, tries to sell herself to Rhett Butler, marries her sister's deluded fiancé for money, and becomes a hard, penny-pinching businesswoman in order to survive and prosper in the unsentimental postwar world. She is uninterested in motherhood and cynical about her three marriages. But what clinches her status as a superheroine is that she is all this and a *femme fatale* too. As befits a romantic movie, Vivien Leigh remains beautiful and fresh through every ordeal; but more importantly, Rhett falls in love with Scarlett not just because she is beautiful, but because she is selfish, aggressive and unladylike—in short, the personification of every adolescent girl's secret dream that she can be selfish, aggressive, unladylike *and* desirable, in spite of the either-or messages she keeps getting in her daily life.

Not that being a superheroine is simple. The complications are played out through Scarlett's relationships with her two men. Leslie Howard's Ashley Wilkes is blond and Hamletesque; Clark Gable is dark, has a mustache, and looks like the bad guy in a western. He is also a lousy actor—when I was a kid I pretended not to notice—but fortunately his role is the kind that almost plays itself. Like the hero torn between the dull but suitable blond woman and the fascinating dark woman who is the wrong religion, race or class and too sexy, Scarlett must choose between Ashley the high-minded gentleman and Rhett the passionate rascal. But here the symbolism reverses itself—the gentleman is the hopeless obsession, the rascal clearly the sensible choice. Furthermore we begin to suspect very

ELLEN WILLIS

early in the game that Ashley is a hypocritical bastard, while underneath Rhett's hard and violent exterior beats a heart of mush.

Ashley is Scarlett's temperamental opposite, the kind of tragic intellectual who not only can't split rails, but broods about it. Scarlett's original infatuation is understandable—Ashley is the only eligible man in her milieu who is "serious," who doesn't prattle on about how exciting the war is going to be or hover over her, craving silly compliments. But her stubborn pursuit is a flight into fantasy. Ashley becomes an abstraction, the unattainable ideal. He is also the object of Scarlett's one-sided rivalry with Melanie. Ah yes, Melanie. I can remember hours of childhood debate about whether Melanie was really as much of a simp as she seemed. As far as I was concerned, the main argument in her favor was that she treated Belle Watling, the prostitute, like a human being, while Scarlett looked down on her like everybody else. But then Scarlett had every reason to feel threatened by Belle—aside from their social class, they had a lot in common. The untainted, unworldly Melanie could afford to be generous. Melanie, the classic Good Woman: selfless, compassionate, loyal, gentle yet brave and resourceful when the survival of her loved ones is at stake; the faithful wife who takes care of Ashley but lets him think he is the strong one; the mother who ends up dying because she can't bear not to bring more life into the world—I say it's spinach! Scarlett thinks so too (though she wavers toward the end; who can hold out against such unremitting, imperialistic goodness?), and her passion for Ashley is bound up with her drive to prove that being the Good Woman doesn't pay. But this is a doomed enterprise; the unattainable man always wants the Good Woman. (The Good Woman, on the other hand, never actively aspires to the unattainable man—she is just *there*.) Finally Scarlett catches on that Ashley has been reserving his high-minded love for his wife, and his ambiguous sexual yearnings for her; that far from being too honorable to desert his family, he has merely been too egotistical to let her off the hook. These revelations occur, conveniently, at the moment Melanie dies and Ashley becomes attainable, which is embarrassing, because Scarlett certainly wouldn't know what to do with him if she had him. So she runs home, away from Death, through a corny symbolic fog, back to Rhett, ready to abandon childish fantasy in favor of mature etc. etc. . . . only to find that Rhett is through.

"Don't you men think about anything important?"   193

The romantic moral of the Rhett-Scarlett love story is that the woman who insists on her own way, and won't surrender to a good man when she finds one, loses in the end. The real, underground moral is that the historical woman must stand alone. To Rhett, Scarlett is a worthy antagonist, the almost-equal woman, the shrew only he can tame. Their romance begins when she almost clobbers him with a vase and peaks when, against her will, he scoops her into his arms and carries her upstairs—the definitive romantic image and the most famous scene in the movie. The taming-of-the-shrew fantasy is a weaselly way of resolving the cultural contradiction between strong woman and sexual woman, tapping our subversive ambition to be both while reassuring men that all women want to be raped. But in *Gone With the Wind* the resolution is only temporary. By encouraging Scarlett to be strong, Rhett starts something he can't finish. In the beginning he uses what he knows about Scarlett —he has overheard her unsuccessful proposal to Ashley and the resulting tantrum—to tease, tempt and bully her into defying the conventions she pretends to observe. Rhett, who makes a fortune from a war he despises, represents the rise of capitalist individualism, the negation of the claustrophobic plantation culture, and he is Scarlett's guide to the new era. By stripping away her Southern-belle hypocrisy and shoving her toward independence, Rhett abets Scarlett's liberation and at the same time controls it, a paradox that amuses him and infuriates her. A recurrent bit of interplay has Scarlett trying to flounce off in a rage and getting her hoop caught on something, whereupon Rhett gently detaches it, smiling his pseudo-inscrutable Clark Gable smile. He even joins the army after the war has been lost, just to get one-up on Scarlett, who expects him to deliver her safely to Tara; instead he gives her a gun (she ends up using it to kill a soldier) and leaves her to go it alone—on his terms. Later he traps her into propositioning him, knowing he is going to refuse.

But something goes wrong; Scarlett gets out of hand. She has learned Rhett's lessons too well. Her single-minded mania for getting what she wants even surpasses his. And she persists in wanting Ashley. Rhett becomes more and more demoralized; the inscrutable smile gives way to violent outbursts. The romantic heroine and the historical heroine are at odds: Scarlett is not about to be dominated, and Rhett is not about to live with her if he can't be number one. When she finally decides she wants him, he must regain the upper hand by rejecting her. He leaves this monster, the self-willed female he has helped to create, and goes in search of the old, genteel Southern values he once scorned. Again he forces Scarlett to make it on her own, really on her own this time. For now, anyway, being her own woman means doing without the man she wants. Still, as she puts it, "Tomorrow is another day!" Scarlett not only survives but walks off into the sunrise, smiling through her tears.

Gone With the Wind is the stuff of romantic myth even when it is saying, in effect, that romantic myths stand in the way of survival. It builds around a series of stock romantic images, affirmed on one level, denied on another. The myth of the Old South is destroyed, graphically by the war, rhetorically by the opportunist Rhett Butler; the portrait of Ashley as helpless throwback is pretty cutting. But at the same time there are all those loving shots of magnificent estates, elegant gowns, huge ballrooms, gracious ladies, and later tragic ruins, all the nostalgia for the golden days of a leisure class and its happy slaves. Scarlett sees Tara as her ultimate source of strength and even Rhett, in a triumph of class background over ideology, returns to the womb at the end. Good blacks are loyal servants who wouldn't dream of letting Lincoln free them; bad blacks insult white women or wear suits and ties and hang around with the Yankees. Scarlett's maid Prissy is played for laughs as a superstitious idiot. (In one scene, though, she flashes a wonderful fuck-you look behind Scarlett's back. I've always wondered if that look was in the script—I have a feeling it wasn't, or at least wasn't meant to come out quite that way, but I can't be sure.) Here the ambiguity turns sour, for some stock images are vicious. But at its best—in the portrayal of Scarlett—*Gone With the Wind* reflects the double vision of women, who are at once hooked on romantic fantasy and profoundly cynical about it. Scarlett is both; that's why I love her. Yesterday is another day too.

20. *Ask Me No Questions and I'll Tell You . . .*

JUDITH CRIST

WHEN FACED WITH the inevitable—I reach for that desert island. The inevitable, for movie critics, is the question of favorites, that eternal question, in private or in public, of "What's your all-time favorite? Which movie do you like best? What's the greatest movie ever made?" The search for an answer is in part for an open-sesame to the soul (let alone the standards, stupidity and small-mindedness) of the critic, and in part for confirmation of the questioner's secret selection. It is, I suppose, the cineaste's film-blot test, a quickie Rorschach to define terms for the ensuing dialogue. It's as scary as the "Who-do-you-love-best-in-the-whole-world?" inquisitions of childhood.

My immediate answer is that desert island and the pretty movie-problem posed thereon. You have been shipwrecked and cast away on the island with, of course, food and drink, a screen and a projector and (admittedly there's a Big Movie Mogul in the sky) one movie. And until rescue comes, you will have to watch this one movie over and over and, quite possibly, over. What would the movie be?

I have long opted for Orson Welles's *Citizen Kane,* a film I have seen about forty times and still watch with absorption, inevitably finding some nuance, some technical facet or creative insight that I had not quite been aware of before. Beyond its stature as a milestone movie, changing the face of so much of film to come, it stands for me as a probing American document in its specifics, its social and psychological penetration going beyond those specifics of a man within his time and place. And yet, that choice once made, I find myself wanting a double-feature for my isolated movie-worshipping, with Jean Renoir's *Rules of the Game* offering, in that far more sophisticated and subtle Continental manner, with a more complex wit, constant refreshment and an "expansion" of detail with each re-viewing. And then, of course, one would want a Chaplin and a Fellini and . . . no, not for me the limitations of that desert-island movie, when you get right down to the situation.

Kane and *Rules of the Game* were on the Top Ten list I contributed last year to *Sight and Sound's* ten-year poll of international film critics. There, much as I am forced to do in the annual ten-best journalistic film-critic ritual, I settled for genre, for the film that seemed to me the quintessence of its type and its author's body of work. In no particular order, I included Chaplin's *City Lights* (the embodiment of every aspect of that great man's art); Renoir's *Grand Illusion* (not double-*hommage* to Renoir but my appraisal of it as the ultimate—and root—war film); Fellini's *8½* (the essence of Fellini as well as the milestone portrait of the creative psyche); Resnais's *La Guerre est Finie* (the filmmaker's triumphant technique in blending past, present and future joins with his brilliant consideration of the revolutionary surviving beyond his passion); Kurosawa's *Ikiru* (a social commentary, a deeply moving human drama and an existential affirmation of a man's life made meaningful); Bergman's *Winter Light* (the most chilling of his philosophic considerations of a heart devoid of love for God or man); Bondarchuk's *War and Peace* (in either its separate foreign-language segments or the cut two-part English-voices-over versions, the finest cinematic spectacular and a great and noble translation of a literary masterpiece); and Huston's *The Maltese Falcon* (the root of the twentieth reincarnation of Sydney Carton via the tough-'tec).

And my eleventh film would have been *Children of Paradise*, my twelfth *All About Eve*.

This was in 1972. And within a year I had discovered two replacements: for *Winter Light* I would now substitute Bergman's most recent work, *Cries and Whispers*, for its expanded technical art and broader, deeper probe of the delusions of human relationships; and for the Kurosawa I would substitute my belatedly encountered *Tokyo Story*, Yasujiro Ozu's 1953 masterpiece of the generational continuum and of the minutiae of human relationships. And what will next year bring? And what of all the "masterpieces" (after all, some critics manage to discover one a week, so let's think sparingly of the term) that one has not encountered even in several decades of ardent moviegoing?

The *Sight and Sound* selections, admittedly, were made on an "international" scale, with an emphasis on the classic, on films viewed and re-viewed and given the perspective of time. There would be quite another list were the "favorite film" question popped, champagne-cork fashion, on December 31 and refer to the year past. Over the past ten years, my favorites, per year, were *Tom Jones* (and that was the year of *8½* as well); *Dr. Strangelove, or: How I Learned to Stop Worrying and Love the Bomb; Darling; A Man for All Seasons*; *Bonnie and Clyde* (the year too of *La Guerre est Finie*); *The Lion in Winter* (the very least of its many virtues, trivially enough, was that it was the first of the hundreds and hundreds of "castle" movies of my lifetime that didn't make me suspect that there was a tidy lavatory, a proper heating system and a Disneyland tour guide just around the next archway); *Oh! What a Lovely War; Five Easy Pieces; A Clockwork Orange*; and beyond *Cries and Whispers* that year, *The Sorrow and the Pity*, the finest documentary film in my experience. And at this writing, in mid-1973, Lindsay Anderson's *O Lucky Man!*—his remarkable collaboration with Malcolm McDowell as star and David Sherwin as scenarist to create the *Candide-cum-Tom-Jones-cum-Pilgrim's Progress* of our time in his own terms and brilliantly high style—may well stand as my choice for this year.

And still I can't leave the past decade at ten or twelve listings. What of Olmi's *The Sound of Trumpets*; Anderson's *This Sporting Life*; Monicelli's *The Organizer*; Losey's *The Servant*; Bryan

198   JUDITH CRIST

Forbes's *Seance on a Wet Afternoon*; *To Die in Madrid*; *Juliet of the Spirits*; *Cat Ballou*; *The Shop on Main Street*; *Loves of a Blonde*; *The Battle of Algiers*; Welles's *Falstaff* (or *Chimes at Midnight* as it was also titled*)*; *Yellow Submarine* and *The Two of Us*; the Perry's *Last Summer* and *Trilogy*; Visconti's *The Damned*; Tony Richardson's *Hamlet*; Chabrol's *La Femme Infidèle* and Robert Downey's *Putney Swope*; *Investigation of a Citizen Above Suspicion*; Donald Shebib's *Goin' Down the Road*; *Women in Love*; Fellini's *Satyricon* and Bergman's *The Passion of Anna*; *McCabe and Mrs. Miller*; *The French Connection*; *The Hospital and Sunday Bloody Sunday*; *The Discreet Charm of the Bourgeoisie*; *Slaughterhouse Five*; *Cabaret* and *Sounder*?

And then there are, so dear to a critic's heart, the "neglected" favorites—a neglected film being, of course, one the critic admired and few others (at least at the time) appreciated. The film I "tout" most often (when invited to one of those show-and-tell sessions beloved on campuses or in church basements) is Arthur Penn's *Mickey One*, made in 1965 but more pertinent by the year in its consideration of our paranoia, our guilt for not being innocent, our flight from the unknown in hopes of getting a word from the Lord, an answer to problems we lack the courage to confront. One wit expanded for me the theater shibboleth ("Satire is what closes on Saturday night") to note that in film "allegory is what never gets to play the nabes." Today, I choose to think, the nabes would be jammed with those who, in this double-level, brilliantly cinematic film, would toss the allegory aside to revel in Warren Beatty's portrayal of a nightclub entertainer, "a Polish Noel Coward," on the lam from the syndicate.

So too, I choose to believe, would audiences today appreciate Joseph Strick's *Ulysses*, with Milo O'Shea as Bloom in an adaptation that makes one realize, in the rereading, that Joyce wrote a scenario in the form of a stream-of-consciousness work. After all, that year produced the then-neglected and politically avant-garde *The President's Analyst*, a satire right on target in its total commentary that had the gall to kid the FBI and the gun-totin' Amurrican family and to cast the phone company as supervillain—and it has been served up to delight television audiences a mere five years later. Audiences will, I am convinced, grow up to Robert Altman's

Brewster McCloud, a remarkably disciplined and original surface-mad core-sane fairy tale of a boy building wings in the labyrinth of the Astrodome, a comedy-fantasy of man's dream of flight and freedom. Altman's later *Images* will also come into its own, not only because it is an exquisitely visualized work (the Czech cinematographer Vilmos Szigmond was responsible too for Altman's *McCabe and Mrs. Miller* and *The Long Goodbye*, as well as for *Deliverance* and *Scarecrow*), but also because it succeeds completely on each of its various levels as a psychological thriller, a portrait of a marriage, a probe of a woman's psyche and a study of schizophrenia—its success in large part due to a magnificent performance by Susannah York. The touter takes comfort, ultimately, in knowing that a film exists, whether or not its audience has found it. And Joseph Anthony's *Tomorrow*, the first film to capture the very heart of William Faulkner's place and people, with Robert Duvall eloquent as one of his inarticulate creatures, is there to be found.

And still I have not scratched the surface of my favorite films. I was brought up on the Hollywood factory product of the thirties and forties, child of Loew's Paradise indeed, lover of tag lines and schmaltz. To this day I will sit dotingly through *The Roaring Twenties* just to see Gladys George clutching the fallen James Cagney to her bosom on the church steps (of course it's snowing) to sum it all up with "He used to be a big shot"; or watch *White Heat* to see Cagney shriek out, "Top of the world, Ma!" as he and those gas tanks go up in flames and Edmund O'Brien, down below, declaring, "He finally got to the top of the world—and it blew up in his face." And Lew Ayres's reach for the butterfly in *All Quiet on the Western Front*, Margaret Sullavan's fatal walk across her sanatorium room in *Three Comrades*, Bette Davis's final nap in *Dark Victory*—the very retrospect chokes me up, even as Karloff's clutch at the little girl's flowers breaks my heart. I still don't see those all-too-apparent wires manipulating the bat in *Dracula*; I still cherish the illusion, not only that Ruby Keeler could dance, but also she was even prettier than Dick Powell in all those Busby Berkeley extravaganzas, and I laugh myself silly over *Horsefeathers* (or any other Marx Brothers madness), *A Slight Case of Murder* and *The Thin Man*, *The Lady Killers*, *Big Deal on Madonna Street* and *Only Two Can Play*. Who can play favorites? I'm past my thirtieth viewing of *All About Eve* and I'm nearing the twentieth-time mark with *The Quiet Man* and *High Noon* and *The Wizard of Oz*; I've lost count on *Witness for the Prosecution, Holiday, The African Queen* and *Marty* and *Bad Day at Black Rock* and *Nightmare Alley* and all the great-movie-star vehicles. And how can one fail to have favorites among the perfectly awfuls, the movies made admirable by the absolute perfection of their awfulness—whether it's all the Old-Southness of *Kentucky*, or Joan Crawford's eternal welling of tears in *Autumn Leaves*, or Peter Finch's bravura hammery in *The Legend of Lylah Clare*?

A favorite movie? In Chipsian fashion—I've had hundreds of them. How indeed can a nice nonsectarian movie critic have so catholic a taste?

You ponder it. I've got that desert island in mind and am slowly but surely collecting my repertoire. So far I've got *The Bank Dick, Casablanca, The Maltese Falcon, Mickey One, All About Eve, I'm No Angel*, selected short subjects—and with the acquisitions I have in mind, I'm planning to charter the *Queen Elizabeth 2* to bring the movies ashore once I get myself cast away on the properly equipped desert island. That way I'll even have room for some coming attractions.

21. Tokyo Story: The Virtues of Mannered Simplicity

FRANCIS X. J. COLEMAN

MOVIES TEND TO BE like most of our acquaintances: we don't like them very much, but we always end up talking about them. But upon occasion an acquaintance works his way into our friendship, subtly, without our knowing or willing it, and we are suddenly startled to discover the reality and genuineness of it. Something like this happy surprise occurs when a film lays a claim to our attention not because it is entertaining, erotic, sensational or cinematically clever, but because it has the substance of genuine art. It is both generous and universal. Such a film is *Tokyo Story*, directed by Yasujiro Ozu, who with Kogo Noda wrote the story and the screenplay. The photography is by Yashun Atsuta.

Few films ever succeed in making their way into the circle of our close friends: they have a way of growing and redeveloping in our memories, returning suddenly into our consciousness with a strange familiarity. Such films make us perceive the world in a new way, and our perception is importantly altered. For my own part, *Rules of the Game, The Red Shoes, Sunrise* and *The Diary of a Village Priest* fall into that company.

202

It is the common lot of great things and of great art to be more readily describable in terms that are negative rather than positive. It is easy to say what *Tokyo Story* is not. Though it is impossible for a film to be apolitical, *Tokyo Story* is only minimally political; it reflects the social values of bourgeois industrialism in Japan during the 1950s. It is not a religious or historical or biographical film. It is not psychological in that sense of reeking in Freudianisms that we are forced to accustom ourselves to in the West. And, happily, it is decidedly not an art film.

The plot is of the simplest. It contains neither suspense, nor reversal of fortune, nor a crime to be discovered, nor a wrong to be righted, nor anything that, if recounted to someone else, would be of interest. In short, the plot is drawn from most persons' lives. An old couple living in the southern Japanese port town of Ornomichi decide to journey by train to Tokyo, where they have never been, to see their children and their widowed daughter-in-law. The old father, played by Chishu Ryu, and the old mother, played by Chiyeko Higashi-yama, are of modest means and origin. They suppose that their children, whom they have not seen for some time, are more success-ful than they actually are. The parents arrive in Tokyo and take a cab to the house of their son who is a doctor; this part is played by So Yamamura. The house is more humble than they had anticipated, and their son's practice is limited to a nondescript suburb. The son and his wife are too caught up in their own affairs to be more than formally hospitable. The daughter, played by Haruko Sugimura, is also married and runs a beauty shop; her time is even scarcer, and her patience with the old parents even more limited.

Only their widowed daughter-in-law, played by Setsuko Hara, shows the couple any kindness. She takes a day off from work to show them around Tokyo. But because neither the son nor the daughter wants to put them up any longer, it is decided to send the old couple to a spa. After a few days there, they decide to leave because of homesickness and the vulgarity of the other persons at the spa, which appears to be a hotel for newlyweds of the lower orders. The old couple return to Tokyo, to their daughter's rooms behind the beauty parlor. She explains that they cannot stay because it is her night to entertain the other beauticians. The old mother goes back to the little flat of her widowed daughter-in-law, where she sleeps on the mat that had once been her son's. The old man sees a few former acquaintances, gets drunk, and because none of them will take him in, stumbles back to his daughter's flat. The old couple leave shortly thereafter by train for Ornomichi. On the way back the old mother falls ill; they are forced to stop a few days at Osaka. The children are notified of her condition. It worsens. The children and the daughter-in-law come to Ornomichi, as does another son who writes for a newspaper. The doctor and the beautician must leave the next day, as must the journalist son. The old man is left with his youngest child, a girl who teaches school, and his widowed daughter-in-law, who must also return to Tokyo. The schoolmistress listens in her schoolroom for the Tokyo-bound train. It is evident that she too will shortly leave the old man. It is important to notice that we learn the names of almost none of the characters, and that these events can hold our attention for one hundred and thirty-nine minutes.

What is first of all remarkable about *Tokyo Story* is that, despite the commonplaceness of pitting one generation against another, no generation is put beyond reproach or mythologized. No earlier time, the perennial refuge of those who would be miserable in any time, is idealized at the expense of another. All generations are equally selfish, opportunistic, self-pitying, self-satisfied and self-righteous. Only the decor changes, and the wardrobes. Although there are several industrial images that recur throughout the film—the smokestacks silhouetted against the drab sky, the endless tenement houses, the freighters in the harbor—still the film does not bear the hackneyed theme that the cause of mankind's woes is industrialization. Even though there is always a box of Rinso soapsuds in the apartment of the widowed daughter-in-law, the film eschews the equally tired theme that the recent cause of the world's woes is the "Americanization" of the world. Countless films have antiposed industrial images against the serenity of nature. But *Tokyo Story,* as a supreme mark of both its artistry and its honesty, simply subsumes the products of a technological era into the ceaseless comings and goings of people and other forms of vegetative life. In the scene following his wife's sudden death, the old father is observed standing in a black kimono on the terrace. He comments that it was a

FRANCIS X. J. COLEMAN

beautiful sunrise, but that he fears that they are in for another hot day.

Tokyo Story is far from being self-indulgent. Images play over the surface of the screen but are not allowed to grow soggy and redolent with sentimental associations. The music, written by Takamori Saito, is Pucciniesque, faintly verging on the saccharine. But the long and impressive view of the steles crowding over the hillside in the cemetery, which occurs close to the end of the film, is not nostalgic, only faintly wistful. It is saved from bathos because the hillside of steles is treated cubistically. The only character who is allowed nostalgia is also the most complicated character in the film, the widowed daughter-in-law. She mentions that her husband used to drink too much and bring his friends home after midnight. He was killed in the war. Now she has nothing but her job. Her nostalgia and her feeling of loss for her dead husband are jaundiced by guilt: she did not love him, or more accurately, she was disappointed in the emotion or behavioral symptoms of love. Or perhaps even more accurately—since the widowed daughter-in-law is hardly a disappointed romantic—she did not even discover with him the formal happiness and pleasures that accrue from love. She weeps, of course, and keeps his picture in her little flat, though he died eight years before. But she weeps not because she believes herself to have lost something of great value, but because she fears that another marriage would give her the same dissatisfactions, and at the cost of her privacy. She feels guilty because she has doubts about the ideal of marriage that she believes she ought to have. She asserts, after her mother-in-law's death, that she is as selfish and as self-seeking as everyone else. Because she has no life of her own, other than her arid job, she has more time for her dead husband's parents when they come to Tokyo. She has little to cling to, and in part out of guilt and in part out of fear, she clings to traditional values such as deference to the old. But a genuine trace of love, perhaps not for her dead husband, but for anyone who would adequately fulfill the role he had played—"Sometimes at night I wake up and know that there must be somebody elsewhere, somebody"—but this realization makes her feel more guilty, for she has touched upon a sentiment which is also the burden of the film: the dreadful replaceability of mankind. It is not so much for her late husband that she yearns, but for anyone of his type or general kind. The notion of the particularity of love seems to be violated.

The widowed daughter-in-law is the major character, not because she is any more moral, any more beautiful, or any more endowed than the others, but simply because she is more self-aware. She becomes the apologist for the others. The youngest daughter says, "Isn't life disappointing, though?" "Yes," replies her widowed sister-in-law, "but that's what it is." She proceeds to make excuses for her brother and sister-in-law.

This is a film without villains, and therefore without heroes. Ozu's view of things implies that in reality there are no heroes or villains. While sightseeing, the old parents look with vague interest at the Imperial Palace. The guide announces that it was built five hundred years before. It was one sight among others. There is not the usual and noisy juxtaposition of sedate temples against buses, throngs, and airplanes. All these are all only appearances, or only realities; for even the Indian notion of Maia is inapplicable, because there is nothing behind the veil.

In *Tokyo Story* what seems to give form to the ceaseless shufflings of generations is art. Not to sound too ponderous: it is always a question of a pagoda or landscape or decorum. But immediately Ozu—and this must be attributed to his genius as a filmmaker—deftly moves on to an image of train tracks or telegraph wires—sometimes even superimposing the two. So it is not a question of "art" or of the past, but simply of aesthetic form. Only form has the grandeur of momentary immobility—like the old man's sunrise after his wife's death. Form provides no salvation, for there is nothing "beyond" in this film. There is no solace, for each generation is as viperous and decorous as the one preceding. Happiness is fragile and fleeting. But form gives a kind of stillness and perfection that is both part of this world and apart from it. In the world of Ozu and Noda, only self-awareness, as expressed in art or in someone's life, has intrinsic value. It is as though the formal perfection of the film, with its cinematic, measured *largo* pace, attempts to show what is of intrinsic value.

There is humor in the film, but of a gently cruel sort. Irony—the self-defense of the weak—is absent. *Tokyo Story* might be viewed as an exercise in self-control, an attempt to keep up appearances.

FRANCIS X. J. COLEMAN

For the old couple the exercise becomes a vaguely mystical, stoic resignation. Humor arises whenever the mask is suddenly ripped away or whenever a clash occurs between two different roles of conventions. The beautician daughter cannot wait to ask for her mother's linen summer kimono and shawl at the funeral dinner. When her parents first arrive in Tokyo she says to one of her clientele, once they are out of earshot: "Oh, they are friends from the country." The most amusing scene is one of the most painful: the neighbor who comes by after the old woman's death to console the old man succeeds only in insisting how lonely he will be.

Although the widowed daughter-in-law's guilt is the most deftly portrayed, all of the characters reveal shades of the same feeling. The doctor, the most intellectual in the film, feels the most metaphysical guilt: he feels guilty for not feeling guilty. A moment after the word comes that his mother is critically ill, he is overheard calling to a pet of some sort or another in the little garden. He strictly carries out his filial obligation, feeling nothing but annoyance. The old father is a dull, kindly, ordinary man with an easy conscience. He is tenuously defined even by his roles of husband, parent and old man in retirement. He is self-centered in the sense that his imagination is too weak to give him more than a hint of other persons' existence. A momentary blur of guilt passes over his face after his wife's death. "I wish I had been kinder to her now," he mumbles. Though a handsome old man, his autism and shuffling manner make him unhandsome and mildly pathetic as a person. The cyclic rhythm of the entire film is reflected in the microcosm of the old man, for his drinking recurs again at the end of his life. He has no hangover after his debauch with his half-remembered acquaintances. His remembrance of his wife will be equally short-lived, and his loneliness will be like wondering where the mislaid umbrella might be.

The beautician's guilt is shown by her chiding the old man for drinking a little cup of saki at the funeral dinner. She tries to palliate her guilt by believing that no one could accuse her of being ungrateful to an old father who is only a drunkard.

Even the old mother, who is spiritually the only beautiful character in this film, feels a kind of guilt in imposing upon her children. She feels another kind of guilt because her thoughts, on the night she sleeps on her dead son's mat at her daughter-in-law's are more with him than with her. She weeps. After her death, the old father tells the widowed daughter-in-law that his wife had said it was the happiest night she spent in Tokyo. He counsels her to remarry, which might placate part of her guilt. She adheres compulsively to the old Japanese custom of faithful widowhood.

The younger son feels guilty about not arriving before his mother's death. "No child can serve his parents beyond the grave," it is remarked. The funeral drum drives him away from the rite. He feels his mother's shade growing dimmer and dimmer.

The young schoolmistress anticipates her guilt. Her widowed sister-in-law explains that becoming independent of one's parents is an inevitable part of life; the young woman will inevitably feel guilty when she takes the train to Tokyo.

The aesthetic inevitability of the film is aided by Ozu's frequent use of symmetrical images and antiphonies. The same woman who bids the old couple bon voyage at the beginning of the film comes by to console the lonely old man at the end. A baseball suit is seen fluttering on a clothesline at the beginning; later, schoolchildren are heard singing "My Old Kentucky Home" in Japanese. The old lady forgets her umbrella in the park: her husband reminds her of it. She forgets it later at the flat of her daughter-in-law, who hands it to her, smiling. The old couple's sandals are observed sitting in front of their screen door at the spa. The widow gives a bank note to her mother-in-law; the old man gives her his dead wife's watch. The cemetery is seen at the beginning and at the end. The film then opens out like a series of balancing panels in a great screen, until the viewer realizes that the structure of the entire screen is itself symmetrical. For in the first half of the film the parents are on their way to see their children; in the last half the children are on their way to see their parents. In a list of imagistic antiphonies such as this, the film might seem forced, artificial, or even precious. On occasion, it is. For example, the schoolmistress looking at her watch only a moment before the widow, returning in the train, looks again at her dead mother-in-law's watch. But usually, because of wide spacing, and above all, the subtleness and casualness of the symmetries—like leaves falling from a tree—they appear natural and provide aesthetic coherence.

208   FRANCIS X. J. COLEMAN

The surface qualities of the film are also textured with elaborate variations on ordinary elements of experience: smokestacks, train-tracks, clotheslines, tenement houses, cemeteries. The visual texture is unobtrusive, matlike in quality. Viewers used to confusions and vagaries of color can only be surprised to see how much visual depth and nuance can only be obtained in black and white. The textures of things seem even more eloquent because of the restrictions imposed by the medium. The viewer, moreover, is left less passive—and surely passivity is one of the dangers of film as a form of art—because we are forced to recall, however involuntarily and subliminally, the textures of things like rice, silk, linen, stone work, human skin, and the water of rivers and of the sea. We are presented with only muted greyish reminders of such sensations, so muted and distilled that they become themselves almost symbolic. It is Ozu's muted touch that renders the most common things universal, though never with the heaviness of touch of a filmmaker like Antonioni, with whom Ozu has sometimes been compared.

What also gives the film its peculiar Japanese texture is the angle from which scenes are shot. The viewer is placed a little below eye-level, as though sitting on a "tatami," or grass mat. The camera is immobile and uncompromising in its reportage of both human beings and things. There are no cinematic sleights of hand, or fade-outs, or dissolves, or that most awkward technique known to the film—the flashback. Only the few panoramas of nature—mountains with rivers, the sea with a few distant islands—widen the viewer's picture and give him a sense of openness. All action takes place within interiors—the beauty shop, the tavern, and the train station, where the action is treated as if on stage. One of the most brilliant sections in the film is a hybrid between interiority and panorama. From a viewing station the old couple, with their widowed daughter-in-law, are viewing Tokyo, laid out before them. To emphasize the interiority, Ozu interrupts the image with a figure descending the stairs, thereby momentarily leaving the old couple—giving once again that dreadful sense of inexplicable loss—only to refind them a moment later a few steps higher, vaguely viewing Tokyo veiled in industrial smog.

It is difficult to fault Ozu's aesthetic eye; it is of wonderful purity and coherence. He refuses to loiter histrionically over details or to sentimentalize. But there is a concession made to popular taste in one scene in particular that has a disruptive, kitschlike quality to it. The old mother is observed walking with her little grandson in a field of weeds and common flowers. He is making a bouquet while the grandmother is asking him what he wants to be when he grows up. Like his older brother, the little boy is ill-bred and selfish; he does not even reply to the old woman. Although the episode is important to anticipate her later death and her fear of not knowing where she will soon be, the scene is too easy and too easily touching. It is one of the rare slips in the purity and innocence of the film, for we become conscious of Ozu's art, which is always death to art. The scene is too well-arranged, self-conscious and obvious in the sharp juxtaposing of the old woman with her grandson. In a few other scenes Ozu and Noda slip into this easy and slightly sentimental filming whenever they omit the third element in the play of generation against generation, or some physical object like an urn or a tree. But the steady, simple grandeur of the film, together with its all-pervasive humanity, almost makes one forget such rare concessions made to commercial art.

The humanity of the film is revealed in the careful sorrows of small lives. After returning from the noisy spa, the old couple begin to unpack a small parcel of painfully tied packages of various sizes, containing gifts for their children and doubtless their grandchildren. This time the old woman forgets where she puts the hot-water bottle. The doctor whispers to his wife that they need not include fish in the *sukiyaki*. The most harrowing image of all is an infant seen only momentarily under heavy gauze in its bassinet, a mere object in a corner of the scene, but a human object. It is the youngest entity in the film—it is difficult to tell what to call it—that will continue the endless cycle of generations. Life is continuously undoing and doing so many that the idea of one more human entity lying under heavy gauze sleeping or dreaming (or whatever its state was) leaves one numb. And the incense coils keep smoking on the floor. And the electric fans keep whirring in scene after scene, half-observed.

It is the incessantness of life, neither banal nor interesting except for its aesthetic form, and its influence upon the penumbra of consciousness, that ultimately sustains the entire film. Activity is con-

FRANCIS X. J. COLEMAN

stant—people carrying pails to mop up, people setting out their garbage, people riveting and typing and telephoning—and we must hear every digit composed on the telephone. Trains moving and boats moving and the smoke coming out of chimneys, and therefore the continuous and stultifying activity of keeping things clean. Frenzied dusters are working hectically in the little beauty shop, pole after pole of clothes are seen flapping in the sunlight. Hair must be coiffed, patients demand attention—there is something about the film that can only be expressed by enumerations, in a curious way like the rational review of essential ideas that Descartes recommends in his *Discourse*. For the day-to-day performance of these activities, pointless individually, give a point to the entire activity of life, or make it tolerable.

Like much greater art, *Tokyo Story* is a moral tale. But "moral" and "morality" must be construed in a sense broader than what is meant by words like "ethics," or "right" and "wrong," or "good" and "bad." Morality connotes "mores," social conduct, nuances of behavior, together with all the bonds and strands that hold human beings together—in couples, families and societies. The most important bond is finally the one that holds each person to himself, even though we can define ourselves and be happy only in the company of others. Self-preservation, therefore, is not to be opposed to altruism, since our own happiness is so intimately related to that of other persons. And consequently selfishness—for *Tokyo Story* is also a study of selfishness and the varieties of guilt that it engenders—is, to a measure, self-preservation. But self-preservation inevitably entails the preserving of those we love, or those to whom we have a filial obligation. Morality has its own symbiosis. Violence is done to each when any particular one tries to live by himself, and especial violence is done to the one who is concerned only with his own self-preservation. Such a state is surpassed only by the child who tries to serve his parents beyond the grave. All the characters in the film are haunted by their moral obligations to their parents and to their offspring, for they all realize that their self-preservation—or the positive values of their own selfishness— are intimately linked with their duties to others.

Only the widowed daughter-in-law is suicidal; she puts too great a stress and importance on her obligations to her parents-in-law. She is too self-sacrificing because she is afraid to be selfish and to preserve herself or to have genuine womanly desires. Her morality is a form of self-abnegation and suicide. The great paradox of her character, the most significant paradox in the film, is that conventional morality, or the ethics of formal obligation and self-sacrifice (she cancels her work more than once), is no more than a form of self-death and morbidity. The widowed daughter-in-law smiles most, suffers most, does most for others, and is conventionally and formally the most ethical and righteous. Yet she is the most morbid character in the film. Not that her goodness is a mask; rather, it is a gauze that covers her fear to love another man. She feels guilty about feeling that her husband was so ordinary. Even her parents-in-law admit that he had not come up to snuff. But, as they convince themselves in regard to all their children, he was better than most. They count themselves among the fortunate. It appears that self-deception is essential for self-preservation.

To conclude this review, and to give what I find is the ultimate impression left by Ozu's *Tokyo Story*, let us return to the most haunting words uttered in the film. The young schoolmistress asserts, "Isn't life disappointing, though?" The widow agrees. But given Ozu's mannered realism, it is certain that he must disagree. Although there are disappointments enough in life, such as parents' disappointments in their children, yet to say that life itself is a disappointment is only a posturing of adolescence. For of that which is other than life we can say nothing. It is only unfulfilled longing in this life that leads us to be so sweeping in our disappointments. For here we are, and there is the temple of Osaka.

22. Psycho Therapy

RICHARD CORLISS

For far too long, respectable film critics approached the challenge of compiling a "ten-best" list with Kierke-gaardian fear and Caligariesque trembling. The interior monologue usually went like this: "What will my colleagues think? What will my intellectual readers think? How can I defend film as an art if I include any Hollywood product among the received masterpieces? After all, *Potemkin* (which I admire but don't really like) is the very stuff of cinema—but *Now, Voyager* (which I love but am afraid to admire) is only a movie!" As a result, the typical "ten-best" list wound up looking like screening selections for an undergraduate course in Seminal Cinema 101. And the *Now, Voyager*s of the film world were relegated to a mind-closet containing all of the critic's secret sins.

With the advent and gradual supremacy of the *auteur* theory—which among other things posited that it was intellectually OK to respond emotionally to Hollywood movies, things loosened up a bit. *Sight and Sound*'s all-time "Top 10" of 1972, a collation of eighty-nine critics' subjective, idiosyncratic, personal choices, ac-

213

tually boasts a comedy (*The General*) and, as runners-up, a mystery (*Vertigo*) and a western (*The Searchers*). But *Psycho*—if nothing else, certainly the most popular and frightening horror film ever made—is hardly to be found. It appears on only four lists. *Potemkin* received four times as many votes, *Citizen Kane* eight times as many.

I was one of the four lonely souls who favored *Psycho*. (For the record, the other Hollywood talkies on my list were, in order of release date, *His Girl Friday, The Lady Eve, Citizen Kane, Casablanca, Letter from an Unknown Woman,* and *The Searchers*— all of which I've written about in a book on American screenwriters called *Talking Pictures.*) From the first time I saw *Psycho,* at age sixteen in the Avalon Theatre on the South Jersey coast, the film admirably fulfilled its Saturday-matinee horror-movie function: it scared the shit out of me. And it still does. Whatever academic pleasure I might have derived from analyzing *Psycho*'s shower sequence on a movieola for this essay was overwhelmed by a purely physical discomfort at reliving an experience that still sets my stomach seismograph aquiver every time I step into a strange shower stall.

If the effect of *Psycho* was merely to upset the viewer's stomach, and not his mind, it might qualify as a "favorite movie"—the kind described, by those who know little and care less about films as art, as a "hot fudge sundae," with a few sprinkles of ground glass to aid indigestion—but it would not be a masterpiece. My hope here is to persuade the reader on both points. And if the tone of this piece seems unnecessarily dispassionate, please chalk it up to my need to retain the proper critical distance from a most unsettling movie.

There are, to be sure, reasons for the film's exclusion from most of the *Sight and Sound* lists. *Psycho* is not what humanists would call an exalting film, a hymn to the indomitability of the human spirit. Dwight Macdonald thought it "a reflection of a most unpleasant mind, a mean, sly, sadistic little mind"—presumably that of the director, Alfred Hitchcock. John Howard Lawson called *Psycho* "a cold and brutal film, almost devoid of human feeling." Charles Thomas Samuels, a semidetached admirer of Hitchcock, wrote that "The key to *Psycho* is less Sigmund Freud than Richard Strauss," and found the director's best films (presumably including

RICHARD CORLISS

Psycho) "devoid of meaning" and "peopled by mere containers of stress." Some critics were prepared to accept *Psycho* as a well-told sick joke (Leslie Halliwell: "psychological horror comics") or a sadomasterful exercise in technique (Penelope Houston: "for Hitchcock, part of the fascination lies in seeing what he can get away with")—but little more. Certainly not a great film.

Nor is *Psycho* an unimpeachably "personal" Hitchcock film. "I don't care about the subject matter; I don't care about the acting," Hitchcock says, summarizing critics' objections to the picture. "The subject was horrible, the people were small, there were no characters in it. . . . My main satisfaction is that the film had an effect on the audiences, and I consider that very important." For Hitchcock, the challenge of filmmaking seems to be that "the Japanese audience should scream at the same time as the Italian audience"—hardly the most exalted of cinematic ambitions. Indeed, when viewing *Psycho,* one can sense a communion of forces not completely under the director's control, or even within his sphere of interest: the superb ensemble acting, the power of metaphysical suggestion in the old-dark-house genre, the complex weave of character and dialogue, of Grand Guignol and Grand Motel, of horror and compassion. As Robin Wood, in his definitive essay on *Psycho,* says of Hitchcock, "he himself—if his interviews are to be trusted—has not really faced up to what he was doing when he made the film."

The influence of the Hitchcock persona on his films is so inclusive, and so intrusive, that critics have a tendency either to accept or reject it wholeheartedly. But it may be closer to the truth to take the famous TV-personality Hitchcock, with the arch, ghoulish diction, the Buddha silhouette, and the whimsical signature tune ("Funeral March of the Marionettes"—not a bad title for some future Ph.D. thesis on Hitchcock's masterful manipulation of characters, actors and audiences), as the director's own defense mechanism against earnest exegetes who would ascribe more moral weight to his films than he himself would care to allow.

Like so many other American directors—truculent John Ford, languid Howard Hawks, generous George Cukor—Hitchcock feels palpably uneasy when confronted with any grand critical statement of his themes. And we may say that again like Ford, Hawks and Cukor, Hitchcock is a conscious craftsman but an unconscious artist. The craftsmanship of *Psycho*—its classical yet often audacious mise-en-scene—is certainly Hitchcock's triumph; the artistry, however, is just as surely the result of that communion of forces I spoke of earlier, and Hitchcock must share the credit for *Psycho's* surpassing brilliance with novelist Robert Bloch, screenwriter Joseph Stefano, cinematographer Robert Burks, composer Bernard Herrmann, and Hitchcock's unsung cattle company of actors: Anthony Perkins, Janet Leigh, Vera Miles, John Gavin and Martin Balsam.

In this Age of the Omniscient Director it's unfashionable to say it but, especially for Hollywood movies with a beginning, a middle and an end (in that order), the Beginning is the Word; the direction of camera and actors is the middle; and the film is the end result. Since Hitchcock is known to work meticulously on both his stories and his story-boards, and since the "Hitchcock film" is a known and respected quantity unlike, say, the "Bloch novel" or the "Stefano screenplay," critics generally assume that the Master creates his films out of whole shroud. Bernard Herrman, who composed the music for every Hitchcock film from *The Trouble with Harry* to *Marnie,* disputes this. Although "it's always written that Hitchcock created *Psycho*," the film was actually "written from Robert Bloch by Joseph Stefano." This fact doesn't make Hitchcock any less accomplished a *director;* it merely disqualifies him from being an *author* in the sense that Chaplin or Bergman or Godard or Bruce Conner is.

More important, it doesn't make *Psycho* any less spectacular a film achievement. Our purpose here, after all, is to celebrate, not to arbitrate in the great Writers Guild tradition. We shall leave to some twenty-first-century Pauline Kael the task of establishing Joseph Stefano as Hitchcock's Herman J. Mankiewicz. Whatever creative combustion produced *Psycho* (and I'd identify the crucial elements as Stefano's screenplay, Hitchcock's direction, and Perkins's performance, in roughly equal proportions), we are more interested in savoring the effect of that sublime chef d'oeuvre rather than determining who's the chef.

Critics who couldn't see anything "exalting" in *Psycho* were, in a way, right, for the film's movement is one of descent—a forward-tracking shot into the dark, the decaying, the forgotten fruit cellars of the mind. And it is perhaps *Psycho's* most secure claim to great-

RICHARD CORLISS

ness that it makes us suspect the normal mind as well as sympathize with the psychotic one. In this light, the film's title, which suggests an abnormal state of mind, looks deceptive: it should more appropriately be *Schizo*. If the film has any "message" to impart, it is that we are all composed, actually or potentially, of two, three, many personalities, generally in friction and occasionally in harmony. Norman Bates/Mother Bates is the central schizophrenic character, but not the only one. *Psycho* is loaded with doppelgangers.

Some viewers have noticed how the close facial resemblance between Janet Leigh (who plays Marion Crane) and Vera Miles (who plays Marion's sister Lila) helps underline their similarities of character. Both are strong-willed, adventurous and tenacious. Both are exasperated by the complacency of the hero (Marion's lover Sam, played by John Gavin). Both seem sensible. But Marion's adventurousness draws her into a reckless forty-thousand dollar theft; her tenacity takes her through the Arizona desert toward Sam in Fairvale, California; her preoccupation with the circumstances of her theft leads her off the main highway, onto a back road and into the Bates Motel. Clearly, what happened to normal Marion could have happened to her normal sister—it very nearly does—and, just as possibly, to normal us.

Norman Bates, who manages that faceless, forlorn motel, first seems like Marion's polar opposite. Norman is tall, angular and remote, like his home on the hill which looms ominously over the row of cramped bungalows below; passive and staring, like the stuffed birds in his office; clumsy, defensive and excitable, like the unbalanced child he still is. And because he realizes all of this, we respect him, sympathize with him. "I think we're all in our private traps," he tells Marion. "Clamped in them. And none of us can ever get out. We scratch and claw, but only at the air, only at each other. And, for all of it, we never budge an inch." When Marion remarks, apropos her own problem, that "sometimes we deliberately step into those traps," Norman replies, almost serenely: "I was born in mine. I don't mind it anymore."

As he talks on, Norman's self-consciousness begins to resemble self-awareness; his passivity suggests years of productive introspection; his childishness approaches the clarity of a childlike vision. Marion senses all this, and reacts accordingly: she decides to return herself and the money to Phoenix. Her low-key conversation with this fragile, odd young man has touched a chord in Marion that we (and she) didn't notice in an earlier dialogue with Sam. Here the discussion deals with essences, not exigencies; with needs, not desires. We may remember at this point that, in her frustrating conversation with Sam, Marion had ruefully mentioned that a dinner together would have to be "in my house, with my mother's picture on the wall." We will recall how the harsh lighting in the car Marion bought on her flight toward Fairvale made her eyes and mouth look foully rodentoid. On further viewings we may see how Marion's utterly perverse and guilty smile, as she contemplates her employer's avaricious agony over the lost cash, prefigures Norman's cadaverous grin of complacent dementia at the end of the film. We may even realize that the change of the heroine's name from "Mary" in the book to "Marion" in the film makes her name more closely an anagram of "Norman," and that her randomly bought new car bears the license-plate initials NFB—for Norman (F.) Bates?

What we can't help noticing in this scene—which comprises ten minutes of Stefano's richly naturalistic dialogue, almost none of it borrowed from the book, during which Hitchcock flipflops back and forth between Norman and Marion to keep them in pathetic, potentially dangerous isolation—is that these two very different people have connected. They have exchanged something: perhaps something less than their identities, but certainly something more than excerpts from two varyingly desperate autobiographies. Norman has indirectly changed Marion's mind; and Marion has, just as indirectly but much more literally, changed Norman's. As he leaves his office to return to the house, his face freezes into some kind of resolve. Marion's presence has galvanized it into a mask of decisiveness, domination, invulnerability, and an act of will is obviously imminent. He *will* confront his fearsome, nagging mother. No: he *will* become her.

Sam, the film's nominal hero, is nonetheless a kind of psychological anagram to Norman, the same letters that spell a different word. Sam says "I sweat to pay off my father's debts, and he's in his grave." When Norman becomes his mother, he sweats to pay off the debts "she" tells him he owes her; and she *should* be in her grave. Like Norman, Sam is henpecked by a domineering woman, although

218   RICHARD CORLISS

Sam's Marion (and later Lila) is healthy, while Norman's mother is sick. An hour into the film, both are dead, but both continue to exert compelling pressures on their men. Marion's and Mother's personalities live on: Marion by "inhabiting" and "directing" Lila, Mother by "possessing" Norman. As Sam, late in the film, looks across the Bates Motel office desk at Norman, we see (even if Sam doesn't) that Norman is Sam's fun-house mirror image—is what Sam, under other circumstances, might have become, just as Lila might have ended up like Marion.

Three things bind this quintet (Marion, Lila, Sam, Norman, Mother): sex, money and death. Indeed, the first third of the film suggests that "sex + money = death." We meet Sam and Marion one Friday afternoon in a cheap hotel, at a time of day when love can only be expressed through some deadly quickie sex, and in a place where you have to pay by the hour for the sex you get. The conversation is moored in a swamp of money problems: debts that the dead have piled up and that the living must make good, debts that Sam's dead father owed and that Sam owes his "dead" (well, at least departed) ex-wife. Marion and Lila's mother is, presumably, dead, but she keeps an eye on them via her "picture on the wall." (Sam: "And after the steak, can we—turn mama's picture to the wall?" From his own parental experience, he should know better.) And what is the most fulfilling pleasure Sam can offer Marion? "When I send my ex-wife her alimony, you can lick the stamps." Marion's reply is earnest, lascivious and not quite ironic: "I'll lick the stamps!"

Just about everybody in *Psycho* is obsessed with sex, or money, or death, or all three—including the viewer, who, throughout Marion's flight is led to believe she must be another guilty-innocent Hitchcock protagonist. The lewd millionaire, whose forty thousand dollars Marion later steals, tells her: "You know what I do with unhappiness? I buy it off. Are—uh—are *you* unhappy?" Much of Norman's dangerous isolation derives from the fact that, some years before, a new highway was built to replace the one that ran past the motel; this keeps the tourists—and their money—away, and allows Norman to act out his morbid sexual fantasies. Mrs. Bates, who knows her son to be one of those "young men with cheap, neurotic ideas," assumes that Marion has the same ideas about Norman, and bullies him into a confrontation with Marion that Norman will defer until he can become his mother: "Go tell her you'll not be appeasing her ugly appetite with my food—or my son. Or do I have to tell her 'cause you don't have the guts? Huh, boy? You got the guts?" Even a bit-part woman buying insecticide in Sam's hardware store takes up the theme: "And I say, insect or man, death should always be painless." In this film, of course, death never is—from the little murders of Marion's and Sam's early hopes, to the brutal murders in the shower and on the stairs.

Robert Bloch had disposed of his shower scene with a razor-quick slash of sophomoric gallows humor: "It was the knife that, a moment later, cut off her scream. And her head." Hitchcock's expansion of these two sentences—into a forty-second montage that makes Eisenstein's "Odessa Steps" sequence look like Baby's first steps by comparison—roughly parallels Stefano's exquisite development of characters whom Bloch was content to sketch in crude, pulpy crayon-strokes. Hitchcock may indeed be justified if his sole purpose in filming *Psycho* was to put the shower scene, and a few others, on film. (Ingmar Bergman and Stanley Donen gave similar reasons for wanting to make, respectively, *The Magician* and *Arabesque*.)

One remarkable aspect of the sequence, aside from its stunning technical virtuosity, is the way it breaks Hitchcock's First Commandment: "Thou Shalt Be Suspenseful, Not Surprising." Its sheer lunatic unexpectedness is what gives the sequence its visceral wallop. Not only do we not expect Janet Leigh to die forty-five minutes into the film (although her star cameo billing in the opening credits— "and Janet Leigh as Marion Crane"—tips the director's hand), but we don't expect an utterly irrational, seemingly gratuitous knife-murder in a "suspenseful, not surprising" Hitchcock movie. It's as if the pudgy old possum had been lying back, making glossy comedy-mysteries through most of the fifties, just so he could drive his audience into shock, delirious with this grotesque frisson. And after it he could again relax, letting the audience squirm in the awful anticipation of another horrible surprise.

Instead we are subjected and treated to ten minutes of Norman, the dutiful son, cleaning up his mother's mess. Much has been made of the "identity transference" in this section of the film: how Hitchcock brilliantly manipulates his audience into identifying with Nor-

RICHARD CORLISS

man once Marion is dead. The sequence *is* brilliant, but it is not exactly unique. If we follow any movie character long enough— whether he's a gangster, a Western desperado, a sadistic punk, or a homicidal maniac's son—we begin to be sympathetically involved with him. For one thing, we see him as a lone man pitted against the hostile, impersonal world; for another, we respect his professionalism in getting things done, whether it means robbing a bank, outdrawing a rival gunman, beating somebody up, or sanitizing a bloody bathroom and depositing the corpse (along with the forty-thousand dollars, concealed in the folds of a newspaper) in a convenient swamp. Besides, we've sympathized all along with Norman. The artistry of Joseph Stefano and Anthony Perkins saw to that.

Stefano's major change in adapting the Bloch novel was to turn Norman Bates—fat and forty in the book, and less a Mother's Little Helper than a Mr. Joyboy as incarnated by Rod Steiger in *The Loved One*—into Tony Perkins. Perkins's roles had ranged from the gentle, fumbling Quaker in *Friendly Persuasion* to the neurotic but nice ballplayer in *Fear Strikes Out,* and his screen image was one of an almost masochistic vulnerability. He made the viewer feel like a mother deer eager to protect her gangling fawn, and thus was a perfect icon for the *Psycho* audience's sympathy. As Norman Bates, fifteen years closer to the womb than his prototype in Bloch's novel, Perkins could transform a tensed jaw and a threatening stare into pathetic defense mechanisms against an overwhelming, unfeeling universe. His uncertain pauses, ominous intensity, boyish smiles, too-precise diction, and stammer made us simply *not want* him to be the maniacal murderer. And so, at the end, we could suppress thoughts of his psychotic strength beneath a protective, but not indulgent, sympathy for his neurotic weakness. If we have gone so far as to identify with Norman, we must see what in him is like us. Perhaps he *is* us. "We all go a little mad sometimes," he told Marion fiercely, and then leaned back in his chair, smiled and asked ingenuously, "Haven't you?"

The detective Arbogast (Martin Balsam) has been sent by the insurance company he works for to find the missing forty thousand dollars. Arbogast is a seedy, pushy, sort of Jewish version of Lila; he asks Norman all the questions Lila would ask if given the chance, and here our protectiveness toward Norman wars with our desire to solve the mystery of Marion's murder. In terms of the plot, though, Arbogast is one thing Lila is not: disposable. His doom is determined the moment he asks Norman if he "spent the night" with Marion (the old obsession!), and sealed when, referring to Mrs. Bates, he observes that "sick old women are usually pretty sharp." Mother is always eavesdropping on her son's conversations, and in this one she hears her son implicated with "that woman" and her own (mental) health slurred. Hitchcock does finally manipulate us into identifying with Arbogast, by placing him in several positions of vulnerability—leaning down over the office safe (is the money in there?), turning the corner toward the house (is Marion there?), opening the front door (is Norman there?)—of which the last position, as Arbogast reaches the top of the stairs leading to Mother's room (and Mother *is* there), is only the most fatal.

For the audience, for us, the most vulnerable, fatal position lies ahead. The film has traced a progression—or regression—into the unknown lower depths, from its first shot into the darkened hotel room, through the rainy nighttime of Marion's long drive to the Bates Motel, through the watery, bloody-wet shower, and into the bathtub drain, the toilet, the swamp, the implacably open eye of a dead young woman. Now we descend, with Lila, our last-chance identification symbol, into the fruit cellar. When she finds herself trapped between the two Mother Bateses (the leathery mummy and Norman in drag and death mask), her scream is overlaid with the piercingly high-pitched vibrato that Bernard Herrmann devised to simulate Mrs. Bates's scream; and this finally gives way to Norman's little-boy, countertenor wail as he struggles, for the last time, out of his mother's clothes and into her mind. The "mystery" has been solved. But the last stage in our descent is still to come.

The Fairvale psychiatrist has just finished neatly unraveling the string of plot for us. His monologue is cleverly written but execrably delivered. But whether or not Hitchcock coached Simon Oakland to be quite so inept, we are wary of the psychiatrist. He is a smart-ass. He reminds us of our first impression of Arbogast—unnecessarily aggressive and threatening. If this man could tell us everything we needed to know about Norman, *Psycho* would be a lesser film than it is. Like the actor's reading, the psychiatrist's diagnosis provides the right words but the wrong nuances. Because of Anthony Perkins's performance, *we* know more about Norman than the psychiatrist ever could. Because we see ourselves in Norman, we can see more deeply into him. So it is fitting that we get a final glimpse at, and into, Norman Bates.

The scene is bright in Norman's cell, the walls impeccably white. Norman-now-Mother crouches against the farthest wall, and as the camera approaches in its last tracking-shot, Mother speaks. "It's sad when a mother has to speak the words that condemn her own son. But I couldn't allow them to believe that I would commit murder. They'll put him away now, as I should have, long ago." The shock of the murder scene is gone, to be replaced by genuine terror, because we are looking into ourselves. We feel the classical symptoms of tragic fear and pity—but is catharsis possible here? "They're probably watching me. Well, let them. Let them see what kind of a person I am." At this moment, we become one of *Psycho's* schizophrenic characters: we are both "they" (the watchers) and "he-she" (Norman-Mother).

"I'm not even gonna swat that fly. I hope they are watching. They'll see. They'll see and they'll know. They'll say, 'Why, she wouldn't even harm a fly.' " We may think of the "insecticide" woman ("insect or man, death should always be painless"), and of Marion (with her sinister smile in the car) and, if *Psycho* has moved us at all, of us. This is the ultimate horror of *Psycho,* and the self-awareness we spotted earlier in Norman—which now must be ours—is the only catharsis the film offers. Norman-Mother smiles; the smile dissolves for a split-second into the grinning skull of the dead Mrs. Bates; and the skull dissolves into a shot of Marion's car being hauled out of the swamp, a visual metaphor for the possibility of withdrawing from Norman's hold on us.

Most horror movies, if they work at all, have the acrid tang of well-structured nightmares that exploit the twin fears of impotence and loss of identity. The best ones also create a palpable claustrophobia, trapping the viewer in a world of unrelenting unreason from which the only escape is either perfunctory or problematical. *Psycho* stands alone among horror movies: it is both the scariest and the best made. But it is also something else, something more. It reaches inside us, the way the crane in its final shot dredges the Bates Motel swamp, to retrieve our dead, or simply mislaid, potential for evil. And once this potential is recognized, it can be released. *Psycho* is not only, as Robin Wood has said, "one of the key works of our age," it is also perhaps the most bracingly, *exaltingly* therapeutic.

23. Looking Backward at the Film 2001

COLIN L. WESTERBECK, JR.

They cannot scare me with their empty spaces
Between stars—on stars where no human race is.
I have it in me so much nearer home
To scare myself with my own desert places.
—ROBERT FROST, 1934.

Frost's lines may seem a curious place to begin explaining why *2001* is my favorite movie, but I thought they might dispel some of the cant and McLuhanacy that now surround the film. Despite the claim that Jesus freaks and other exponents of nonlinear living have made on *2001*, Frost's classical, conservative attitude toward man is not so different from Kubrick's. The film begins in the desert places of prehistory, and throughout it Kubrick pokes fun at man's puny vision just as Frost's feminine rhymes do. Like Frost, Kubrick is really after the desert places in man's own nature rather than the empty spaces in the universe. It is the terrible limitations of man himself, not the capaciousness of the universe,

225

that threaten man from beyond the solar system. Frost's poetry offers us a certain wisdom about such limitations. His directive to his readers is a cautionary one: don't be too ready to find out what man's limitations are. Kubrick's film is more adventurous. He takes for granted man's determination to exceed the limits of space and time, but he also assumes that man will prove inadequate to this excess. Like Frost, Kubrick suspects that what lies beyond the original in experience will be some truth about the aboriginal in man himself.

Thus I might begin this essay simply by saying that I like *2001* because it fits into my frame of mind. The film seems to me a shrewd judgment on men and future events. But this is probably as close as I can come to playing favorites here. At best *2001* is *a* favorite of mine, not *the* favorite, for no one who sees a lot of films can feel that one alone dominates all the others. Preferences are always far more relative than the question posed for this book would allow. And besides, what I really hope to explain here is why I think *2001* is a great movie. I assume my explanation will imply—perhaps better than I can say it directly—why I favor the film. A film is great in part because it says the right things at the right time; it is great in relation to the moment at which it is made and as an expression of that moment in people's history. It is because of this that the public responds to the movie. It doesn't make sense, then, for one film to remain a moviegoer's favorite forever. His favorite will inevitably change and change again, and it ought to. Although my favorite movie may change next year, or next week, *2001* will continue to be a great movie. Trying to explain why it will has to be the most durable kind of praise I can offer it.

Trying to do so in these pages has a special appeal since *2001* was widely abused when it premiered, in many cases by critics whose essays on other films can be found in this book. When the film opened at the Cinerama Theater in New York in 1968, the only thing about it that appealed to the prominent critics was its ascerbic comedy. The one important review that was favorable came from Penelope Gilliatt, who seemed to like the film because she saw nothing except black humor in it. She thought it "hideously funny— like *Dr. Strangelove.*" It is indeed like *Dr. Strangelove,* particularly in its middle section when Dr. Heywood Floyd goes to the moon

COLIN L. WESTERBECK, JR.

colony at Clavius. Floyd has the same martial habits of mind as *Strangelove*'s Gen. Buck Turgidson. Floyd relishes the idiotic secrecy of his work. He is genuinely pleased when an associate tells him that his fatuous speech on mission security "beefed up morale a helluva lot." Floyd is also a bit vainglorious. As soon as he arrives at the site of the monolith, he and his co-workers begin photographing each other like a bunch of German officers prematurely celebrating their new empire in front of the Arc de Triomphe. This is the same stuff of which Turgidson is made.

But, at the same time, Floyd is not so odious a man as Turgidson. HAL 9000 may turn out to be a transistorized Gen. Jack D. Ripper, but Floyd is a far less savage caricature than his forebears in *Strangelove*. The reason is that in *2001* man is for Kubrick ultimately an object of pity, not contempt. As a satire the film is more Kubrick's *Modern Times* than a repeat of the misanthropic *Strangelove*. Like Chaplin, the little fellow who is fed by one machine and then eaten by another, the astronauts in *2001* end up the hapless victims of their own technology. Moreover, like *Modern Times, 2001* is a talkie dominated by silent-screen comedy. Dr. Floyd's photographic expedition to the monolith is an example, as is his encounter with the Zero Gravity Toilet. But perhaps the sight gag that comes across with the sweetest irony is the scene in which Poole goes jogging aboard the spaceship *Discovery*. The fun made of man here is, after the fashion of silent comedy, pretty warm-blooded. As he passes along the ship's circumferential floor, Poole feints and bobs toward the walls, shadow-boxing with the electronic equipment anchored there. Surrounded by astronautical hardware of his making, man still gestures with the mentality of an ape who hasn't yet thought of picking up a bludgeon.

The jogging scene isn't completely silent, for a Chopin waltz played on the sound track contributes to the joke. Nor is this the only time that music is part of the satire. There is the "Blue Danube Waltz" to which the satellites orbit the earth early in the film; and just before Bowman arrives at Jupiter, as he disconnects HAL's brain, the computer sings "A Bicycle Built for Two." These musical interludes are all old-fashioned and a bit corny in a way that debunks man's achievement in space. The unfamiliarity of what we see is being neutralized because what we hear is a little too familiar.

Yet in Kubrick's use of these tunes something is going on besides mockery. There is also a dramatic effect in the way that waltz time, with its implicitly orbital motion, is suited to the rotating of the satellites. The circularity of the waltzes is suited to the very design of the satellites and of the spaceships, which are all white and cylindrical.

In this symbolism, as in the rest of *2001*, Kubrick clearly intends to be more than funny. "If *2001* has stirred your emotions, your subconscious, your mythological yearnings," he has said, "it has succeeded." He meant that it has succeeded *only* if it has done these things; and as he knows, satire alone would not have been enough to do them. It would not have satisfied his Promethean ambitions as a filmmaker. Some more elemental drama was needed. The monolith seen by Bowman, the apes and Dr. Floyd is an attempt to achieve such drama. The music and the design of the spacecraft are a comment on the limits of human imagination. In man's conceiving, the universal rhythm of time and organization of space are a cycle. It is beyond man's conception for them to be otherwise. Against man's conceptions the film therefore posits a black monolith—something rectilinear, and thus beyond man's comprehension or mastery.

But this opposition of a black rectangle to a white circle is so abstract, so easy to reproduce and impossible to elaborate, that it seems merely bad art. Although I don't think that it is just bad art, whatever art *2001* has is admittedly crude. Consider the cut that Kubrick makes between a bone hurled into the air by an ape and a satellite orbiting the earth. There can be no argument whether this bit of montage is crude. It is. But then the montage in Eisenstein's films is crude in just the same way. Kubrick's editing here is no more sensational than Eisenstein's is in *Potemkin* or *October,* nor are Kubrick's lingering shots of interstellar space any more tedious than are Dovzhenko's long takes of Ukrainian wheat fields in *Earth.* If Kubrick's techniques often seem as blunt and radical as the early Russians', it is because his aspirations for his work are comparable to theirs. Like both Eisenstein and Dovzhenko, Kubrick is searching for images that will move us more profoundly that mere art does. Like the Russian directors of the 1920s and 1930s, Kubrick has the indecent ambition to be more than an artist. As his own remarks suggest, he would be a myth poet instead.

COLIN L. WESTERBECK, JR.

Eisenstein and Dovzhenko could conceive such a vocation for themselves not only because they were working in a new art form, but because they were living in a country that had proclaimed itself the inaugurator of a new historical epoch. Until this century man created his myths out of his past, but the early Russian cinema was part of a national effort to create a myth of the present. Now Kubrick would astonish us with a myth of the future. Eisenstein and Dovzhenko saw Russia's present as a time that would be liberated from her past, and their myth was accordingly optimistic and Olympian. Kubrick's is dark and Titanic. He sees man's future as a time that will fall heir to the past. Since Kubrick does not feel himself in harmony with the institutions of his times, his motives for attempting such mythopoesis are necessarily more private and solitary than those of his Russian predecessors. But the creation of new myths is what all modern artists have attempted one way or another. In order to affect an audience in just the same way that Kubrick would like to, William Butler Yeats once turned briefly from poetry to a moviemaking of sorts: he tried holding up painted images before a crowd to see which ones the people would respond to. Kubrick is doing much the same thing.

The culmination of Kubrick's attempt to project a myth on the future comes when Bowman enters the space-time warp at the end of the Jupiter mission. Kubrick does intend to mystify us here, but he is also unwilling to succeed completely. If we are disoriented in these final sequences, it is not simply because we feel that what we see is opaque and incomprehensible. This feeling alone wouldn't make the film disturbing, for we could go away content that we had not missed anything. But the final sequences also give us the feeling that they are too lucid in a way—that they signify too much to be taken in at such speed. We have that impression given by all myth that the content of the story has suddenly achieved a very intense and undisguised order of symbolism: the action has become a transfigured pantomime, an allegory almost. If only we could slow down this superluminary rush of images. . . . But the fact that intelligible images fly at us too quickly to be understood is part of Kubrick's design upon our consciousness and our unconscious. He would throw us into future shock on purpose. When Arthur Schlesinger first saw the film he remarked that "the conclud-

ing statement is . . . too profound, or perhaps too shallow for immediate comprehension." Like Schlesinger, we are unsure which is
the case. It is this confusion that Kubrick hopes will involve us in
his ending.

One way to get our bearings in the time warp is to see it as an
extension of moments in other Kubrick films. First and foremost, the
time warp is a rectilinear space like the black monoliths. But as
such it is also a corridor—when we enter it the narrow walls are
vertical—and is thus not unlike other corridors we have been made
to travel rapidly in Kubrick films. *In Paths of Glory* Kubrick's camera backtracks through the battlefield trenches in France, giving
way before the advancing figure of Kirk Douglas. Earlier in *2001*
the camera rolled backward in the same way while Poole was taking
his exercise jogging aboard the *Discovery*, and while Bowman
stalked through *Discovery's* companionways going to decerebrate
HAL. In *A Clockwork Orange* this camera movement precedes
Alex through the aisles of his local record store. The only difference
at the end of *2001* is that the usual relationship between the camera and the space photographed is reversed. The camera now moves
forward instead of back; and after the first few seconds, the corridor shifts from the vertical to the horizontal plane.

In essence (if not in immediate effect) what comes tearing out
of the screen at us is also a reversal of a kind: a reverse journey
through evolution. It is as if the reels from a camera present at the
Creation were now being run in reverse. Though we seem to be
traveling forward in space to "Jupiter and beyond," we are figuratively traveling backward in time—as if Kubrick's camera could
now backtrack twelve million years to the Pleistocene era in which
the film began, and beyond. Kubrick and Arthur Clarke both speak
of the present as the electronic epoch, the way one might speak of
an epoch of geological time. The passage through the time warp
begins in a maze of electronic light blips and dismembered grids.
We seem to be hurtling through the inner being of some monstrous
computer.

But then the patterns change from mechanistic to organic
forms. Galactic explosions yield a regression of unicellular, plas-
mic and protoplasmic substances. A shape that is ambiguously either spermatozoan or meteoric moves across the screen, and ends in

230   COLIN L. WESTERBECK, JR.

the inchoate stirrings of a cloud-chamber atmosphere—the sort of atmosphere in which life began. Before that, all matter was inorganic, like the crystalline figures that replace the cloud chamber on the screen. The lifelessness echoes the death images of the desert and of animal skulls that were the first things we saw in *2001*. Penultimately the time warp leads us back into that desert landscape —or rather, into a solarized vision of it—where the apes lived at the beginning of the film. We have in effect passed through all the evolutionary forces before which man has been either the powerless beneficiary or the accidental victim.

Ultimately we find ourselves at rest in an eighteenth-century French room—a room done in a Louis Quinze decor with the appropriate wall panels by Boucher or Fragonard. (While the panels look authentic, or at least like faithful copies, Kubrick makes most other appointments a modern imitation that is too abstracted and stylized to pass for genuine period work.) Like a tracking shot in a corridor, this room is a recurring touch in Kubrick films. We have seen such rooms before in *Paths of Glory,* whenever Col. Dax meets with the villainous Gen. Broulard. And we are to see similar decor and wall panels again at the casino theater in *A Clockwork Orange,* when Alex and his droogs engage in some ultraviolence.

The style of Louis's France represents to Kubrick both the aesthetic refinements and the corruption of all high civilizations. Kubrick believes that they all belong here, at the end of Bowman's journey and closer to the blind, dumb origins of life than we usually imagine. In this setting Bowman himself devolves to helpless infancy. In one way Kubrick is only reminding us of the simple paradox that the age of man is relative. But he is also making his final cinemetaphor out of Relativity Theory's "time-dilation factor," which is the implication that time slows down as the speed of light is approached. Hypothetically a further conclusion must be that if the speed of light were exceeded, time would be reversed. Traveling beyond the speed of light, a man would return to his point of departure earlier than he left it. In the closing sequence of *2001* the unborn fetus that hurtles through space is Bowman's. According to a Kubrick aide, its resemblance to Keir Dullea, the actor who plays Bowman, is quite intentional. This fetus, with its expression that is at once both terrified and mindlessly serene, confirms the irony of the film's subtitle, *A Space Odyssey*. Man will be a diminished presence in space, not an epic hero.

At the end the monolith remains an unsolved mystery, a force of nature that is implacable and wholly indifferent to man. Because he knows that people won't try a movie they suspect to be depressing, Kubrick as a rule avoids commenting on this or any other sobering aspect of his film. He steadfastly maintains that *2001* is committed to the ideal of technological "progress." But in a *Playboy* interview done soon after the film opened, Kubrick unexpectedly acknowledged the dark side of his imagination which the film's ending reveals. After giving out his usual public-relations line in response to predictable questions, he was asked one personal question: Why does he refuse to travel by airplane? Although the question was only a throwaway about his private bugaboos, his lengthy answer ranged over the whole subject of technology and the relation of man to nature. His answer also contradicted most of what he had said earlier in the interview. He eventually came to the conclusion, already drawn in the fetus's gaze at the end of *2001*, that "the most terrifying fact about the universe is not that it is hostile but that it is indifferent."

The ending of *2001* is what most bothered the legion of critics who panned the film. Richard Roud could have been speaking for the whole club when he said that Kubrick "just hadn't thought it through." What Roud shares with other critics is the ability to attribute to the film any incoherence that exists within himself. *Time* magazine echoed that the film "leaves doubt that the filmmakers themselves knew precisely what they were flying at." Andrew Sarris thought the film "a disaster, because it is much too abstract to make its abstract points." Pauline Kael decided that Kubrick had assembled all the film's sets and paraphernalia, "never even bothering to figure out what he was going to do with them." And John Simon complained that the film must be pointless because "the slab is never explained."

I can't help wondering whether these critics would be better satisfied by Arthur Clarke's novel than they are by the film, whose scenario is, by Clarke's own admission, ninety-five percent Kubrick's work. The novel and film are both based on a 1950 Clarke short story called "The Sentinel." The story is about two space explorers

232   COLIN L. WESTERBECK, JR.

who find an impenetrable monument on the moon, and finally succeed in exploding its mysterious shield. At this point one of the two says of the monument, "And as to its purpose, here is my guess." Whereupon he explains that he thinks disturbing the monument triggered a signal to the extraterrestrial civilization that erected it. "Perhaps they wish to help our infant civilization," he philosophizes. "But they must be very, very old, and the old are often insanely jealous of the young."

I'm not a sci-fi buff, but I believe Clarke's story fairly typifies the genre. There is always a rational explanation that clarifies everything in the end. All mysteries have perfectly logical solutions, most of which can be rendered in mundane platitudes like "The Sentinel's" wisdom on the galactic generation gap. The novel that Clarke made out of *2001's* screenplay is in sensibility the same as "The Sentinel." In fact, in the novel the extraterrestrial presence is even more anthropomorphic and sentient than in the short story. As opposed to Kubrick's black monoliths, Clarke's monoliths are transparent. It is an appropriate difference. At the end of the novel Clarke has the star-child, as he calls it, destroy some orbiting nuclear weapons that man has placed around the earth. Apparently, however, a few readers were confused enough to think that the earth was destroyed too. When Clarke heard of this, he considered stopping the presses so that he could rewrite the ending and eliminate all doubt whatsoever from it. But he really had nothing to worry about—we have the word of NASA astronaut Col. William A. Anders on this. Col. Anders has compared the novel with the film and reports, "Though I enjoyed the film very much . . . I was somewhat confused by the ending of the third part. This was cleared up when I read the book." Since they share Col. Anders's aversion to ambiguity, perhaps some of the critics who disliked the film would also feel more comfortable with the novel.

But whether a lot of critics hated *2001*, or I like it, is now somewhat beside the point. Again, playing favorites does not seem to me a very helpful act of criticism anymore. *2001* is an important movie, like it or not. The fact that the film has made money is not what counts, for pure kitsch can do that. But kitsch is entirely predictable. It lives down to our easiest expectations: it can arouse no controversy. Unlike *Gone with the Wind, The Sound of Music* and most of the two or three dozen other blockbusters in its tax bracket, *2001* is not a film whose meanings are obvious. Moreover, it is a film that surprised its viewers. It understood something about them that they had not understood, and this is what makes it an important movie. In this respect *2001* might be classed with *Little Caesar* or *Stagecoach, Easy Rider* or *Bonnie and Clyde*. Aesthetic merit is not the issue in the long-run reputations of these films either. What all of them have in common is that they transformed a popular convention. *2001*'s ability to do this has had a lot to do with the extranarrative elements of the film, which is why critics who attacked it for poor storytelling misjudged its appeal.

The landscape in which the film was shot has much to do with its power. I suspect that something very similar accounts for the impact that *Stagecoach* had on its audiences. I was born too late to make the premiere of Ford's film; but when I see it now, the shot in which I can sense how impressive the film must have been to its original audience is the one where the coach first heads out into Monument Valley, passing beyond the fence that marks the perimeter of the town. By itself the story told in *Stagecoach* was too sentimental, just as Kubrick's story may prove too cynical. But as the first movie that Ford made in Monument Valley, *Stagecoach* dazzled a public that had thought itself completely bored with westerns. *2001* gives its audience a new view of space much the way *Stagecoach* gave moviegoers a new view of the West.

Like Monument Valley in a Ford film, outer space in *2001* becomes a mythical landscape. Saturation television coverage of the Apollo program has rendered space travel stupifyingly dull, especially for the generation of Americans who will be most affected by it. It turns out that what the youth of America wants is a chance to feel there might be some adventure, some human commotion or drama, in all that technology and empty space; *2001* gives our TV astronauts, those technocrats jibbering "pads" of numbers, a place among classic American heroes. The heroes that we have acquired in movie houses have always been men who live on the outer edges of society—way out West, in the underworld of gangsters or, more recently, in the underground of motorcycle bums. Our heroes have

234   COLIN L. WESTERBECK, JR.

been empire builders, men who have a lot to do but little to say, and nothing to say about themselves. Out of more than two hours running time, *2001* has less than forty-five minutes of dialogue. It is almost a half hour before the first word is spoken in the film. In their quiescence, as in other qualities, *2001*'s astronauts have been put out on the mythological fringes of our experience so that our imaginations can cope with them.

But Kubrick has also done more than create our farfetched heroes anew: he has had the audacity to show us why they must ultimately fail. It seems that a great many of the American people were ready to entertain such a suggestion—more ready than even they or Kubrick had supposed. This shock of mutual recognition between a moviemaker and his audience does go beyond art. A work of art tells us something about the artist who made it. It is the statement of an individual consciousness, and we respond to the otherness we sense in it. But *2001* tells us something new about ourselves. It is a statement of the collective unconscious: it brings to consciousness for us what was before known only to our collective unconscious. This is what our greatest movies have always done.

24. The Inevitable Movie

PARKER TYLER

A<small>RT,"</small> <small>PAUL VERLAINE FELT OBLIGED</small> to explain to his young worshipers, "is to be absolutely oneself." And criticism? Is it not an art—is it not creation? Modern opinion tends to say that true intellectual activity above a certain level is creative. If that be conceded, it could follow arguably that criticism is an art— an "art" in more than a colloquial sense of that abused word—and so, to be a master critic, it is necessary to be absolutely oneself. . . . If Verlaine, that is, was correct. The more I think about the matter, the more convinced I am that he was. In the present day, this opinion might look a bit facile. Don't existentialist habits of thought make it easy to translate from one system of values to another, and above all, to simplify objective problems by referring them back to the subject's dominant motivation, even to his pure self-interest? Thus one should be careful. Yet should one not—above all, the poet and the critic—always be careful? *Care* has become another fashionable philosophic concept, closely associated with existentialism as it is. On higher levels, care implies philosophic reflectiveness on all important matters. Care is veritably a measure of the seriousness with which one regards life—one's own and others'.

Asked to testify in this book devoted to favorite movies, I could not help arriving at the thought that prompted the above paragraph. Is it really truthful to select one movie—that is, one work of film art—and exalt it credibly, eloquently, convincingly, as an object superior to all others of its medium? How much of an intact object can the film work be when it is the subject of true criticism? The latter problem has nagged me during my whole career. Regarding any question of the singular best, one might demur on grounds of finding an embarrassment of riches, so that, torn among a large number of candidates to be thus honored, one would be reluctant to name one's favorite because in certain details it might be less fine, less "perfect," than one of its rivals—some other "favorite movie." There are so many movies—so many factors, if not favorites—that it is hard even to recall and to tabulate everything. A critic determined to conquer this problem could well be in for a good deal of labor. The labor, for all that, might do him good. It might remind him that film criticism, as honorably and as well as he may practice it, perhaps lacks (even in *his* hands) basic and coherent standards —true constants, true measures of greatness. Turning his critical searchlight inward, a critic bent on making his selection might learn that he feels not completely equipped to reach a very confident result . . . is timid about an ultimate commitment.

So scrupulous a critic seems bound to speculate that it would be an easier thing to select, say, the ten or twelve best films of his lifetime acquaintance. At least, he could then point to outstanding examples of the film art that represented its most valuable trends, provided (for the film art) a pattern of exemplariness. Yet I truly think such an alternative for the original problem, however worthy as a separate project, would be an unfair evasion. I find something basically challenging about the deceptively simple, and singular, proposition: "What is your favorite movie?" Insofar as the question be not an excuse for interesting speculations, a display of personal tastes or some pyrotechnics, it goes deep—deep enough to challenge *my* basic integrity. In short, the question has gotten to me in the most loaded sense of that slang expression. It is a lot like the question "Do you believe in God?" or "Do you believe in immortality?"

If you don't brush it aside, you have to think. It abruptly evokes the ultimate realm we variously term truth. Common reference is made to "the moment of truth," but I fear this is the habit of a morally negligent, inadequately thoughtful society. Can something compacted of truth be put in either a "moment" or a "movie"?

If film critics and observers of film critics were induced to be quite candid as to the present problem, they would have to concede that much too much time is spent by professional critics in what justly is to be called, I think, the juggling of opinions. For anyone professionally obliged to keep up with film production, there are at least two or three films a week to be assessed; films which his occupation technically does not allow him to miss even if he does not write about them all. He has to see them and file away their ratings so as to be ready for associating them with similar works and future works by the same hand. A disconcerting element of the historic present is the pace at which taste and its tacit values tend to change—to change even at the elite level. Besides, "elite" is itself a rather suspect word in a time when to be called "Establishment" is to be automatically suspect as an agent of oppression, reaction and even chauvinism. Maybe there's something un-democratic now, even un-modern, about being a *critic*!

A critic's pride—and certain film critics are aggressive upon this point—is, at least implicitly, to have standards of taste and a clear moral conscience: he doesn't flatter, he won't yield to pressures crude or subtle, he declines to cater to popular taste or just to something new because it is, or pretends to be, "new." Yet the more this brave attitude is tested on a continuous level, where a critic must expose his judgments of movies every day, every week or month, the deeper the conscionable critic gets into commitment, irrevocable commitment. The more he disciplines himself to write regularly and with conviction, the more precise he is in formulating his opinions, the less free he is to revise his judgments in the future.

How many film critics, for example, obliged to write up daily or weekly opinions, find it practical to measure movies by historical values, that is, by abiding standards as set by movies since the beginings of the art? A pivotal point is that to select one's favorite movie—the greatest of all time or whatever—one would plausibly have to have a well-developed sense of the art's historical achieve-

PARKER TYLER

ment, a ready file of highly distinguished films which have won their superior place through known, established values. But for such a group of films to exist in a critic's purview, he would have to be an initiate of comparative criticism in full historic perspective. It strikes me, from what I know of contemporary critical opinion, that however shrewd and sensitive are the best critics, truly comparative —or as I would say *historical*—film criticism is a shadowy and little practised thing. Most volumes of film criticism are either information surveys, collections of necessarily rough reflections or simply columns of reprinted reviews; there is very little show of definitive, really definitive, essays. Moreover, even the most important works of film aesthetics and theory are weighty in generalities, hopelessly thin in specificities. Yet how else than by a system of truly historical rating of individual films can a specific film be chosen above all others as the best exemplar of its art?

I will be surprised if many of my colleagues contributing to this volume come up with a single favorite identified with perfect conviction. I rather fancy some will procrastinate (on critical grounds naturally) and that at least three or four will speak of leading candidates rather than a supreme, unrivaled winner. Am *I* procrastinating? Not really. I am cautiously surveying what I think is the true perspective of this problem. Just to speak of favorite movies in the plural tempts one to point to trends, fond memories, grounds for high rank without reference to order or percentages of merit. Still, one has second thoughts. . . . According to how much "gone" one is on the movies, how much of a real buff, the embarrassment of riches provides a true playground for fine shades—and for wallowing. Perhaps even that old romantic lover of the movies, James Agee, would find himself, were he alive to contribute here, in solemn quandary, and like the *réligieux* he was about the movies, would pause to reexamine his conscience. At the end of which pursuit, he might come up with something rather less speculative than this contribution, but having a conclusion neither satisfying nor quite positive.

Faced with this crisis, a film critic might well review his own past as well as the past of the film art. How much and how finally can he adhere to each printed opinion of current movies since he set up shop as professional opinionator? The film art is a great deal like Pop Art, which as a culture commodity is hardly more than a decade old. Of course, the movies are over seventy. Yet they bear the scars administered by lofty disdain from aesthetes and other arbiters. Like Pop Art again, the movies prevailed without more than tolerance (a lot of it mute or skeptical) from many recognized art experts. Originally a few large philosophic souls, such as Elie Faure, hailed the movies' wonder, but not without attributing to them a mythic grandeur by which (according to Faure) a clairvoyant camera recorded history as both past and future as well as present. Perhaps he was somewhat inspired by Jules Verne, the early science-fictionist. If alive today, Faure might well pick *2001: A Space Odyssey* as the supertrip film of his clairvoyant camera, even though he knew *2001* is actually a studio-contrived fiction, based on childishly reconstructed human history.

Faure's vintage essay—"The Art of Cineplastics"—was admirably adventurous.[1] Yet I think all films resembling his vision of the goal of film art would have to be written off by really conscientious critics facing up to the present task. This writing off considerably reduces the field of choice. Personally, I'd retain pure fantasy films of quality, such as *The Cabinet of Dr. Caligari*, the best Dada-Surrealist films (Buñuel, Dali, Clair) and Cocteau's films, even though that filmmaker, with his mythfilm-in-mufti, *Orpheus*, went glaringly public. Which stirs up a still troublesome tension: that of the critical position that commercial film should be separated from avant-garde and experimental film, including today's valid underground works; a necessary corollary, then, is to decide how pure and legitimate, art-wise, commercial films ever managed to be. In turn, this must prick the critic's conscience and make him ask himself: What price professionalism in the film art? Has it had to sacrifice too much to popular taste, to the mass market?

Under such insistent scrutiny, some of one's foremost candidates for "the best" might well show wilting edges at first recognizance. Duly one recognizes classic film directors, the pioneers, the developers—D. W. Griffith and von Stroheim; Abel Gance with his multi-screened historical epic, *Napoléon;* Jean Renoir with his early, inventive filmic sensibility; Orson Welles, rising in post-Depression days as the great American film buffs' darling, responsible for

[1] Reprinted in *Film: An Anthology*, edited by Daniel Talbot (Berkeley: University of California Press, 1966).

PARKER TYLER

one of the world's most popular films among critics, *Citizen Kane.*
In Europe, we had the pre-World War II Germans and Frenchmen:
besides René Clair and Carné, Pagnol with his *Marius, Fanny, César;*
the elegant maverick Jean Vigo; of course Renoir with *Grand Illusion* and *Rules of the Game;* and Lang, Pabst, Murnau, von Sternberg; then the Russian school, Eisenstein being (I think) clearly
at the top with *Potemkin,* the aborted *Que Viva Mexico!* and the
curtailed but magnificent *Ivan the Terrible;* also, Dovzhenko and
Pudovkin. Then, in a wave, came the postwar Italian neorealists,
Rossellini and De Sica, with Visconti, Fellini and Antonioni soon
to surface; more lately, Pasolini and Bertolucci at his more mature
stage; further afield: the best of Bergman, Buñuel and that uneven
Frenchman, Bresson. The brilliant Japanese were spearheaded in
the Western Hemisphere by Kurosawa's arrival with *Rashomon.*
Then there was the unique case of the poetically gifted Indian,
Satyajit Ray. Granted, works by all the above are historical quantities. They are in the archives. Yet how do they hold up in the light
of today? If one really sits down just to be serious, rather than to
make a ten-best list, it can be the tenderest, most embarrassing of
critical predicaments. Nothing, I think, disintegrates so quickly as
a film under the pressure of really serious, really competent,
criticism.

By now, I have mentioned by name only (counting von Stroheim)
three American directors. Of course, a patriotic school of film buff
criticism still swears by Griffith's epics—too well-known to mention
—and by von Stroheim's *Greed.* Yet, to me, time's perspective
seems more and more cruel to the pretensions of these epics of
Griffith—certainly so in the light of the film art as technically
and stylistically expanded since his primitive era. It is hard to
isolate a surviving virtue in them, one that looks really intact, aside
from that matrix of montage: his narrative cross-cutting. On the
other hand, the poetry of the intimate *Broken Blossoms* (as absurd
and naive as it looks from certain angles) survives as perhaps
Griffith's purest and best work; next best: *Way Down East*—yes!
despite everything. As for *Greed,* it is incomparably its director's
best and deserves to be included in any exclusively American list of
superlative films. . . . Nor do I forget that there are still Americans
dear to the patriots and the buffs. Surely King Vidor deserves to be

remembered for *The Crowd* and the remarkably coherent and articulate *Hallelujah!*, which, by the way, is a dignified "black film" by a white director; in fact, the first of its kind. By my scale of values, most American directors tend to get on the list by the fun route—by doing more or less amusing charades or pure zany comedies, the best of the latter being surely (as films) those of the Marx Brothers. And naturally there is Chaplin's *oeuvre,* though I think that he himself, as a creative clown, is (like many another American comedian) distinctly better than his films *qua* films.

Well I know, too, that museum archives in the United States are bursting with vintage films aside from those of Griffith and von Stroheim, Vidor, John Ford and John Huston—I add the last two because, for me, two of the most memorable American films are Huston's *The Maltese Falcon* and Ford's *The Informer.* Yet I cannot see that the heavy repertory which American films have gained since museum directors began taking them up can show anything to compete with the parallel repertory of foreign films, of which I just gave a summary outline. To the classic foreign repertory must be added works by a brilliant Hungarian, Miklós Jancsó, and a gifted Brazilian, Glauber Rocha. I say this while bearing in mind that schools of taste sponsored by buff critics recognize not merely other "classic" American directors but also new and current ones— men as recent as Kubrick and Cassavetes, the Maysles, Peckinpah, Dennis Hopper and Arthur Penn—even (if one has an ear pressed to the ground) Peter Bogdanovich. *Easy Rider* has already "made the list" if only because of its use of the hippie lifestyle. Well, time may do strange and ghastly things to that movie as well as to its inspiration. Personally, I would put Cassavetes's *Faces,* and especially his earlier film, *Shadows,* above the work of other younger Americans of today.

If hitherto I have not mentioned certain foreign directors, Truffaut or Resnais or Godard, or any English directors at all, it is quite consciously and on purpose. I know too well some of them occupy places on lists as well as in archives. Resnais's case seems to me tantalizingly ambiguous if only because after doing something as impressive as *Hiroshima, Mon Amour,* he could do something as trivially flashy as *Last Year at Marienbad;* at his very best, Resnais does not rank with the best Europeans. I am quite unpersuaded of anything solid or truly creative about the facilely gifted Truffaut or the facilely gifted (and often very bad) Godard. Merely mentioning these two brings up the towering issue of the *auteur* director as a leading criterion of merit. Hitchcock, one of Truffaut's influences, is one who wields an *auteur's* signature without its making his films a bit better than they should be. The same goes for Carol Reed's best melodramas. I am sure that the worthiest English films, whether or not indelibly *auteur,* are certain obscure and probably forgotten works, not the dazzlers whose directors are famous in the world of commercial films and consequently ornaments of the archives. Phalanxes of interesting and intelligent films by Englishmen exist, but almost none stand out for their *auteur* stamp or any other great filmic or stylistic quality. Many of these are adaptations of well-known plays: by Shakespeare, Shaw, Wilde—and I think of Noel Coward's *Blithe Spirit.* (Ken Russell? The less said about *his auteur* qualities, the better.) Only determined buffs, far-gone addicts, even recall who directed this or that play adaptation. Everyone remembers Laurence Olivier's *Henry V* but would its director be remembered if Olivier hadn't played King Henry?

To have evoked so many difficulties and handicaps over the problem in hand brings in train (for me) the impulse to sweep them all away and become simple—even if this means throwing away conscience. Some might claim I have been beating about the bush and stirring up an extraordinary amount of dust. That thought may have a grain or more of truth in it. But, if so, it merely brings us back to the beautiful dictum of Verlaine with which I began. I think, in fact, that Verlaine's dictum brings us to the *inevitable* movie: the movie of the film critic's career autobiography, the movie that lies in print and will never go on film. . . . Verlaine said that toward the end of his life, not the beginning. If a critic is just going to speak from the heart—to indulge his blessed memories of pleasure gained in the movie house and to hell with standards!—the case presents an altogether different aspect. Surely I am not the only one engaged with film from the side of professional criticism to have soft spots for this film and that—and for very particular and personal reasons.

I cherish deep inclinations for suavity and sophistication in dealings with human truth at its deepest level. For this quality, what can compare, as to drive and technique, with the integrated comedy, satire and pathos of Renoir's *The Rules of the Game*? For sheer worldly nuance and easy poise, it is probably unique in film history. I am the more moved that this film is by Renoir who, despite *The Rules* and several almost equally fine films, eventually allowed himself to make one of the stupidest errors in film history: *Picnic On the Grass*. But I am in a mood to brush aside all Achilles' heels. In general, the French have been very good at the game I mean, especially with themes such as homosexuality which are widely considered offbeat. Films such as Delannoy's *This Special Friendship* and Jacqueline Audry's *The Pit of Loneliness* (a plague on the title!) create a very attractive style of sentiment, a very attractive style of narrative —things parallel with literature—without being conspicuously filmic. Then I feel impelled to rescue certain films from undeserved oblivion or merely an esoteric reputation: films that nevertheless are uniquely meritorious. I think, in the esoteric category, of Jean Genet's brief, very pure *Un Chant d'Amour* and of Curzio Malaparte's *Forbidden Christ*, which I imagine few of my colleagues even recall. Yet both these works have the rarest sort of sensibility to appear on film: something intact, independent, aesthetically *right*.

Of course, I hereby abandon any ideal of perfection, filmic or otherwise. Perhaps in our very imperfect and insidiously corrupt world of commercial film, where opportunism and gaudy novelty are so powerful at this date, one should opt (even faced by this task) for what is rare, and rarely pure. For example, all one has to do is compare that incredibly insensitive whale of an epic, the Soviet Union's recent version of *War and Peace*, to Eisenstein's *Ivan the Terrible*, to realize that the latter is virtually unique in filmdom for achieving one of the main qualities of epic work: majesty. And I urge myself to add: *sheer* majesty. Despite its rigid stylization, its relentless theatricalism, Eisenstein's *Ivan* is marvelously articulated and attains an heroic intactness fully as heroic as it is intact. . . . Well, I hope the reader agrees that I have found a way to be personal, subjective, even egotistic, without sacrificing my responsibilities to this occasion.

I don't want to leave the page without mentioning another crush I could never forget. It was (or rather is) a film made in Paris during the German occupation in World War II and so, to some extent, must be suspected of collaborating—even if in the name of art—"with the enemy." If it failed, one wouldn't, now, even want to accuse it. But it succeeded. I mean Marcel Carné's *Children of Paradise*. A special fillip is added to its charm—what I think of as its high charm—when one considers that it is saturated with Paris itself, and historic Paris at that, and is surely as discreetly French as it is Gallically discreet—and surely, gently, directly poetic. . . . In the last chapter of one of my early books, I wrote a summation of my attitude in terms of an impossible "scenario," bringing together in one order the themes and actions of all the films I had treated interpretively in the foregoing pages. I titled it "Scenario for a Comedy of Critical Hallucination." With different material and a more straightforward and compendious aim, I have done the same thing here with the total of all the movies I've written about. So to call it "The Inevitable Movie" seems . . . inevitable.

25. TV Favorites

HOWARD THOMPSON

I LOVE MOVIES. God help me. I review them.

After many years, most of them in the Movie Department of *The New York Times,* I have never been able to decide whether this passion—there must be a better word—is a help or a hindrance. But there it is, and there I stood about two months ago, on the banks of the Upper Nile, marveling at the cavalcade of paintings and stone chiselings adorning Karnak Temple, the grandest pile of ruins in the world. The frozen images seemed poised for movement. Too bad, I thought, that the ancient Egyptians couldn't have recorded themselves with a camera. And sweet irony, not too many years before, a Hollywood troupe, equipped with the best of color camera equipment, had recorded all this in a magnificent still-life canvas, only to paste against it a feeble, creaking plot labeled *Valley of the Kings.* It starred Robert Taylor and Eleanor Parker.

The picture is now on television (which is what I am edging into), duller than ever but glowingly worthwhile because of those backgrounds, especially on a color set. TV does curious things to movies. It's a curious kind of artistic sieve.

Many favorite pictures that I am going to tick off here won't be on any other best list in this volume. I will deal only with the movies shown on television, films that for various reasons have given me the most satisfaction and pleasure. They represent one of my beats on the *Times,* the daily coverage of movies beamed in the New York metropolitan area— about 250 weekly over seven channels— most of them with my very short comments as to merit. By now I must have seen about eighty percent of them all; when I haven't, I march over to a card index (maintained by my own two hands) and make out a new card based on a *Times* review by someone else. I'm not beholden to do this, for I may have seen the film and simply don't agree with a colleague. When a brand-new movie that I haven't seen comes up on TV, I simply give a hint of the content as supplied by the station, such as "Dog bites man" or vice versa, or "Heiress stalked by killer."

So here we go, with Thompson's favorite TV flicks. Let me hastily add that they do not represent my choice of the best movies of all time. Some films actually improve when shown on the home box, some classics sag; there are even some that seem better because of —not in spite of—commercial intrusions.

What are my critical standards? For one thing, fairly clear eye-sight, although late watching and rewatching (as with *Shanghai Express* the other night till 5:00 A.M.) often leaves me cockeyed. What, I ask myself, is the movie trying to do, and is it doing it well? Are there compensations that balance flaws? What about a big beautiful *Becket*? Emotionally intriguing, yes, and a gorgeous tapestry —but a thudding bore after three hours of royal and clerical wind. Another big, beautiful, expensive film, *Lawrence of Arabia,* was infinitely better, but it only touched the root of the Lawrence enigma —and after all that time.

A review is obviously one person's reactions. I try to keep my writing simple and clear, a suggestion made to me by my rock, Bosley Crowther, when I first joined the *Times.* I've never had better advice. When the operation of movie-capsule coverage for our daily television listings started about seven years ago, the comments had to be boiled down to pinhead size because of space. Brevity, I think, is still the soul of readability. Even though I wrote it, I didn't mind the label I slung on *Patton* recently. It seemed to fit:

"Aces." For the pure hell of it, and for some pure acting, I added, "Viva Scott!" And did a real platinum-plated stinker like the Taylor-Burton *Boom!* rate more than *Burp!*? Anyway, not according to *The New York Times* TV listings.

Two more things, briefly. I try to write for people, not the wise ones, the cultists or other critics—just people out front watching, same as myself. I think a critic's prime function should be that of a shopper's guide on the advisability of spending time and money in a theater. At home, before a TV set, it's time, of course.

I have been asked how the *Times* movies-on-TV capsuler sees them. The answer is—usually flat on my prat at home, an apartment in Greenwich Village, with a color set in the living room and a tiny black-and-white one in the bedroom. Sometimes I commute to test. *Black Narcissus,* with those British nuns in the Himalayas, is one beauty that holds up minus color. *The Red Shoes,* the most beautiful ballet film ever, simply does not—nor indeed how could it?

I am one nut, having a bathroom and simply liking to stir occasionally, who does not mind the intrusion of commercials if they're strategically placed and don't gobble up too much footage.

Some movies demand absolute concentration; if they're as good as the old *Shanghai Express* was the other early morning (I hadn't seen it since 1932), you don't want to miss a minute. Should one read a book and watch TV simultaneously? This one does, depending. I split not long ago between a biography of Tolstoy and an old Laurel and Hardy, shifting from one to the other. I finally put the book down, laughing and lassoed by the comics. It's possible to watch *Suez* and *In Old Chicago* with half an eye, closing in for those sandstorm and fire finales, the real meat of each. But something like *The Hurricane,* a better movie, should be absorbed altogether, I believe.

Anything that sits me down good and hard on the living-room floor in front of the set has got to be good. I may get up and prowl around a bit, but not for long. One trick I have learned after starting a black-and-white favorite in one room and ending the night lying in bed and watching the picture taper off, is not to let prone comfort trigger wishful thinking.

Don't, I tell myself, especially if the movie is lousy (and doesn't everyone?), start wondering why the stations don't show this picture

HOWARD THOMPSON

or that one—such as *Anne of Green Gables, They Won't Believe Me, The Old Maid, Only Yesterday* (introducing Margaret Sullavan), *The Southerner, Our Betters, They Knew What They Wanted, Susan and God, Blithe Spirit, Cavalcade, The Scoundrel, Three Comrades*, the early Durbin delights, *Idiot's Delight, Star of Midnight, Whipsaw, Sequoia, Roxie Hart, Miss Fane's Baby Is Stolen, Madame Du Barry, The Match King, Grand Canary* and *So Ends Our Night*. And so, often, does mine.

Most of my favorite films on TV are of the thirties, forties and fifties, simply because I find them more interesting than the later output. For my money, there's too much aimless, subjective soul-searching in the guise of art. With films finally recognized as a genuine art form (and how long it took!), how many genuinely towering movies now stand clearly outlined on a horizon that is challengingly wide open in realism and permissiveness. Let's give them time. Meanwhile, the older films, reflecting an aura of innocence for their day, telling stories with a beginning, a middle and an end, and with a breed of stars I find far more compelling than most of today's crop—these are the ones that hook me night after night at home on television. I can't resist, for instance, *Hands Across the Table*, a 1935 romantic comedy with Carole Lombard as a money-minded Manhattan manicurist, Fred MacMurray as an impoverished society playboy and Ralph Bellamy as a crippled, kindhearted millionaire. This is pure, antiquated boy-meets-girl froth but with a kind of rakishly sweet flavoring that just misses blandness. The playing by the three leads and a nice supporting cast is easy and genial. So is the smoothly turned direction of Mitchell Leisen. Possibly this is his best piloting ever. Above all, I believe, there is the natural, bubbly dialogue of Norman Krasna's scenario, based on a Vina Delmar story. This is a grand nightcap at home. If you haven't already, try it for same. The *Times* says, "Delicious, delightful and delovely."

Another favorite, with the great Lombard, is *Twentieth Century*, (1934), a screamingly funny and biting farce, brilliantly pairing the lady with John Barrymore as two former lovers and show-biz personalities playing cat-and-mouse on a train. The other passengers—a press agent, a maid, a business manager and some stranded members of a Passion Play company, along with a genteel little nut

—are almost as amusing. Howard Hawks's direction has it all shrewdly in hand, and Ben Hecht and Charles MacArthur, fortunately adapting their Broadway success, added a two-scene prologue that neatly sets up the action.

Except for that final, meandering half-hour (when I spin the dial), I'll stay up any time for *The Awful Truth* (1937), with Irene Dunne (in the funniest, slyest comedy-playing of her career) and Cary Grant as an estranged, sophisticated couple heading toward reunion through some bright situations and even brighter dialogue supplied by director Leo McCarey and scenarist Vina Delmar, who, wonder of wonders, are supposed to have penned the script piecemeal, often minutes ahead of shooting time. It worked.

Then there's *Ninotchka* (1939) for plain, pure champagne— and for the great Garbo, immensely abetted by the charming Melvyn Douglas and Ina Claire. This picture has everything, not the least of which is Ernst Lubitsch's marvelous direction, and a pearly, literate script by Charles Brackett and Billy Wilder. But take my advice. Don't overdo it. Man cannot live by champagne alone. Ten viewings is enough, at least for a while.

So is another favorite Lubitsch romp of mine, *Trouble in Paradise* (1932), with Miriam Hopkins and Herbert Marshall as a pair of jewel thieves, Kay Frances as their rich quarry and a devastating opening that nobody but Lubitsch could have concocted. It starts with the camera aimed squarely at the fat behind of Venetian garbage collector making a scoop from his gondola. Then off he poles, singing "O Sole Mio," and the camera floats upward to the brightly lighted terrace of an expensive hotel where trouble begins in paradise.

The *Times* capsule comment for this next one, exquisitely directed by Rouben Mamoulian, more or less speaks for itself: *Love Me Tonight* (1932), with Maurice Chevalier, Jeanette MacDonald, Charles Ruggles, Myrna Loy. Lovely old valentine, oozing charm and fine Rodgers-and-Hart. Dig that opening, plus the great *Isn't It Romantic?* sequence, and the obscure *Nothing but a Tailor* and *Poor Apache*.

And now two Samuel Goldwyn specials, both 1936 productions, both strong, brilliant dramas for adults, holding up beautifully now. Once you dial in on *Dodsworth*, which has Walter Huston, Ruth

Chatterton and Mary Astor as Americans roaming prewar Europe, you're unlikely to let go. Best of all, in Sidney Howard's adaptation of his own play (from Sinclair Lewis's novel), masterfully directed by William Wyler, is the riveting candor and skill of Miss Chatterton as an aging, selfish woman. Curiously, a compromise ending, changing the book, seems logical.

The strange truth about *These Three* is that Lillian Hellman's own simple, heterosexual triangularization of her calumny theme from the play, *The Children's Hour*—to appease the censors, what else?—added, and still adds up, to a stronger, more credible film than a later version with the original Lesbian theme at least implied. In this first version Miriam Hopkins, Merle Oberon and Joel McCrea are excellent—William Wyler again is at the helm. Bonita Granville is strikingly effective as the abominable, rumor-spreading youngster in the girls' school, but it is little Marcia Mae Jones, as her terrified pawn, who does the most memorable work.

William Wyler, who mus be my favorite director, had much to do with the brilliance of *The Letter* (1940), which has as fascinating a performance as Bette Davis ever gave, including *All About Eve*, which I'll touch on later.

For this one—and four scenes in particular—I'll rush home, or drop everything or sit up late any time. First is that opening, with the camera establishing the ambiance of a rubber plantation on a sultry night, an abrupt shooting on a nearby porch with the pistol-holding woman, Miss Davis, whirling to look up at an emerging moon. Then there is the meeting between Miss Davis and her victim's former mistress, Gale Sondergaard. Then Miss Davis's confession of adultery to her shattered husband, Herbert Marshall; watch her closely, as she sits, waiting, barely moving her fingers. The wind-up, when the killer-heroine is vengefully murdered—justice triumphs here, supposedly for the censors—has been called the film's only flaw. I challenge this, at least now. As we see her go prowling through a garden, knowing danger lurks, I think that such a woman might have masochistically welcomed punishment. Anyway, what a picture!

Another rubber plantation, with little art but brimming with grand, yeasty fun, is the one in *Red Dust* (1932), with Clark Gable, Jean Harlow, Mary Astor and Gene Raymond. This vintage, tin lizzie of a drama is shorter, more entertaining and infinitely more suggestively steamy than John Ford's remake, *Mogambo,* tooling around television these nights like a big African Cadillac, with (again) Gable, Ava Gardner, Grace Kelly and Donald Sinden aboard. And the Gable-Harlow *China Seas* (1935), which also had Rosalind Russell and Wallace Beery adding color and punch to a bulging, trouble-bound passenger freighter of yore, is in some ways even better.

Grand Hotel creaks a bit around the edges on TV, even with that cast. But not its all-star sister or brother, *Dinner at Eight* (1933). If ever a picture meshed, floated and finally soared primarily because of star chemistry, it's this one, which has John and Lionel Barrymore, Billie Burke, Jean Harlow, Wallace Beery, Marie Dressler, Lee Tracy, Madge Evans and more, every one of them operating at peak level.

Granted, they had ripe fodder to draw on in the adaptation of the Edna Ferber-George S. Kaufman play. But the play, when revived on Broadway several years back without that Hollywood cast, laid a succinct egg, which must prove something.

The Women (1939), another Hollywood improvement on Broadway, is a savage, scintillating movie everybody should see at least once (beware a later, musicalized version titled *The Opposite Sex*) for pure malice. Norma Shearer, Joan Crawford, Joan Fontaine, Rosalind Russell, Mary Boland and Paulette Goddard head up this one, which never wears thin (with TV smoothly extracting an out-of-date fashion show—one cut that makes sense).

Hitchcock's *Saboteur* (1942), which has Robert Cummings and Priscilla Lane in a cross-country chase involving espionage, is one film that seems to me actually enhanced by well-placed, strategic commercials on TV—at least it happened that way the last run-off. For once, the breaks seemed like natural intermission curtains in an otherwise unrelievedly episodic chain of events.

For that matter, some movies actually seem to improve in transferring from a big theater screen to the more intimate home box; pictures such as *The Old Man and the Sea, Porgy and Bess* and the antique *Dead End.* In each case, the stagey atmosphere is minimized, the drama rendered more vivid and intimate.

I am running out of space but not favorites, which requires

HOWARD THOMPSON

shifting to capsule gear. *Three Strangers* (1946), a wonderfully adroit, engrossing yarn with Geraldine Fitzgerald, Peter Lorre and Sidney Greenstreet; *A Tree Grows in Brooklyn* (1945), possibly Hollywood's finest drama of a growing girl, with a luminous portrayal by young Peggy Ann Garner; *Make Way for Tomorrow* (1937), Hollywood's most moving and skillful study of old age, with Beulah Bondi and Victor Moore; *Viva Zapata!* (1952) and *On the Waterfront* (1953), both with Marlon Brando and director Elia Kazan in peak form, and who could ask for anything more?

There are some TV regulars that are so good and so well known that the titles suffice, such as *Red Shoes, Stagecoach, All Quiet on the Western Front, All About Eve, Lost Horizon, Sunset Boulevard, The Maltese Falcon, David Copperfield, Pride and Prejudice* and the first *Mutiny on the Bounty*. And *Citizen Kane,* although some Kane addicts shriek at the thought of commercial breaks and hold out for a theater revival. Not I. And is it superfluous to suggest that any and all Astaire-and-Rogers musicals are worth seeing, at least in part? My favorites, primarily for the Gershwin and Kern scores, are *Shall We Dance?* and *Swing Time.*

And I absolutely must cite two love affairs I have kept up on television for years with two British beauties, Noel Coward's wondrously moving and touching *Brief Encounter,* and his great drama of World War II, *In Which We Serve.*

There are periodic rumbles from within that the TV industry may soon be running short of movies. What's the problem? There are enough beauties and plain good ones on hand already. Just roll 'em around again, boys. I'll be watching.

26. Auteurism, *Hawks, Hatari!* and Me

STUART BYRON

I DON'T HAVE FAVORITE *movies* so much as I have movies which I consider the best, or most representative (or even the most *favored*) of my favorite *directors*—a situation which makes me an unabashed *"auteurist,"* an application I accept without the slightest embarrassment. No critical credo has been more idiotically misunderstood as has *auteurism,* but its main tenets—or at least those which caused the greatest controversy—can, I think, be reduced to three: (1) the director is the author of the film; (2) directorial careers, their total outputs, are more important than individual films; and (3) certain Hollywood directors, when examined in light of the first two tenets, can be proven to be as cinematically interesting, emotionally rich and philosophically complex as European directors of "art films."

None of these propositions seem as startling today as they were twenty years ago when first developed by the critics associated with the Paris magazine *Cahiers du Cinéma* (among them such future directors as François Truffaut, Claude Chabrol, Jean-Luc Godard, Jacques Rivette and Erich Rohmer), or even as they were ten years ago when introduced to America by such critical pioneers as Andrew Sarris, Peter Bogdanovich, Eugene Archer, Rudi Franchi and Marshall Lewis. And it should be noted that there is at least one division of *auteurism*, mostly centered in England, which subscribes to the first and third of these postulates but not to the second, conceding only that good directors are more likely to make good films than are bad ones, but insisting that each film must be judged only as a thing unto itself and without reference to the director's other movies.

Auteurism exploded with a bomblike force everywhere in the world in the early sixties. In most European countries, after the initial shock wore off, it was absorbed rather easily into the critical mainstream, already-established reviewers becoming semi-*auteurists* if they never could equal the enthusiasm of younger purists. In England or Sweden or Italy today it would be considered odd if a critic did *not* think Alfred Hitchcock a great director and Samuel Fuller a near-great one. In the United States, though, there has continued to be great resistance to the whole idea, especially among the Morningside Heights intellectuals, largely, I believe, because the films and directors most in contention are *ours*; the anti-Hollywood phobia will, perhaps must, die last in its home country. And so objections continue to be raised.

Isn't filmmaking, especially in Hollywood, a "collaborative" art? No, it isn't, for at least three reasons—one objective, one qualitative, one subjective.

Objective: Auteurism resurrected only a limited number of Hollywood directors, and those it resurrected were, except in an extremely limited number of cases (and even those are only partial exceptions), men who directed not only actors and cameras but also writers. Of course ninety percent of Hollywood direction tends to be hackwork, but Ford and Lubitsch and Sternberg and Borzage happen not to be in that ninety percent; they chose their projects at early stages, and told their screenwriters what they wanted (they often wrote their scripts themselves but declined screen credit, due to a combination of union rules and Hollywood custom). Those occasional articles in *The New York Times* championing scriptwriting against *auteurist* claims are simply irrelevant to the argument. Moreover, no one has yet to produce a single magazine article (much less a book) which proves a continuity or depth to the work of *any* Hollywood scriptwriter to equal the studies devoted to a score of American directors. The burden of proof, indeed, is now on the anti-*auteurists*; I await the study of Ben Hecht or Dudley Nichols which will find in their work anything approaching what Robin Wood found in Hitchcock or John Baxter in Ford. Of course, scriptwriters affect directors, but only as colors or styles affect painters—as things to *use* toward a personal vision. John Ford has a "Dudley Nichols period" and a "Frank Nugent period" the way Picasso has a blue period or a Cubist period. And saying that the "look" of Ford's films depends on their different cinematographers is saying no more than that a Beethoven piano étude sounds different from a string quartet.

Qualitative: In general, the best acting and the best cinematography are done for the best directors. Nonetheless, enough exceptions abound in film history to give pause. There is such a thing as great photography in an otherwise undistinguished film, as such men as Gregg Toland and Leon Shamroy and Conrad Hall have proved. And there are actors who have created screen personae who can transcend direction: Dietrich and Garbo and West and Brando and Bogart and Belmondo.

But it is a question of degree. Acting and cinematography are arts, but they are *minor* arts—like still photography or cabinet-making. Compared to direction—which can encompass moral and historical and poetical factors of the greatest dimension—they are limited in what they can do. It is a matter of cultural priorities; Chippendale has its place, but it isn't beside Rembrandt. People who prefer Bogart to Hawks are like people who prefer antique shows to museums. Of course, stars create "myths" and "national dreams," but that's part of the history of sociology, not of aesthetics.

Subjective: If operagoers stopped listening to opera libretti *through* the music written for them, most opera houses would close their doors permanently within six months. Not that, say, Da Ponte is bad (great composers, like great film directors, tend to prefer good writers to poor ones), but Da Ponte's *Don Giovanni* would hardly be worth a revival once every fifty years, much less each season as part of a permanent repertory. The problem is a thorny one; the history of opera supports the view that the composer had the final say whenever a dispute with a librettist arose. But even if this were not so, even if it could be proven that Da Ponte and Mozart were equally responsible for their works, the fact remains that they live because of a kind of *collective subjectivity* developed over the years on the part of critics and audiences. We see *Don Giovanni* as Mozart's because if we didn't it wouldn't give us as much pleasure.

All sorts of valuable theories have been advanced as to why the cinema is a visual or director's art. To take an example close to hand, I was recently impressed by an argument advanced by my colleague William Paul who, in the context of a review of *Portnoy's Complaint* in *Rolling Stone,* convinced me that the novel is the art of reaction while the film is the art of action, and that therefore the former is a writer's and the latter a director's medium. And although it may be true that the stage director can contribute casting, lighting and blocking to a playwright's art, the balance "tips" in favor of the director of a film because he has all these *plus* camera movement, editing and framing. And there is the historical factor to take into account: the cinema having begun as a silent, purely visual medium, the tradition developed early that the director had the last word over the writer, whereas the opposite situation obtains on the stage.

Yet all of this seems to me to be begging a question—a question rather frightening in its dimensions, but one that must be faced. The fact remains that the play is permanent while the production is transient, and *that* is why one must try to see through the production to the play. Direction *can* be essential in the theater; the *locus classicus* of the recent past, I suppose, is Elia Kazan's mounting of the original 1957 production of William Inge's *The Dark at the Top of the Stairs,* which convinced almost everyone (Robert Brustein a notable exception) that it was a good play, a judgment which falls apart whenever the play is staged by anyone else. Yet Kazan's magic has no ultimate meaning in the history of dramatic literature; it has disappeared and can only be reproduced by Kazan himself, an unlikely prospect. Against this stands a concrete and hard-to-deal-with fact: films are frozen forever on celluloid.

And they are directed. Again, *qua* script. I believe that the screenplays written for Ford and Hawks and Hitchcock are superior to those written for lesser directors. But it doesn't matter. A "bad" script which has been transmogrified into something rich and strange is as *meaningfully* "bad" as is Kazan's staging of Inge is "good." We don't watch the script, we watch the script *through* the director's eyes.

Now—and here is my essential point—we don't have to do this; we can, if we wish, ignore everything the director does, despite all that has been written about how the screen is inherently or naturally "visual." It isn't. This is a point difficult to prove, since even a great novel turned into a screenplay, or a stage play which has to any extent been "opened up" for the screen, is not precisely what it was as source material. But there are a few more or less "pure" examples, most recently Sidney Lumet's *Long Day's Journey into Night,* which carried no script credit whatsoever because this greatest of all American plays was filmed word for word. And it was awful, most notably in its casting and playing; a film which depends on slow revelation of character cannot be cast and played in close-up in such a manner that all is revealed from the start (which is why what seemed miscasting in Mike Nichols's *Who's Afraid of Virginia Woolf?* worked out so well). And *Long Day's Journey* was mislit, miscut and misshot. And yet we could, if we wish, ignore all of this, and just listen to the words, and declare it a great film. Which is precisely what a number of respected critics did. In the end, one is tempted to ask: "So what? We already *had* the play. Is *Otello* a great opera because it is based on a great play?"

No, the fact is that if we choose to watch a film visually, choose to watch it as a director's art, it is for the same reasons that we choose to watch opera as a composer's art. We *choose* to. First, because we want to see something done in a new and irretrievable way. We have come to watch an opera or a film, not a play or a novel. And second, because the proof is in the pudding. Who, forced to choose between brass and gold, would select the former? If Da Ponte, through Mozart, provides a transcendental experience that Da Ponte alone does not, why deny yourself the pleasure of that experience?

The original *auteurists* felt as though they had stumbled upon an undiscovered gold mine. Considered merely as scripts, the films of certain American directors seemed little better than the dime and popular novels on which they were based or which they resembled.

STUART BYRON

Seen through their directors, the films seemed works of genius. And here was the beauty part: you didn't have to throw away the "art films"; it wasn't Bergman *or* Hawks, but Bergman *and* Hawks (though, for a later faction of *auteurists,* it became Hawks and only Hawks). For the same money, you got twice the pleasure. Since most people, including critics, enjoy pleasure, critics in most countries sought to seek out the mysteries of *auteurism,* to join in the collective subjectivity at looking at Hollywood films. Why torture yourself? Not so to the Establishment critics in the United States. Despite the great many articles and books which have provided depth analyses of American directors, Stanley Kauffmann and Pauline Kael and John Simon refuse even to test the waters, to give them a try. I can only conclude that they are a bunch of cultural masochists.

This same "pudding-proof" applies to the director's-career-versus-individual-works question. Actually, of all the objections initially raised against *auteurism,* this question seems the most dated today. Film versus career never made for a serious argument in any country other than the United States, and for obvious reasons: it was here that the New Criticism of Ransom and Brooks, with its emphasis on "the poem itself"—a necessary corrective to the simplistic biographical criticism of the immediate past, but no more than that —was invented, and in 1960–62 it was still in its heyday. No one nowadays takes New Criticism to Brooks's extremes; if anyone did, she or he could never write books on individual writers and could never use words like "Faulkneresque." The fact remains that artists create great individual works *and* create worlds and languages of their own; how to relate these to each other is always in flux in our minds, and all we know is that our Housmanesque hairs stand on end while shaving *both* when we think of "Ode on a Grecian Urn" and when we think of Keats's work as a whole. Even in the days of the first *auteurist* assault, New Criticism was questionable enough that few hesitated to say "Pirandellian" or "Miltonesque" where applicable. Yet so pervasive was the "collaborative effort" view of filmmaking in 1962 that, incredible as it may seem today, such words were unknown even for foreign directors; one just didn't say "Dreyeresque," for example. Today, when even middle-brow critics throw around "Bergmanesque" and "Fellinian" with abandon, the pudding-proof reigns supreme: our hairs stand on end when we think *Persona* and when we think "Bergman," and who would want it otherwise?

The singular masterpiece by the author who never again achieved greatness has never lasted long in critical esteem; presently one pays more attention to the recently rediscovered late Tennyson than to "The Rubáiyát of Omar Khayyám" or "The Hound of Heaven." The same process is beginning to take place in film history: even diehard anti-*auteurists* find "minor" Murnau or Lang more interesting than Robert Wiene's *The Cabinet of Doctor Caligari* or E. A. Dupont's *Variety*, two one-time "masterpieces of German expressionism" by directors who never again produced anything memorable. A minimum of resonances from other films by the same man seems necessary for one of his works to attain classic stature.

This part of the *auteur* controversy, inasmuch as it still exists, has boiled down to the commercial Hollywood cinema, for it seems that one cannot appreciate the greatness of Ford or Hawks or Leo McCarey until one has seen a lot of their films. My own experience confirms this: one look at *Rules of the Game* and you know Renoir's great; but it takes one look at each of ten Fords or—and this is crucial—ten looks at *one* Ford before the same conclusion is reached about the American director. And in trying to understand this paradox, a strange analogy occurs to me, an analogy that places the most commercial of art forms alongside one of the most esoteric: one undergoes a similar learning experience in regard to poetry.

It is a commonplace that the modern poet creates his own world and his own language with its own connotations. Wallace Stevens is an exemplary example. To one who has never before read him, a poem like "The Emperor of Ice Cream" is baffling at first reading. Who is this "emperor," a word that makes no sense in its usual literal or metaphoric meanings? Now there are two common ways to go about finding out. The first—which is the more usual, since it requires less patience—is to read some more Stevens poems. From "Sunday Morning," for example, one might get a vague impression of an atheistic world in which man has created his own heaven in the guise of imagination, and a reading of "To

STUART BYRON

the One of Fictive Music," with its explicit references to a "goddess" of art, might make the poet's usage of deities suddenly click into place, at which point the meaning of "emperor" becomes immediately clear. Alternatively, one could read and re-read "The Emperor of Ice Cream," eliminating all the possible misinterpretations, until the right one comes to mind.

Just as the modern poet appears at first to be writing nonsense, so the commercial Hollywood director seems at first to be filming clichés. But in perhaps a score of them, a complex world view is just as "hidden"—and just as exhilarating to discover—as in Wallace Stevens, though it's sure to consist not only of language but of modes of acting, camera placement, scripting and editing. Though I think that great directors, like other great artists, tend to be consistently great, I also think that each of their great films can stand on its own, gaining only in resonance and understanding by reference to other works. Even John Simon, forced to see *Hatari!* ten times, would understand its greatness.

Truth to tell, Hawks is not my favorite director. If I were forced to rank them, he'd place fourth, behind Ford, Renoir and Robert Bresson. But Hawks holds a special place as a rallying cry of *auteurism* because, of all those directors considered really great by *auteurists,* he is the most "commercial" (Ford, Lubitsch, Sternberg and the other "pantheon" names are conceded to have made a great film or two even by Establishmentarians). Truffaut and the original French *auteurists* sometimes termed themselves "Hitchcocko-Hawksians," and as Joseph McBride has pointed out, when *auteurism* first hit the United States a critic could always get a laugh by defining these strange creatures as the people who liked Howard Hawks. Moreover, it is through Hawks that most people "come to" *auteurism*; it is usually while watching a Hawks film that one "sees the light" (*auteurists* are fond of biblical expressions). William Paul and Jon Landau describe such experiences, and it was mine also; sitting at the Museum of Modern Art during the summer of 1962, watching the retrospective organized by Peter Bogdanovich, I couldn't understand the excitement over all those seemingly simple action films and comedies. And then one day (I think it was during 1935's *Ceiling Zero,* but it might have been 1939's *Only Angels Have Wings*), it all suddenly hit me: at once I understood even the films I had seen—and dismissed—days before. I was hooked on a certain philosophy of cinema and for good. Though I discovered John Ford the next year, and finally decided he was the greater of the two great American action directors, Hawks holds a special autobiographical place in my heart.

Simple action films and comedies—that's what Hawks's films seem like at first. Among the former can be found groups of men who fly or test planes (1930's *The Dawn Patrol,* the aforementioned *Ceiling Zero* and *Only Angels Have Wings,* 1943's Air Force); race cars (1932's *The Crowd Roars,* 1965's *Redline 7000*); pioneer in the Old West (1948's *Red River,* 1952's *The Big Sky*); preserve law and order in frontier towns (1959's *Rio Bravo,* 1967's *El Dorado,* 1970's *Rio Lobo*); catch animals (*Hatari!*). In the earliest days of the Hawks rediscovery, it was common to note in these films a unifying plot element of male "professionals" who were "doing a job," and thus consign Hawks to a kind of tight-lipped existentialism *avant la lettre,* relating him to Chandler and Hammett—and, at best, Hemingway. The problem with this approach was that it left out or could not account very well for a good half of the comedies—those in which there were few elements of male camaraderie or professionalism—nor for such seeming aberrations as *Scarface* (1932), *The Big Sleep* (1946) and *Land of the Pharaohs* (1955). Still another quasi-Freudian view identified "maturity" as a main theme, and explained the comedies by noting that in them characters are reduced to "infantile" behavior.

There is something to each of these notions, and surely one measure of a great director is that his work can sustain varied interpretations. Still, neither of them located in Hawks that sense of history which, to me, is the mark of the great director. Here, of course, one must be ultimately subjective: a great director, to this writer, presents through his films a world view so thematically and stylistically complete that one feels at times that he is an Atlas precariously balancing the globe on his shoulders. His best film is the one that most realizes this view.

With Hawks one must begin, I think, with comedies like 1938's *Bringing Up Baby,* 1949's *I Was a Male War Bride* and 1952's *Monkey Business,* in all of which Cary Grant becomes not so much "infantile" as associated with a lower form of life. He is, in *Bringing*

262   S T U A R T   B Y R O N

Up Baby, an anthropologist working with dinosaurs who eventually gets involved in a hunt for a lost leopard—becoming finally, *like* a leopard, on all fours. In *War Bride,* as a French general trying to emigrate to the United States, his final degradation is to wear a wig made from a horse's mane, and in *Business* he drinks a potion meant for laboratory chimps. And as Robin Wood has astutely pointed out, *Scarface,* whatever its stature as a classic gangster film, should really be classified with the comedies because its mobster protagonist, Paul Muni, becomes more and more ape-like as the film, and his downfall, progress—a transformation suggested totally by acting and lighting. In each case, then, the Hawksian "loss of dignity" is a step downward in the evolutionary scale.

It is my proposal that Hawks should be understood as a Darwinian without regrets. The descent of man is, for him, the essential knowledge of (as one of his film titles has it) the *Twentieth Century.* Man's superiority to, and yet relationship with, the animal world is his limitation and glory. He locates the glory more specifically in technology—Hawk's continuing metaphor for mankind's mastery of all nonhuman environments, be they animal, vegetable or mineral. In all the dramas, there is a "nemesis" to be conquered —space in the airplane dramas, speed in the racing stories, land or water in the epics, animals in *Hatari!*; when the nemesis is human, as in *The Dawn Patrol* or *Rio Bravo,* he is a "villain" of such abstractness—characterless and usually dressed in black—as to be almost non-human. All these nemeses, it seems to me, are but symbols of man's evolutionary past.

This vision leads, on the positive side, to a kind of atheistic humanism. God is dead, all we have is other men—but what a glory is man! And it *is* a vision—a realization through story structure, acting and camera placement. It is the way the groups of men are presented—casually, with small gestures of trust in each other, the dialogue frequently overlapping to communicate the unity of the group. It is the way death is accepted stoically—each man has attempted to master the environment, and his unity with the race in that pursuit is his monument. The way characters *care* for each other—how, for example, in *Rio Bravo,* the alcoholic Dean Martin, first seen groveling on the floor after coins in a western saloon (precisely like a primate), is brought to moral strength by friend John Wayne; in a classic scene, Wayne continues passing cigarettes to Martin until the latter is able to light one. The way new characters, men and women, are assimilated into the group, and the way old and seemingly useless ones are kept in it. In the dramas there is usually also the central image of technology, about which Hawks has a few illusions, since it can be represented by as benign an invention as the riverboat in *The Big Sky* or as menacing as the dynamite in *Rio Bravo*.

There are the neutral elements to this Darwinism—such as the frequent need for newer group members to prove that they are "good enough," a kind of natural selection. In several films a character who has lost a finger or hand loses the girl to his more "perfect" competitor. Yet none of this ever seems ugly, and Hawks is never the "social Darwinist" or believer in progress, since, to him, all technology is on the same plane, from the pyramid-building in *Land of the Pharaohs* to the bomber-flying in *Air Force*.

But there is a negative side to all this, too. God is dead—and Hawks does not avert his eyes from the implications of this. For if we can take comfort from the contrast with our evolutionary past, we also must recognize that we are living in a spiritual void. The race cars in *Redline 7000* constantly circle the same track—and as Hawks shoots it, the empty oval inside becomes a symbol of the godless nothingness outside. The frequent shots of the train exterior whizzing through the black night in *Twentieth Century,* the barren mountain peaks against the sky during the climactic flight of *Only Angels Have Wings,* the sound of the church bell completely obscuring any religious purpose during the first gunfight in *El Dorado*— all these are acknowledgements of a void. Hawks's frequent admission in interviews that he doesn't understand what the title *The Big Sleep* means, and the discomfort of critics with the most obvious solution—"death"—can be clarified by the proposal that the monicker means "nothing," a thought which also justifies the famous fact that the film seems eminently satisfying even though no one can follow the plot; human *activity itself* is holding off "nothing" in *The Big Sleep.* The most unpleasant protagonist ever created by Hawks is the king in *Land of the Pharaohs* who has a pyramid built to insure his "immortality." For if God to the Christian does not give but *is* love, then to the atheist Hawks technology does not give but *is* immortality.

With the instinctiveness that makes him a great curator but a lousy critic, Henri Langlois, director of the Cinémathèque Française, once entitled an article "Hawks Homme Moderne" and then didn't explain in the body of the piece just what it was that made Hawks so "modern." And yet one can understand this failure, for almost nothing of Hawks's ultimate concerns is ever made *verbally* explicit. According to the Kaels and the Macdonalds and the Simons, such a modern world view didn't enter the cinema until Bergman and Antonioni came along with their explicit verbalizations that God is dead and there's a void out there. Yet I think it's arguable that, inasmuch as he has no nostalgia for religion, Hawks is more starkly modern than Bergman (or for that matter, Wallace Stevens)—and that he can only be compared thematically, among the major modern figures, with Samuel Beckett.

Now, as I've mentioned, there are *auteurists* who believe that this implicitness makes Hawks a greater filmmaker than Bergman. I am not one: I consider Robert Bresson, for instance, greater than Hawks despite the fact that he makes his viewpoint verbally clear; and I think that the still young Bergman, given a satisfactory "late period," could outdistance Hawks. To those *auteurist* extremists who actually dislike Bergman and Antonioni, I am forever quoting two thoughts of W. H. Auden: "Those who condemn didactic poetry can only do so because they condemn didacticism and must disapprove *a fortiori* of didactic prose," and "Too exclusive a taste is always an indiscriminate taste. If a person asserts that he worships Donne but abhors Pope, or vice versa, one suspects that he does not really appreciate his favorite." To Kael and Simon I say: to worship Bergman and not Hawks is not to appreciate your favorite.

Still, a *little* didacticism in a Hollywood director never hurts, and it is for that reason that *Hatari!,* his 1962 movie about catching zoo animals in Africa, seems to me Hawks's greatest film. Man's evolutionary past need not be abstracted or sublimated into something else; catching animals is, after all, dealing directly with the lower orders. All the thematic and stylistic elements of professionalism and male camaraderie are present in John Wayne's international team, which includes Gerard Blain and Hardy Kruger:

the testing as to whether a newcomer is good enough, the hostility turning into professional friendship, the caring for one another. But the nihilism is here integrated into the structure of the film itself, which alternates between action-packed daytime exteriors and fatigued game-playing interiors. The compound becomes almost a sectarian "church" in the midst of a void, indicated directly via a series of extraordinary dissolves that punctuate the tension-relax-tension rhythm. The most striking of these is a dissolve from night-time relaxation to the head of a giraffe—a mute, mindless "void" that is *also* ancestor to man. Moreover, the film is explicit in the importance of technology: once, Wayne and Elsa Martinelli, who plays a photographer, pass by African tribesmen tending a centuries-old well; later, Red Buttons builds a primitive rocket which causes a net to entrap monkeys in trees. All technology—from the Dawn of Man to the Space Age—is seen on the same plane, and equally celebrated.

To be honest, though, there are other, more subjective factors which dictate the choice of *Hatari!* as "my Hawks."

The first has to do with women. As a homosexual somewhat involved in the gay liberation movement, I share many of the attitudes of the concurrent women's liberation movement; both, of course, are against gender-defined "roles." Now a debate has arisen as to Hawks's women, who are very special, very consistent in his work, and very much his own. There is a "Hawksian woman," from Jean Arthur in *Only Angels Have Wings* on through Lauren Bacall in *The Big Sleep* and Angie Dickinson in *Rio Bravo,* and ending with the trio of women in *Rio Lobo*. They are aggressive and independent but at the same time hard and masculine. Thus, an argument ensues. Pauline Kael and Beverly Walker, for example, think that Hawks is the ultimate male chauvinist because his women must all be "accepted" into a "male bonding" by learning to act like men. Other feminist film critics, such as Naomi Weiss, declare that Hawks's women eschew role-playing and are the most consistently liberated women on the American screen.

I think that the debate is valid in the case of Dickinson in *Rio Bravo,* usually considered Hawks's most perfect female creation. True, she is independent—but, like most Hawks women, she is a dance hall entertainer, thus someone who earns her living as a

266   STUART BYRON

sex object. And though she changes and "softens," she does so in a way undefined by gender; Wayne "softens" too, in *Rio Bravo*. Elsa Martinelli may not be as great an actress as Angie Dickinson—and there are ways in which the female role in *Hatari!* is a shallower creation than the one in *Rio Bravo*—but two things have to be taken into account. Martinelli earns her living as a photographer, and thus, unlike almost any other Hawks heroine, does a job a man could do (indeed, the men at the compound are expecting a male photographer before she appears). And there are elements in her character which are distinctly feminine—a displayed maternal and gentle instinct in the caring of animals, for example, which has no equivalent in, say, *Rio Bravo*.

My second reason for preferring *Hatari!* over all other Hawks's films is that it is about the movies itself. All great art is ultimately about art, of course, but *Hatari!* is a landmark instance. It is the film that proves that because of the cinema's relationship to reality, you can do *anything* if you are life-like enough. *Hatari!* is really genre-less; it begins as a tragedy (a man has been gored by a rhino) and ends up as a slapstick comedy (elephants knock over food counters in Nairobi). Because he involves us so much in its personalities, Hawks performs this switch with effortless ease. *Hatari!* does not really have much of a plot; it's just "a hunting season from beginning to end," says Hawks.

The film was shot in 1961, just about the same time that Godard and Truffaut were making their first films. The major contribution of the New Wave, it seems to me, was its discovery that personality can substitute for incident. And from whom did the makers of *Breathless* and *Shoot the Piano Player* learn this? From at least two French sources—Vigo and Renoir, certainly. But mostly from Hawks, for whom it had long been a principle. In *Hatari!* as much as in *Breathless*, however, it became a truly radical principal and affected an entire generation of filmmakers. In the early years of the decade, a 65-year-old man and a couple of Parisian youngsters found themselves at the same artistic point—and the rest, as they say, is history.

27. Docks of New York

MARTIN RUBIN

I CANNOT TELL A LIE. *The Searchers* is my favorite film. But the excellent recent article by Joseph McBride and Michael Wilmington in *Sight and Sound,* while certainly not definitive, is sufficiently comprehensive that I feel it will take some time to absorb it before moving on to deeper explorations of this western epic which at its heart is a mystery, in the sense that death or the myth of the United States is a mystery. At the moment, I could envision doing no more than embroidering Messrs. McBride and Wilmington's analysis with specific points that they failed to raise. Such as the fact that the idiot Ol' Mose always appears on the scene just before Chief Scar. Or why Martin Pawley is continually being wrapped up in a blanket, like a cocoon. Or how we are supposed to take Martin Pawley's mixture of Indian blood: is it an impure stain expurgated and then forgotten in the course of the story, or does Ford see a solution to racial tensions in the fractionally interracial marriage of Martin and Laurie at the end—let us not forget that their children will be one-sixteenth Cherokee. Eventually, I envision a grand treatment of myth and style, perhaps along Fiedleresque lines. But all that seems many years or a single inspiration away, and the most sublime film deserves nothing halfway.

As for Mizoguchi's *Sansho the Bailiff*, I'm frankly still a little overawed by it. I am still a very young man, and I must admit that at this time I feel uncomfortable writing about foreign films—I worry about getting the context all wrong. How much do we miss in a Mizoguchi film that we take for granted in the background of a Ford film? But as long as we're dreaming, that article would begin by pointing out that virtually every shot in *Sansho* has a foreground, a background and a middleground. "What else is new?" you might wonder, but take another close look at *Sansho* with that in mind, and you'll see what I mean. It would be a way of beginning to understand the extraordinary *wholeness* of Mizoguchi's world. And I can't forget the final shot, in which the camera cranes up from Zushio and his blind mother to a solitary old man picking seaweed in a cove. Like many good camera movements, this one connects ideas, but on the grandest scale. Here we have the remnants of a noble family, torn by exile and racked by personal tragedy, and here we have a peasant, in whose name it has all taken place; the juxtaposition is unbearably moving. What I've just said represents about one-millionth of *Sansho the Bailiff*. One of these days—

So I'm writing about *Docks of New York*. I feel no compunction about doing so because it seems to me that when a film reaches a certain level of greatness, any calibrated distinctions—Number 1, 2, 3—become academic and largely pointless. This article could have just as easily been about Roberto Rossellini's *India*, a film that opened vast possibilities for the mixing of documentary and fictional forms which haven't even begun to be explored; or F. W. Murnau's *Tabu*, the cinema's greatest exercise in abstraction; or Frank Borzage's *Moonrise*, a film unlike any other, about which I hear too little, and which for pure formal excitement cannot be beat; or Jean-Luc Godard's *Contempt*, in which the director stands exactly on the bridge between classicism and modernism, and we see an entire era of filmmaking irrevocably passing into another; or D. W. Griffith's *Birth of a Nation*, one of those official great films that is actually great, although many critics tend to forget about it in an understandable desire to reclaim Griffith's later work; or even *The Shanghai Gesture*, by our friend Josef Von Sternberg.

I picked *Docks of New York* because it seemed to me that the silent cinema would be neglected in an anthology like this one (apparently I was right), and because Josef Von Sternberg is a director about whom some misconceptions need clearing up—most notably his handling of character. Through *Docks of New York,* I have also tried to define a general style of filmmaking which, although I would never prescribe it, I generally consider the richest. One more thing: I believe that at least once in his life a critic should really *analyze* a film. Just to show he can do it. Just as a mathematician shows he knows the tables, or a dancer shows he knows the old two-step. I picked this opportunity to do so because I assumed that part of the definition of the greatest films would be that they could stand up to this sort of intensive analysis, whereas anything lesser couldn't. The following article is an attempt to see if my assumption was correct.

"It is when the author tries to show his own feelings that he succeeds the least in expressing his personality."
—JEAN RENOIR

Docks of New York (1928), Sternberg's silent masterpiece, is detached, ironic, and contemptuous of its own sentimental plot; yet it is also uncommonly moving, tender, humanistic, and one might even say, sentimental. The actors are directed so rigorously that their roles seem programmed rather than acted—each is allowed a few stylized gestures which are repeated endlessly with variations—yet their performances are among the most brilliant, sympathetic, and emotionally valid on silent film. The film's style is controlled to the point of schematism, yet it is completely nondeterministic, unacademic, and as devoted to the independent evolutions of the characters as a Renoir film.

Like Murnau's *City Girl* (1930), Keaton's *The Cameraman* (1928), and Seastrom's *The Wind* (1928), *Docks of New York* represents the final maturation of the American silent cinema. In these films, command of the medium has reached a point where everything but the most essential has been stripped away. Their form is so refined and controlled that the slightest variations become incredibly expressive.

Thus Murnau, the virtuoso of atmospheric long shots (*Nosfer-*

atu), forceful tracking shots (*The Last Laugh*), and violent lighting (*Faust*), goes on to make *City Girl,* a film which contains two or three tracking shots, no stylized lighting, the most ordinary locales and characters, and which is composed almost entirely in medium shots. When a country boy, in Chicago to sell wheat futures, learns of a stock drop, a tracking shot leaves him isolated at the side of a busy city street. This, the film's long shot, is all that's necessary to provide sufficient motivation for the quickness of his developing relationship with the city girl, which might otherwise seem coincidental and forced. Such a total command of simplicity, restraint, and proportion is usually known as classicism.

What these classical films strip away are plot incidents and photographic "effects." *The Wind, City Girl,* and *Docks of New York* could be plot-summarized by Walter Winchell in a taciturn mood, and their stylistics will not send MacGowan, Montagu, Spottiswoode et al scurrying back to amend their tomes on film technique. The point of this scuttling of visual and narrative props is to liberate character for a realistic development hitherto unknown in film.

Previously, directors usually maintained a one-on-one attitude toward their material. They expressed their attitude directly *in* the world of the film—for example, by maintaining a consistent attitude toward it (Stroheim), by fashioning it directly to their meanings (early Griffith), or by imposing an attitude on it in the form of a character (Chaplin). Toward the end of the silent era, however, the filmmaker begins to express himself *through* the world of the film, which stands apart as a given, a catalyst, a metaphor for reality. Of course, the filmmaker creates this world, but he doesn't have to construct it to directly serve his meanings. Instead, he removes himself from it only in order to involve himself in it anew.

This form of involvement is a style of indirect, rather than direct, observation. Interpretation becomes more important than origination; the attitude of the filmmaker toward his material becomes more existential than descriptive: committed to the irreducible independence of the world of the film, and grounded in the experience (rather than the recording or creation) of existence. Out of this dialectic comes the concept of the Hollywood *auteur,* who doesn't have to choose the story, write the script, or cast the actors in order to make a film which is entirely personal. (The ultimate decadence of this approach is *cinéma verité*.)

The characters are a part of this world, but an independent part. Their relationship to the world of the film is a metaphor (but not necessarily more than a metaphor) for the filmmaker's relation to his material. The characters, the world, and the style of the film are independent entities integrated into a single expression—unlike, for example, *The Birth of a Nation*, where the characters are integrated into the world of the film but their independence is limited.

When Griffith cuts together shots of Colonel Cameron sitting on the porch of his antebellum home in *Birth of a Nation*, the main point is not to acknowledge his existence in the film, but to clarify his *function* in the director's plan: repeated, static setups implant an ideal of the stability of the past for the director to base his subsequent argument on. But when Griffith cuts to a high-angle shot of Lincoln pacing the floor of his darkened dining room in his slippers in *Abraham Lincoln* (1930), he affirms the independence of the character as a man (the slippers, which work against the tone of the rest of the shot), as a part of history (the heroic lighting), and as the filmmaker sees him (the high angle). The quality of the setting—in this case, its spaciousness—establishes it as a constant that unifies and supports all these conceptions, allowing them to co-exist without constricting them. Such a shot would strike a false note in *Birth of a Nation* because none of the characters is integral enough to support it; it would need so much elaboration that it would ultimately constrict the character rather than open him up.

Similarly, it's a long way from Lillian Gish forcing a smile by turning up the corners of her mouth in *Broken Blossoms* (1919) to the even more intense stoic despair registered in her subliminally unfocused eyes in *The Wind*. That's because the earlier film is an admirable parable that works directly on the audience's consciousness, whereas the later film is a study of existence that mingles filmmaker, character, and audience in a common meeting ground of observation and interpretation.

Consequently, most of *Broken Blossoms*'s most effective shots are constructed straight into the camera, while most of *The Wind*'s most effective shots are constructed horizontally and obliquely to the camera. In *Broken Blossoms*, when Richard Barthelmess leans

MARTIN RUBIN

into the foreground before deciding not to molest Gish, he pushes the shot forward in a short, arrested motion that reveals all we need to know about the action; after Gish is raped in *The Wind*, the camera glances off her in sideways panning shots that keep us speculative. The character's independent and evolving interpretation of the event in *The Wind* is just as important as our own or the director's, and, in fact, each one complements, reinforces, and enriches the other.

The intertwining of independent elements in a film results in less clarity but greater depth. It allows a greater subtlety and more unobtrusive directorial manipulation than before. The director's themes are so fluidly embedded in the actions, characters and relationships of the plot that the slightest play of one element against another becomes a means of significant expression independent of prior manipulation of these elements. These late silent films may represent the last flowering of a doomed art, but they also point forward (as the citation of *Abraham Lincoln* has already suggested) to a type of Hollywood narrative sound film that will be influential for the next thirty years. The elements which constitute their extraordinary depth and mobility are precisely the elements common to some of the greatest masterpieces of the sound era—*The Searchers, Rio Bravo, The Wrong Man, The Magnificent Ambersons, Tarnished Angels*—while a parallel series of films with more directly constructed worlds—*Moonrise, Written on the Wind, Rancho Notorious, Shock Corridor*—has a closer link with the films of the early silent period.

So where does Sternberg fit into all this? Most readers familiar with his work will probably see the point about subtlety, since few directors are as demanding in approaching their subjects indirectly, through nuances and shifts in detail. Sternberg himself has said, "It is obvious that the greater a work of art the less are its merits immediately apparent." It is obvious that he applied this maxim to his own work.

But character? Sternberg is known as a creator of surfaces, not characters. Why, one can't even concentrate on a face because of the highlights, veils, bits of lace, nets, mirrors and assorted gimcracks that are constantly distracting the viewer's eye. The director himself has done much to popularize this view, thanks to a confusion caused by his unflattering comments about actors. For example, Olga Baclanova, one of the secondary leads in *Docks of New York*, is referred to by Sternberg in his autobiography as "having no more importance than someone who had to do no more than lift a mug of beer." John Grierson once described one of Sternberg's films as "the most beautiful picture ever produced in Hollywood, and the least human." This critical view of Sternberg was to prevail as his career continued; it was assumed that he steadily perfected the art of key lighting to the exclusion of the human condition.

In fact, Sternberg's detachment from his characters is a measure of respect, not disinterest. This is simply because Sternberg's characters don't reveal themselves directly, like rhetorical constructs, but obliquely, like human beings usually do. For example, the characters in *The Shanghai Gesture* (1941), his greatest sound film, are constantly trumpeting their self-images at each other; but these are constantly belied by their real images, revealed eventually and as a matter of course by the mere probabilities of existence—like the roulette wheel that governs Mother Gin Sling's Casino. In general Sternberg believes that patience and detachment will reveal more accurate fodder for compassion than the involvement achieved by embracing a character spontaneously.

So perhaps the best place to start with *Docks of New York* is with the characters, as incarnated in the extraordinary performances of George Bancroft and Betty Compson. Bancroft's Bill Roberts, a stoker, moves through the film with the easy implacability of a bemused fullback. He has but a single facial expression: an amiable preoccupied look that seems to be continually contemplating something, but whether it's his last glass of beer, the meaning of life, or simply nothing at all is not for me to say. This reflective air counterpoints the robotlike swagger of his massive body and adds a dimension of elusiveness to the character.

Betty Compson's Mae at first strikes one as quite different from Bancroft, but we soon see that this is a case of surface contrasts being used to point up essential similarities, and that major distinctions in personality are caused by the slightest gradations. If Bancroft is characterized by a graceful rigidity, Compson's impression is one of a weary fluidity. Her body is draped languidly on her

MARTIN RUBIN

frame like a dress on a hanger. Her glum, pursed lips shift easily and imperceptibly from an apathetic deadpan to a wan, tentative smile, allowing a glimpse of an infinite reach of emotion which lies somewhere between hopeless optimism and wistful pessimism. A constant in her performance is that her tired eyes are continually shifting around, as if nothing is worth holding their attention very long, and nothing could surprise her—she's seen all that before.

There are a couple of secondary characters of some importance. Mitchell Lewis plays Bancroft's chief, and Olga Baclanova is Lewis's wife. Their function in the film is a combination of plot machinery and a sort of chorus commenting on the inevitable future of the Bancroft-Compson relationship. Their performances are for the most part so repressed that Bancroft and Compson positively seem character actors in comparison. Which, of course, is precisely the point. There exist three levels of characterization in *Docks of New York*: a nearly constant background of completely undifferentiated extras (stokers, pub crawlers, etc.), a sketchily developed middle ground, comprising a grand total of four characters (Lewis; Baclanova; Bancroft's shipmate, played by Clyde Cook; and Hymn Book Harry, played by Gustav von Seyffertitz), and a foreground of two people, Bancroft and Compson. Thus, rather than developing his foreground characters by bringing them out in relief through flamboyant performances, Sternberg keeps them back in murky coexistence with the background and develops them through the subtle and unsuppressibly natural distinctions that maintain their individuality from it. Sternberg's entire style, in fact, can perhaps be best described as a slightly articulated surface.

The film opens in the hold of the ship where Bancroft works as a stoker. The initial atmosphere is one of extreme stylization. Broken dust light and drifting smoke draw a hazy veil over the shots. Backlighting molds the sweating bodies of the stokers into luminous statues. The background, in half-focus, is considerably brighter than the foreground, and reinforces a feeling of overall surface. The scene is composed mainly in diagonal, nonfrontal setups with strong diagonals (iron bars, ladders, grilles) within the shots. And in the corners of nearly every shot, chains swing gently and ceaselessly. These chains, of course, are blood kin to the dredge in *The Salvation Hunters,* the shuttle loom in *An American Tragedy,* the church bells in *The Scarlet Empress,* the roulette wheel in *The Shanghai Gesture,* and the waves in *Anatahan*: concrete manifestations of the monotonous and abstract rhythms of fate. Everything in the opening scene contributes to an atmosphere of indirectness, abstraction, and surface. These attributes are summed up in the final shots of the scene, as the men, anticipating liberty, moon over a wall covered with telephone numbers, girls' names, and crude childlike drawings of female figures—obscure hieroglyphs of desire which nevertheless motivate the major actions for the course of the film.

The next scene introduces the primary location of the film, a waterfront dive called The Sandbar. It's a dive like any other—in a Sternberg film. In other words, it's naturalistic and dreamlike, seedy and abstract, crammed with details yet read as an unassimilable whole. The entire structure seems to exist underwater, murky and in a state of perpetual night. Mirrors and nets abound. Meaningless fights break out about every thirty seconds. A player piano grinds away in a corner. The atmosphere, again, is highly stylized and schematic. The scene opens with a long tracking shot forward, ends with a symmetrical tracking shot back. Fast, straight sideways tracking shots skim over a split-up background of crowded movement. Sternberg's camera movements are rarely inclusive or sinuous or ornate, nor do they shape space or analyze actions: they show space without revealing it: they describe actions without penetrating them.

The subject of the scene is the arrival of Mitchell Lewis into the bar. We see Olga Baclanova dancing in a state of virtual orgasm with a sailor. Lewis saunters over; Baclanova looks over her shoulder. "Meet my husband," she casually informs the sailor. Lewis's glance back is totally noncommittal. "I bet you never expected to see me here," she says, without particular interest. Lewis calmly leaves, stamping out a cigarette.

Here we see Sternberg's deadpan acting style paying off, revealing another layer in the action. Although we first take Baclanova's line at face value, a moment's reflection in the vacuum of nonreaction by the principals gives it a delayed action irony: where else would he expect to find her? And in what other circumstances?

276   MARTIN RUBIN

There are very few surprises in Sternberg's world, upon a moment's reflection.

We next see Bancroft disembarking from the ship through fog and lights. There is an abrupt cut to a close shot of the water by the pier. A form appears in reflection. It jumps. A fine screen of spray breaks the surface of the shot.

Several things of importance are occurring here. On a plot level, the major personal relationship is being set into motion: the person who jumped is Mae (Betty Compson), taking the convention-honored route of waterfront floozies. On a stylistic level, the shot has signaled the end of the first part of the film. *Docks of New York* is rather schematically divided into three parts, each with a different style, which Sternberg is kind enough to mark off with a sort of visual signpost, a shot which signals a major shift in style and emotional development. In each case, the ingredients are the same: surface, water and extreme abstraction.

On a character level, Bancroft's reaction to the event is an amazing thing to see. Without breaking stride or hurrying in the least, he slips off his jacket, puts out his cigarette (the first link between him and Lewis), and jumps in to save Mae. This automatic, almost comic nonchalance sets a pattern for Bancroft throughout the film: the continuity of his actions is never interfered with—neither by himself, in the form of breaking off one motion for another, nor by Sternberg, in the form of cutting. Thus from time to time we see Bancroft performing such tricks as knocking down a rowdy and picking up a glass of beer in one motion and one shot. At one point, while eating a sandwich, he is goaded into fisticuffs. So he enters the fight, but continues eating his sandwich, as though both actions were one and the same. Sternberg simply refuses to analyze Bancroft's actions; his motivations move invisibly under the surface of Bancroft's physical grace and Sternberg's continuous shots.

As Bancroft resuscitates Compson, a group of people congregate. Impervious, without a word, Bancroft gathers her up in his arms and bears her off down the wharf. There follows an extraordinary beauty-and-the-beast shot of Bancroft carrying Compson, silhouetted in a backlit world of nets and fog. For an instant, the characters become Man and Woman, archetypal figures acting out parts in a very old drama of desire, and their stolid unconsciousness of this fact makes the shot all the more moving. Appropriately, this is intercut with a single-take scene of Lewis and Baclanova attempting ominous accord, acting out Bancroft's and Compson's roles for the future, trapped behind a bed grille that engulfs the foreground.

Bancroft deposits Compson in a back room of The Sandbar. Some women tend to her as he waits outside on the wharf. Compson's dress, a wet rag, is thrown out the door. Then another little miracle of character occurs. His face a mask of contemplation, Bancroft scrutinizes the dress, picks it up, and hangs it neatly over a railing. At first, one might take this unexpected, almost out-of-character gesture as merely sentimental: a prelude to the revelation of a hidden gentleness beneath Bancroft's rough exterior. But in the next scene, after breaking into a store to steal a new dress, Bancroft throws the garment down on Compson's bed in a spirit of complete disinterest, goes over to the other side of the room, and tends the fire without looking at her. In fact, this heart-of-gold temptation, although not arbitrarily denied, is played down throughout the film. Bancroft's gesture simply proclaims him as a human being incapable of being understood, and therefore worthy of our attention.

After Bancroft enters her room, Compson observes, "So you're the guy who saved my life"—she says it as if it were a way of passing time between cigarette puffs—"You could have saved yourself the trouble." Bancroft's prognosis: "All you need is a good time." She's unimpressed. "Give me a chance," he says. In a close-up of Compson, her face seemingly unchanged except for her downcast eyes, she looks suddenly tender and vulnerable: another shift below the surface, all the more moving for being so remote and so acutely observed. And also for such a major step in personal commitment (later, we'll see just how major it really is) being glimpsed in such a small detail (but not minor: there are no minor details in a Sternberg film). "OK," she finally replies.

In the next scene, Compson joins Bancroft in the main room of The Sandbar. As they sit down at a table, Sternberg introduces a rather marvelous medium-long shot which dominates the next few minutes. Their table is located right-of-center in the shot, and a long mirror just behind them covers the upper-left-hand side of the screen. This mirror becomes a fascinating visual sideshow, almost

MARTIN RUBIN

a screen within the screen, on which we see a series of colorful and crowded fights break out. It also makes it impossible to concentrate singly on Bancroft and Compson, who are engaged in an extremely important conversation; it forces one to react to the shot as a whole. I can think of no more striking example of Sternberg's ability to use conflicting details to form a unified surface. In this case, the shot clearly remains faithful to the surface of the characters, who are painfully exposing themselves while at the same time keeping up their fronts; it's like watching someone trying to keep a mask on while performing a striptease. (Remember, in *Dishonored,* when Marlene Dietrich, in a gesture of false modesty as the "peasant" girl, lifts up her skirt to cover her face?) A few snatches of the dialogue may convey some of the contradictory revelation/counter-revelation tone of the scene:

COMPSON: Ever been married?
BANCROFT: Who'd marry a guy like me? . . . . You ever been married?
COMPSON: Who'd marry me?
BANCROFT: I've sailed the seven seas, and I've never seen a craft so trim.
COMPSON: Stop kidding.
BANCROFT: I'm not. . . . What did you ever do that makes you worse than me? I'd marry you in a minute.
COMPSON: I'll try anything once.

This disturbing ambivalence of tone is extended in the subsequent marriage scene. Bancroft doesn't exactly marry her in a minute, but the ceremony is a rather hasty and absurd affair. He drags Compson across the saloon, announcing their nuptials. The crowd in The Sandbar looks upon the whole thing as a fitting and hilarious climax to a swell Saturday night. When the minister hesitates because they don't have a marriage license, a gross fat woman volunteers to take over and proceeds to officiate with a beer mug in hand.

However, Sternberg also introduces a few elements in the marriage ceremony which, although they don't undercut its rowdy tone, at least coexist with it. One is the presence of Hymn Book Harry, the waterfront minister, who lends an air of impeccable but unpompous gravity to the proceedings. Immensely skeptical about the whole business, he asks Compson, "Does it mean that much to you?"

All she does is drop her eyes, but that's enough for him—and us; he proceeds with the wedding. We see in Harry's sardonic, compassionate, and slightly moth-eaten dignity the inevitable truth of this "ceremony" (it's just a pretext for a quick lay), and we also see it in the extensive parallels drawn throughout the scene with Lewis and Baclanova. When Hymn Book Harry lectures Bancroft and Compson about marriage being an honorable endeavor, there is a brief insert shot of Lewis looking particularly shifty-eyed. More strikingly, Compson and Baclanova, during the entire ceremony, are always seen together in two-shot, back to back, like mirror images. After the ceremony, Baclanova gives Compson her wedding ring and, in her one unsuppressed emotional moment, impulsively grabs and kisses her, sealing the bond between them.

Bancroft carries Compson outside to the back room, the luminous nighttime-and-water atmosphere recalling the first time he carried her off. A medium two-shot shows them overlooking the water, with a couple of offshore lights indicating the background. Then, as the characters arrange themselves in the shot, they blot out the lights; everything goes totally dark gray, the setting absolutely abstract and bare. Fadeout. End of Part Two.

If the first "transition" shot introduced the aqueous and confusing atmosphere of the second section, the second "transition" shot is an appropriate prologue to the barren look of section three; the style of the third section is as unadorned and realistic as that of the first section is richly stylized, with section two falling somewhere in between. Each one has a primary location: the ship for the first section, the bedroom for the third, with The Sandbar doubling as the center of section two and as a unifying constant in all the sections, changing its appearance accordingly in each one.

This division of styles has no real symbolic or dialectical significance, but merely provides a series of different environments, for the characters to define themselves in, which are appropriate to the current stage of their relationship and our developing acquaintance with them. Thus, the schematic and containing style of the first section sets a convivial and functional stage for setting the plot machinery in motion and placing the characters in a situation where they must respond; the ambiguous tone of the second section accommodates that response in the form of hazard, delusion, and the partial breakdown of roles; and the barren tone of the third section provides an uncluttered space for the characters' most trying moments of self-revelation and morning-after disillusion. The third section also represents a falling away by Sternberg's style in recognition of the characters' ability (and need) to fill that place.

The section opens with a documentary-like exterior of the waterfront. In the bedroom, while Compson still sleeps, Bancroft lays some money on the night table. He turns to go, hesitates, reflects, and shells out a few more bills. Then he leaves.

He goes into The Sandbar, which is somewhat transformed by the natural, shadowless lighting of the section, and sits down at Lewis's table to order breakfast. "You're fired," Lewis informs him. Bancroft keeps eating without a reaction. "One ship's as good as another," he eventually concludes.

The next scene opens with a shot of a man, from the back, entering the bedroom. At first we think it's Bancroft, but as he enters the room we see it's Lewis, and we're suddenly struck by the physical similarity of the two men. In a brief, unstressed detail shot, Compson, now awake, slips the money on the table under a hairbrush, covering the action by getting a match out of a bowl. Lewis makes his proposition: "You know he ain't comin' back."

"You're a liar," Compson replies.

But the previous insert shot, which might go unnoticed on a first viewing, is actually the most important shot in the film. From it we see that not only does Compson know Bancroft is ditching her, but also, from the naturalness of her action, that she has probably known it throughout the entire film. Both sides of her character, her worldly-wise sense of inevitability and her delusive vulnerability, suddenly make sense in terms of this hopeless masque. And it's been so well prepared by careful observation of her performance that Sternberg shoots it not as a last-minute revelation (that is, a reaction shot of Compson) or a voyeuristic glimpse behind the character's back (that is, a reaction shot of Lewis), but as an ordinary detail shot—that is, just another integral and natural part of an ordered environment. In other words, he treats the revelatory moment as a discreet and irreducible message of a coherent personality; he allows his characters their dignity while their illusions are exposed.

Nowhere is Sternberg's obliqueness more subtle, compassionate, and true.

We next see Baclanova ominously slipping into the bedroom. There is a cut, almost a subconscious reaction shot, to Bancroft in the bar. He goes outside and bulls his way through an excited crowd until a cop blocks him outside the bedroom door—the first time Bancroft's motion has been broken in the film. Baclanova confesses to the shooting of her husband. As she is ushered into the police van, she looks back at Compson on the porch.

There follows one of those moments of instinctive, elemental, and subverbal communications which occur in Sternberg's films only between women acknowledging their equal footing—we see it again between Dietrich and the girl she kisses in *Morocco,* between Dietrich and the row of bargirls she accosts in the gambling salon in *Dishonored,* between Dietrich and Anna May Wong after Wong's rape in *Shanghai Express.* Here, the physical world drops out of sight as both women are placed in close shot against completely blank backgrounds—Compson against a bare wooden wall, Baclanova against a field of gray provided by the doors of the van. "I hope you have better luck than I did," says Baclanova, her words unnaturalistically jumping the long distance between her and Compson. "But I doubt it."

After the police depart, Bancroft is left to confront Compson in the most painful scene of the film. "Sorry, baby, sailing in an hour," he tells her. "Never missed a ship in my life." The scene is shot almost entirely in straight-on, eye-level medium shots. Appropriate to this objective camera, the first thing one notices about the scene is that Sternberg refuses to condemn Bancroft for not being moved ("I've never done a decent thing in my life"), or to pity Compson for trying to move him ("You ain't so bad"). Perhaps it would be most accurate to say that Sternberg sympathizes most with Compson, but identifies most with Bancroft.

Accordingly, the point-of-view of the scene, along with its emotional tone (Bancroft moving between callousness and compassion, Compson between passive despair and defiant hope), is constantly shifting. For example, the scene contains the most blatant bit of subjectivism in the entire film—a shot through Compson's tears (complete with vaseline on the lens) as she tries unsuccessfully to

MARTIN RUBIN

thread a needle—but Compson also turns her back to us during two crucial moments when Bancroft starts to leave. The first time, when she finally turns around, she tearfully bids him a stoic goodbye. The second time, she turns and explodes in indignant anger. But what went on behind her back to provoke that difference in response is as mysterious to us as it is to Bancroft, who exits in confusion and remarks, "The nerve of that dame. After all I did for her."

Compson walks out on the porch to watch him leave. As she stands on the left side of the shot, Sternberg superimposes a shimmering surface of water over the right half. The water dissolves out; Compson turns around and relaxes completely. Her final achievement of this state of passivity prefigures Bancroft's evolution in the next section of the film. End of Part Three.

The last section of the film is a reprise of the styles of the first three sections, moving from the ship to The Sandbar to a barren courtroom (which replaces the bedroom). This is only appropriate for a section in which Bancroft finally sees his past, present and future as being identical. As he situates himself in the hold of his new ship, a new chief, identical to the last, comes down and gives the identical order: "Get going." Bancroft, in the manner we have come to know and love, calmly walks over, hands him the shovel, and leaves.

Sternberg's characters usually reach this point where, although still uncomprehending of their fate, they are no longer blind to their roles in it. The results of this consciousness can be affirmative (the end of *Dishonored*), defeating (the end of *Anatahan*), or a mixture of both (the end of *Morocco*—or of *Docks of New York*). But awareness is seen as a value in itself, regardless of the nature of its consequences; it's like an island of self contained within, yet at the same time distinct from, an ocean of relentless otherness.

The last scene opens with a long shot of a very barren courtroom. The judge is an automaton who seems to intone without variation, "Thirty days. Next case." In his solemn demeanor and position in the shots (upper center), he strongly recalls Hymn Book Harry— appropriate for what is in effect the re-"marriage" of Bancroft and Compson, and ironic in its sense of parallel and sameness.

Compson is being tried for possession of the clothes Bancroft stole for her. When she's led off to serve her sentence, Bancroft, previously unseen, steps out of the crowd of spectators. As he confesses ("I had only one night ashore and wanted a good time"), he looks alternately penitent and sardonic, and Compson looks alternately disgusted and dependent. After receiving his sentence, he tells her, "Sixty days ain't a long cruise."

"I guess I'd wait forever," she replies, without delirious enthusiasm.

So Bancroft hasn't missed his ship after all; one ship's as good as another. The only thing in the film that has changed is the characters' self-knowledge. If for no other reason, this is why their independence has been so necessary; their evolving interpretation of the events has been the subject of the film. A small distance for a film to travel, one might think. But in a world view where the process of life is seen as integrating oneself with the meaningless rhythm of the universe (of which personality is a predictable part), this semitragic consciousness is the only way of maintaining a semblance of individuality, and the only way of eking out a mode of existence which is other than absurd. The last shot of *Docks of New York* is a trackback to long shot, returning us to the perspective of the shot that opened the scene. In the background, we see Bancroft being led off, while in the opposite corner Compson watches him leave. In no other shot in the film have the characters been placed so firmly and irrevocably in their environment, yet in no other shot have we been so acutely conscious of their presence. *Docks of New York* is perhaps the most beautiful film of the American silent cinema, and the most human.

MARTIN RUBIN

NOTES ON CONTRIBUTORS

PETER BOGDANOVICH directed *Targets, The Last Picture Show, What's Up Doc?* and *Paper Moon.* He has written on film for *Esquire,* and is collaborating with Orson Welles on the latter's autobiography.

STUART BYRON, a former film publicist and *Variety* reporter, is film critic for Boston's the *Real Paper.*

JAY COCKS reviews movies for *Time.*

FRANCIS X. J. COLEMAN, an associate professor of philosophy at Boston University, was film critic for the defunct quarterly *Modern Occasions.* He is the author of the novel *Philip the Draftsman* and the forthcoming *An Academic Affair.*

RICHARD CORLISS is the editor of *Film Comment.*

JUDITH CRIST, formerly film critic for the *New York Herald Tribune,* is currently reviewing for *New York* and *TV Guide.*

DAVID DENBY is film critic for the *Atlantic.*

STEPHEN FARBER is the Los Angeles editor of *Film Quarterly* and formerly film critic for the defunct newspaper *LA.* He is the author of *The Movie Rating Game.*

RICHARD GILMAN, a contributing editor of *Partisan Review,* is a professor of playwriting and criticism at Yale Drama School.

ROGER GREENSPUN teaches film at Rutgers University, and formerly reviewed for the *New York Times.*

PETER HARCOURT is Director of the Department of Film Studies at Queen's University in Kingston, Ontario.

MOLLY HASKELL reviews movies for the *Village Voice.*

DWIGHT MACDONALD began writing on film in 1929. He was *Esquire's* film critic from 1960 to 1966. His essays and reviews have been collected in *Dwight Macdonald on the Movies.*

JOSEPH MCBRIDE, a reporter for the *Wisconsin State Journal* in Madison, is editor of *Focus on Howard Hawks* and author of *Orson Welles.* He has published film criticism in several journals, including *Film Quarterly* and *Sight and Sound.* McBride plays a film critic in an Orson Welles movie-in-progress entitled *The Other Side of the Wind.*

JONAS MEKAS is a filmmaker, *Village Voice* columnist and director of Anthology Film Archives in New York City. His *Village Voice* columns have been collected in *Movie Journal: The Rise of a New American Cinema, 1959–1971.*

WILLIAM PECHTER is film critic for *Commentary* and author of the collection *Twenty-four Times a Second.*

RICHARD ROUD is Director of the New York Film Festival and Managing Editor of the forthcoming *Critical Encyclopedia of the Cinema.* He was film critic for the *Manchester Guardian* (1963–69), and has published numerous articles and books on film.

MARTIN RUBIN is Film Programmer at the New York Cultural Center in New York City. He co-authored *The Director's Event* and has contributed articles on film to the *Village Voice, Movie* and the *New Journal.*

CHARLES THOMAS SAMUELS teaches English and film at Williams College. He reviews films for the *American Scholar* and is author of *A Casebook on Film* and *Encountering Directors* (a collection of interviews with eleven leading directors).

ANDREW SARRIS, an associate professor of cinema at Columbia University, has reviewed movies for *The Village Voice* since 1960. He has written several books on film (*Confessions of a Cultist, Primal Screen*) and is the author of the screenplays of *Promise at Dawn* and *Justine.*

RICHARD SCHICKEL, former film critic of *Life,* now reviews for *Time.* He is working on a biography of D. W. Griffiths.

JOHN SIMON is a drama critic (*New York*) and film critic (*Esquire*). His film reviews and essays have been collected in *Acid Test, Private Screenings* and *Movies into Film.*

HOWARD THOMPSON reviews movies for the *New York Times.*

PARKER TYLER is the author of several film books, including *Underground Film: A Critical History, Magic and Myth of the Movies* and *Screening the Sexes: Homosexuality in the Movies.*

COLIN L. WESTERBECK, JR., reviews films for *Commonweal.*

ELLEN WILLIS is rock critic for the *New Yorker* and writes on movies for the *New York Review of Books.*

ROBIN WOOD has done a number of books on directors. He teaches film at the Berkshire College of Education in Reading, England, and reviews for the (London) *Times Educational Supplement.*

INDEX

Index

289